MARTIN LUTHER

Prophet to the Church Catholic

by

James Atkinson

THE PATERNOSTER PRESS

WILLIAM B. EERDMANS PUBLISHING COMPANY

AUSTRALIA:
Emu Book Agencies Pty., Ltd.,
63 Berry St., Granville, 2142, N.S.W.

SOUTH AFRICA:
Oxford University Press,
P.O. Box 1141, Cape Town

British Library Cataloguing in Publication Data
Atkinson, James
Martin Luther: prophet to the catholic church.
1. Luther, Martin—Influence 2. Public
worship—History 3. Liturgies—History
I. Title
264   BV176
0 85364 377

First American edition published 1983 through special arrangement
with Paternoster by Wm. B. Eerdmans Publishing Co.,
255 Jefferson Ave. S.E., Grand Rapids, Michigan 49503

Library of Congress Cataloging in Publication Data
Atkinson, James, 1914—
Martin Luther: prophet to the Church Catholic.

I. Luther, Martin, 1483-1546. 2. Christian union.
I. Title.
BR325.A83   1983   230'.41'0924   83-16462
ISBN 0-8028-1260-0

Printed in the United States of America

CONTENTS

PREFACE

THE FOLLOWING PAGES are an expansion of the Didsbury Lectures delivered at the College of the Nazarenes in Manchester, 1981. I thank the Principal, the staff, the students, and the public for the warm and critical way in which they received them, and in particular for the encouragement and support of Dr. Tom Noble throughout the series.

Readers will readily see the structure of the book. Part Two is the essence of the work, by which the book stands or falls. It shows what Luther can say to the Church today, and it was this part that was delivered at Didsbury in an abbreviated form. Part One shows the lamentable way Luther has been devalued for four hundred years, but it also shows the revaluation now taking place. No exercise could give the Church in its entirety a deeper spiritual and theological revival than a fresh look at the rejected monk of Wittenberg.

I thank Miss Mary Long, former secretary of Latimer House, the Evangelical Research Centre at Oxford, for typing the entire manuscript and showing such interest in the contents. Her help is deeply appreciated.

JAMES ATKINSON

PART ONE

THE CATHOLIC PERSPECTIVE ON LUTHER

CHAPTER ONE

CATHOLIC DEVALUATION OF LUTHER, 1517–1939: The Period of Hostility and Destructive Criticism

IT TOOK ROMAN CATHOLICISM a long time to come round to giving Luther a cold and careful look. For over four and a half centuries, since the night that Luther nailed up his Ninety-five Theses against Indulgences on 31 October 1517, Roman Catholicism took an unrelenting line of vicious invective and vile abuse against Luther's person, while virtually disregarding his vital and vivid religious experience, his commanding and irrefutable biblical theology, and his consuming concern to reform the Church according to the teaching and purpose of its founder, Jesus Christ. It is one thing to offer criticism; it is quite another to hurl scurrilous abuse: the former creates and maintains some relationships; the latter will deaden and destroy any relationship that exists.[1]

It was not until 1939, when Joseph Lortz, then Catholic professor at Muenster, published his fine two-volume study of Luther, entitled *Die Reformation in Deutschland* (1939-40), that the first ray of hope of any creative theological dialogue between Catholicism and Protestantism lit the dark horizon. The work was so scholarly and so informed that it was found to subserve a highly significant and irenic critique of Luther and Lutheranism. Later in this volume we shall consider this book along with the books of the other Cath-

---

1. A useful summary account of the Roman Catholic attitude towards Luther is given in Gordon Rupp's *The Righteousness of God: Luther Studies* (New York: Philosophical Library), 1953, pp. 3-55. For a detailed comprehensive survey, see Richard Stauffer's *Luther as Seen by Catholics*, trans. Mary Parker and T. H. L. Parker (Richmond: John Knox Press, 1967); this text is even more valuably detailed in its German version, *Die Entdeckung Luthers im Katholizismus*, to which I am much indebted.

olic theologians who have since begun to engage in a respectful encounter.

Immediately after the publication of the Ninety-five Theses in 1517, there arose a strong counterattack from the Dominicans, while Luther's bishop began the process to inhibit and silence 'the audacious monk of Wittenberg'. The Dominicans were the champions of orthodoxy and of the absolute power of the papacy, and Professor Wimpina of the University of Frankfurt-on-the-Oder, wrote 106 theses for Tetzel the indulgence seller in refutation of those of Luther. They bear no trace of original thought, but simply reiterate the conventional scholastic teaching on the subject: they are dismal reading indeed. In response to the Dominican efforts, the Pope instructed Gabriel della Volta, the General of the Augustinian Order, to restrain Luther.

Sylvester Prierias, the Master of the Sacred Palace of Rome, entered the lists against Luther as early as 1517 with his *Dialogue on the Power of the Pope*. Himself a Dominican, Prierias supported Tetzel during the indulgences debate and hastily compiled some documents against Luther. He later published the rather feeble book *Errors and Arguments of Martin Luther* (1519). Alveld, Murner, Emser, and other lesser lights also attacked Luther. It is now widely admitted, not least in Roman Catholic circles,[2] that the papal case suffered badly in the early stages by being put into such incompetent hands. Luther always felt this most keenly: he frequently called for his case to be met and answered at the scholarly and spiritual level at which he had raised it. The two exceptions were John Eck, whom he was to meet in Leipzig in 1519, and Cardinal Cajetan, whom he was to face in Augsburg in 1518. Nevertheless, Eck, brilliant theologian though he was, proved vile and abusive, and Cajetan, brilliant and spiritual though he was, handled Luther by authority rather than argument. To his friend John Lang, who had befriended him at Augsburg, Luther wrote at this time, 'If this work is of God, who will prevent it? If it is not of God, who will make it prevail?'

It was during and after the Disputation at Leipzig (1519), when the brilliant and redoubtable John Eck debated the Wittenberg theology with Luther and Karlstadt, that the opposition to Luther took significant shape. John Eck (1486-1543) was by far the ablest op-

---

2. By Hubert Jedin, Hans Küng, and others.

ponent Luther ever had. The young prodigy Eck entered the university at the age of twelve, and by the age of twenty-four was professor of theology at the University of Ingolstadt; he held the chair till his death. He was a man of immense learning in philosophy, theology, Hebrew, and Greek, with a prodigious memory and a great flair for debate, in which his ready wit and swift repartee made him the most masterly disputant in all Germany.

It was in 1517, when Luther published his Ninety-five Theses, that Eck attacked him. In the famous Disputation at Leipzig (1519) Eck and Luther debated the primacy of the pope and the apostolic origin of the office, as well as penance, purgatory, indulgences, and the power of the priest to grant absolution. Eck cleverly led Luther into admitting that his theology was simply that of Huss, who had already been condemned by council at Constance in 1415. Why, Eck asked, did Luther not use his great gifts to strengthen the Church, rather than to attack it and to revive heresy? Eck elaborated his position in the debate in a subsequent volume *On the Primacy of Peter against Luther* (1520). It was he who was largely responsible for promulgating the papal bull *Exsurge, Domine* (1520). He continued to hound Luther, and during the next six years published eight major works against the Reformation, the most important of which was his *Enchiridion locorum communium (1525).* [3] It went through an edition a year for some fifty years, and before the century was out, ninety-one editions had been printed.

It would not be possible or fair to attempt to summarise this learned work, though it is perhaps permissible to indicate the scope of its attack. The work deals with the following principal areas of dispute between Catholics and Protestants: the Church and its authority; councils; the primacy of the pope; the heretical use of Scripture; faith and works; all seven sacraments; church order; feasts, fasts, worship of saints, indulgences, purgatory, burning of heretics, and private masses; vows and celibacy, free will; and transubstantiation.

The book is a highly learned work, teeming with Scripture references. On every issue, Eck begins with his biblical authorities,

---

3. Eck, *Enchiridion of Commonplaces of John Eck against Luther and Other Enemies of the Church*, trans. Ford Lewis Battles (Grand Rapids, Mich.: Baker Book, 1979). This is a valuable translation of an important piece of Catholic polemic. A critical edition of the original text is being prepared by Professor Frankel of Geneva for the *Corpus Catholicorum*.

passes on to the Fathers, Church decisions of Councils, papal decretals, and the like, and concludes with a rehearsal and refutation
of the counterarguments. He is a consummate controversialist with
an unbelievable store of texts at his fingertips from scriptural, patristic, and conciliar authorities. He has received heavy criticism
from Protestant controversialists for his alleged coarseness and immorality, but we cannot be blind to the historical evidence before
our eyes of a devoted and brilliant scholar, utterly single-minded in
defence of his Church, completely committed to pastoral care (as
his *Cure of Souls* and hundreds of published sermons testify)—a
man who never spared himself and who in his published works left
behind a memorial that few have equalled.

It was not only the Lutherans who received Eck's attention.
The Swiss, too, were engaged. In 1526 Eck attacked Zwingli and
Oecolampadius for their teachings on the Eucharist. At Baden, supported by Thomas Murner, he engaged on a great Catholic/Protestant
disputation.[4] Eck presented propositions on transubstantiation, intercession of the saints, images, purgatory, baptism, and original sin.
Out of this debate came Eck's *On the Sacrifice of the Mass* (1527)
as well as other treatises and sermons.

He was active, too, at Augsburg, where Melanchthon presented
the *Confessio Augustana* to the Emperor and his theologians and
advisers in 1530. He was one of the authors of the *Confutatio Ro-
mana*, (rewritten five times at the insistence of the Emperor), to
which Melanchthon's *Apologia* (1531) was a reply. The *Confutatio*
expressed agreement with the Lutherans on the issues of civil government, the return of Christ in judgment, the cause of sin, and
only partially on free will. The main areas of disagreement included
the following: communion in both kinds, the marriage of priests,
the mass, confession, fasting, vows, and the authority of bishops. It
was during this period that Eck also published his 'Refutation of
Zwingli's Articles'.

Eck made a complete translation of the Bible in 1537. At the
various colloquies that took place in 1540 and 1541 (Hagenau,
Worms, and Regensburg), he maintained his hard line against the
reconciling Catholics Contarini, Gropper, and von Pflug. Out of

---

4. See Beresford James Kidd, ed., *Documents Illustrative of the Continental
Reformation*, (Oxford: Clarendon Press, 1911), pp. 458-59.

these conversations came his last works, *Apology* (1542) and *Replica Eckii* (1543); he died soon after in 1543. He had also published a four-volume collection of his *Works against Luther*.

Following all this, the Franciscan friar Augustine von Alveld wrote a scurrilous, abusive attack on Luther. Because it was in Latin and addressed to clergy, Luther ignored it. But when Alveld addressed the same thing to the laity in German, Luther replied instantly in what was to prove an important book, *The Papacy at Rome* (1520), in which he 'welcomed the opportunity to explain something of the nature of Christianity for the laity'. In this tractate Luther enlarged his doctrine of the Church (as we shall see later), but in it he was also aiming beyond Alveld to Cajetan, whom he had already met at Augsburg in 1518, and also to Sylvester Prierias and Jerome Emser. Emser, a prebendary serving Duke George at Leipzig, now stirred up controversy against Luther after the debate there.[5] The same debate stimulated the Strasbourg friar Thomas Murner, who wrote some thirty-two books against Luther, few of which achieved publication.

It may be worth noting, for it says a lot about Luther, that throughout his long life of controversy, when contumely and insult were heaped upon his person continually, he was always quick to defend Christianity, but never himself. As he put it on one occasion, 'Whoever will, let him freely slander my person and my life. It is already forgiven him. God has given me a glad and fearless spirit, which they shall not embitter for me, I trust, not in all eternity.' Nevertheless, when the Gospel was at stake, Luther outmatched every opponent when it came to language. His words burned holes in the pages.

Perhaps Luther's most influential antagonist was John Cochlaeus (1479-1552). Cochlaeus was influential not on account of any special ability, but because his life of Luther, *Commentaria de actis et scriptis Martini Lutheri*, set the tone for almost all the Roman Catholic biographies that have appeared from the sixteenth to the twentieth century on a deplorably low level. A parish priest of Frankfurt, and later canon of Breslau, he was strongly influenced by the

---

5. A convenient account of Luther's handling of this debate may be found in *The Works of Martin Luther*, ed. Henry Eyster Jacobs (Philadelphia: Muhlenberg, 1943), 1:329-36.

Renaissance, and in the early stages came out in actual support of Luther. It was when Luther burned the papal bull of 1520 that the humanist Cochlaeus shrank back from the incipient Reformation movement, considering Luther a revolutionary rather than a reformer. He took an active part in the discussions at Worms (1521), when, after Luther's official condemnation, he sought a *modus vivendi* between Luther and the Catholic party.[6] When such a rapprochement proved unattainable, Cochlaeus parted from Luther with tears in his eyes, saying that he would continue to write against Luther and to fight for the Church to the utmost of his powers and to the end of his days. This he did. With unbridled and calumnious polemic, in total disregard of Luther's genuine religious experience, of his unchallengeable biblical theology, and his pure concern to reform a secularised and corrupt Church, Cochlaeus raged against Luther. He carried on his self-imposed campaign to the end, quite heedless of historic evidence, maintaining printing presses at his own personal cost, virtually giving his life and his all in defence of the Catholic Church, all the while remaining ironically unappreciated for his efforts.

There can be no doubt of the sincerity and conviction of Cochlaeus, but neither can there be any doubt that it was he who poisoned the well of historical studies. Roman Catholic historians have drawn their prejudice against Luther from this polemical source, which in its animosity has an almost total disregard for objective truth and historical facts. Denifle, Grisar, Cristiani, Paquier, and Maritain (to cite only the most famous and influential) have all drunk deep of this poisoned well—too deeply—and lesser historians have adopted their position. We shall never break through into the light until the entire Church, Catholic and Protestant together in a total catholicity, seeks genuinely and honestly to do Luther historical justice. There are clear signs that this movement is beginning, particularly among German Catholics, as I will try to make clear in this volume.

Even the Catholic scholar Joseph Lortz says that Cochlaeus argued from false presuppositions, and had written to put an end to the false opinion about Luther current among Catholics—that is, to 'the gross error that Luther had been a good, devout and saintly

---

6. See my *Trial of Luther* (New York: Stein and Day, 1971), pp. 169-72.

monk, more versed than any one in holy scriptures'. Lortz quotes Cochlaeus:

> Luther is a child of the devil, possessed by the devil, full of falsehood and vainglory. His revolt was caused by monkish envy of the Dominican, Tetzel; he lusts after wine and women, is without conscience, and approves any means to gain his end. He thinks only of himself. He perpetrated the act of nailing up the theses for forty-two gulden—the sum he required to buy a new cowl. He is a liar and a hypocrite, cowardly and quarrelsome. There is no drop of German blood in him. . . .[7]

For a century the polemic raged and was carried on by both sides in the vilest language imaginable. The Franciscan John Nas produced a series of attacks that culminated in his *Anatomy of Lutheranism as It Was Instituted by the Devil*, which achieved an air of authenticity by virtue of its numerous quotations from Luther's writings. This was followed by a weightier volume entitled *Anatomiae Lutheri*, from the pen of Johann Pistorius, a court physician who made a pretense of literally dissecting Luther in order to reveal the seven devils that demonstrably had possessed him.

This kind of writing, which sought to substantiate the hints and insinuations of Cochlaeus, nauseated both Jesuit and Protestant alike, and eventually lapsed. Becanus, Bellarmine, and Bossuet elevated the discussion at least to discuss theological and historical matters. John Adam Möhler produced an impressive critique of Protestant theology in his *Symbolik* (1832), while his colleague Dr. Döllinger maintained the traditional repudiation of Luther, though in a less offensive manner. Johannes Janssen produced a massive scholarly work entitled *The History of the German People at the Close of the Middle Ages* (1876), wherein, with fine documentation, he depicted the Middle Ages with its own surging lifestyle, grappling with its problems, but being disastrously interrupted by the Protestant Reformation.

The Luther Jubilee of 1883 saw the launching of the definitive edition of Luther's works and the foundation of the Society for the Study of Reformation History (*Verein für Reformationsgeschichte*). There followed the publication of notable research sources and also some enduring studies from a generation of fine Luther scholars,

---

7. Lortz, *The Reformation in Germany*, trans. Ronald Walls (London: Darton, Longman & Todd, 1968), 1:296.

such as Köstlin, Enders, Brieger, and Buchwald. In 1899 Ficker began to edit the text of Luther's earth-shaking *Lectures on Romans* (1515-16), which had long been forgotten. Scholars were now seeking the real historical Luther, not approaching him through centuries of confessional and polemical Lutheranism, but rather from the original source material.

Into these agreeable developments Father Heinrich Denifle intruded with the most violent attack on Luther that had appeared since Pistorius's in the sixteenth century. What made the book so devastating and destructive was that Denifle was an archivist at the Vatican, a man of immense reputation in the world of scholarship with weighty and valuable work to his name. He claimed that his massive work, entitled *Luther and Lutheranism*, was based on impeccable source material, and indeed, it contains thousands of quotations from Luther himself. Denifle had not only steeped himself in Luther, but had also had the unique advantage of being able to use Luther's hitherto unpublished *Lectures on Romans*, a copy of which the Vatican possessed, but which Protestantism did not.[8] He declared that at the beginning of his research, he had studied Luther and Luther only, and that it was only when he had a complete grasp of Luther that he turned to secondary sources. This may well be true, but it should not be taken to imply that Denifle brought an open mind to his studies. He does not admit the validity of the Protestant conviction at all, and expressly says so in his preface.

Denifle has two principle theses: the first is that Luther was so vile that he could not possibly be an instrument of God, that he was an impostor whose reforming zeal was but a cloak to his own moral decadence; the second thesis is that this so-called reformer made no discovery at all in the theological realm, that he was not only a liar, but an ignorant liar—too ignorant of the true medieval context to understand the prevalent teaching of the righteousness of God.

To defend the first thesis, Denifle accuses Luther of buffoonery, hypocrisy, pride, ignorance, forgery, slander, pornography, vice, debauchery, drunkenness, seduction, corruption, and more: he is lecher, knave, liar, blackguard, sot, and worse. Rupp describes such lan-

---

8. In fact, the Protestants were in possession of a copy, but unaware of the fact: it lay neglected and forgotten for years in a Berlin museum.

guage as belonging to criminal pathology.[9] Such accusations are seriously drawn up, and in the guise of scientific objectivity have deceived many: they are dictated by blind anger. He cries out towards the end of his book, 'Luther, there is nothing divine in you!'[10] At the end he appeals to Protestants, 'Have done with Luther; return to the Church'.[11]

To defend his second thesis, concerning Luther's theological incompetence, Denifle argues that Luther was contaminated with nominalism, and had shown himself utterly unable to understand the golden age of scholasticism. In a volume of sources published the following year, Denifle analyses no fewer than sixty-six commentaries on Romans from the time of Augustine onwards, in an attempt to bring out Luther's errors on justification and his ignorance of medieval tradition. Unfortunately for Lutheranism, no Luther scholar of the day could match Denifle's mastery of the Middle Ages or his knowledge of the religious life for use in preparing a response. When the Protestants eventually did reply, Denifle simply dismissed them, referring to the 'inferior mentality' of Protestants (men such as Harnack and Seeberg!) and describing them as symptomatic of 'the bankruptcy of Protestant Science'.

Denifle's thesis has wreaked irreparable harm to the Catholic understanding of Luther, and has exercised an astonishing influence on Catholicism in general and on Catholic scholarship in particular, which one might have thought impervious to such impassioned and biased thinking. Nevertheless, if it has had a primary destructive effect on Catholicism, it has had a secondary constructive effect on Protestantism. In the face of such excoriating and execrable criticism, Lutheran historians renounced once for all any suspicion of hagiography, and set about rediscovering the true Luther — the man overwhelmed by the amazing grace of God and his love for man shown in Christ, the man of profound, childlike prayer, the man captive to the Word of God (and perhaps the finest biblical expositor of all time), the prophet to and reformer of the Catholic Church that he loved and to which he was wholly given. To the great gain of Luther scholarship, Protestant scholars devoted themselves to the

---

9. *Righteousness of God*, p. 23.
10. Denifle, *Luther and Lutheranism*, 1904, p. 763.
11. Ibid., p. 860.

most painstaking and critical study of the early Luther, to a period that had been treated superficially by nineteenth-century scholars, but that has now been treated exhaustively under the most critical historical scrutiny.

Denifle's second main thesis had the effect of convincing Protestant theologians that it was urgent that they seek a better understanding of medieval scholasticism.[12] Lutherans have tended, and still tend, to begin the Reformation with Luther. This is valid enough in a limited way, but a prerequisite to understanding Luther is to see both the theology *and* the church practice of his day that caused his protest. Lutheran theologians have, with a few distinguished exceptions, been weak on medieval scholasticism as well as on patristics: they have lost the source of tradition characteristic of scholars of other communions (e.g. the Roman, the Greek, and the Anglican). It was Karl Holl more than anybody else who brought about the new understanding of and approach to Luther in the 1920s, who established a new school of new scholars, men who have since then brought Luther studies forward so that the movement is now called the 'Luther renaissance'. Holl showed convincingly that Luther created not only a rediscovery of the thought of Augustine, but also a new understanding of God.[13] The movement initiated by Holl has been maintained with distinction by Robert Stupperich (a student of Holl), Gerhard Ebeling, Heinrich Bornkamm, and many other distinguished scholars too numerous to mention. It is still a vital movement, though reduced in numbers and largely limited to scholars.[14]

Owing to the excesses of Denifle, Roman Catholic scholarship moved to a much calmer appraisal of Luther, though one no less critical. The brutal frontal attack of Denifle was replaced by the smooth insinuations of the Jesuit professor Father Hartmann Grisar

---

12. Indeed, this has been my contention for the past twenty-five years. It also seems to me that Luther's protest most properly begins with the earlier *Disputation against Scholastic Theology* (1517), rather than with the ninety-five theses against indulgences.

13. See Karl Holl's *Gesammelte Aufsätze zur Kirchengeschichte*, vols. 1-3 (1928; Darmstadt, Wissenschaftliche Buchgesellschaft, 1964-65).

14. See, for example, Walther von Loewenich's exceptional *Martin Luther: Der Mann und das Werk* (Munich, 1982), and Martin Brecht's detailed original work *Martin Luther: Sein Weg zur Reformation, 1483-1521* (Stuttgart, Calwer, 1981).

in his chilly *Martin Luther,* [15] which even goes so far as to insinuate that Luther could have had syphilis. Grisar also repeats Denifle's main thesis, namely, that Luther was incompetent to teach on justification; he contends that this incompetence derives from a wrong attitude toward good works, a hostility to 'holiness by works'. Furthermore, he argues that Luther's view did not have its origin in his study of either Romans 1.17 or in any theological source, but in his own immorality — that in order to justify his loose life and to excuse his renunciation of the monastic ideal, the apostate monk had no other course than to become the apostle of salvation without works.

Grisar does not go as far as Denifle in arguing Luther's moral turpitude; he even refutes a number of fables and calumnies (though he breathes new life into others). He further demolishes Denifle's criticism of Luther on the matter of the understanding of *concupiscentia*: Denifle had interpreted Luther completely in sexual terms, whereas Grisar shows that Luther understood the word as the 'I' in every man that sets itself against God. [16] Where Grisar goes beyond Denifle is in asserting that Luther was a neurasthenic and a psychopath. He sees him as the victim of bad heredity, a maladjusted misfit entering the monastic life because of some traumatic experience during a thunderstorm when a student. Grisar argues that Luther was simply a neurotic man who spent his entire life unhappy and guilt-ridden.

Grisar's intent was to ruin Luther's reputation, and among those who accept him as an authority without reading further, we may suppose that he succeeds altogether too well. Nevertheless, not all Catholic scholars have been convinced. Friedrich Heiler said of Grisar's work that it was not an essay in understanding Luther, but an attempt to rule out Luther's person and liquidate Luther's work. Hubert Jedin, Adolf Herte, and Yves M.-J. Congar have expressly stated that Grisar was wrong in his understanding of Luther and wrong to argue that Luther was a spent force. Rupp writes of Grisar and Denifle, 'Anybody who cares to work through their thousands

15. Grisar, *Martin Luther, His Life and Work*, ed. Arthur Preuss, trans. E. M. Lamond (London: B. Herder, 1930).

16. See Holl, 1:137-38, in which it is suggested that Luther understood the word as *Ichsucht* and *Selbstsucht* (i.e., self-love or egoism, not sensuality). Cf. Philip Watson's *Let God Be God! An Interpretation of the Theology of Martin Luther* (Philadelphia: Muhlenberg Press, 1949), pp. 16-17 and p. 20, n. 41.

of pages will emerge knowing that he has heard all that can plausibly be said against the character and work of Martin Luther'.[17]

THE ENGLISH SPEAKING WORLD

With an article on Luther in the *Catholic Encyclopaedia* (1910), H. G. Ganss brought the views of Denifle to the English-speaking world. He declares that Luther inherited a wild temper from his father, who was an irascible man almost carried to murder by his fits of temper. Ganss also denies that Luther ever had a true vocation to the monastic life, and suggests that in the monastery he became the victim of inward conflicts. He also claims that Luther was unfaithful both to the rules of his order and to the teaching of the Church, and that this infidelity brought on very deep depressions of a mental and spiritual kind. Ganss attributes Luther's consequent despair to a false understanding of the Roman teaching on good works, and describes his break with the Church as the product of reforming zeal that degenerated into political rebellion. The reformer is portrayed as a revolutionary who, in the enforced leisure of his sojourn at the Wartburg, broke down under sensuality; it is alleged that in his book *On Monastic Vows*, Luther pleads for an unbridled licence.

Ganss presents Luther's irascibility in pathological terms, and describes him as disheartened and disillusioned in his old age, dejected and despairing, tortured in body and spirit, abandoned by friends and colleagues alike. He assembles his portrayal of Luther in terms of 'The Accusers': it is all a matter of revolt, apostasy, a fall — the unhappy end of a monk unfaithful to his vows. There is nothing of Luther's searching biblical theology, of his glad-heartedness in Christ and joy in the Gospel, of his deep prayer life, of his compelling power as a preacher, of his invincible faith. He speaks of Luther in his sojourn in the Wartburg as beset by sensual temptations, and yet makes no reference to the fine books he wrote there during his captivity of some nine months, books such as his *Refutation of Latomus*, not to mention his magnificent and influential

---

17. *Righteousness of God*, p. 26.

literary masterpiece, the translation of the entire New Testament, which in itself would have been a life's work for any other mortal.

P. F. O'Hare, in his *Facts about Luther*, reintroduced Denifle's and Grisar's case to the public on the four hundredth anniversary of the Ninety-five Theses (1917). He presents Luther as the son of a murderer who after an unhappy childhood entered the monastery without any real vocation to monasticism. He suggests that Luther never understood Augustinianism or monasticism, and that as a monk he experienced long fits of melancholy and depression. O'Hare follows Grisar in making Luther a sick man of abnormal mentality suffering morbid spiritual maladies, a man mentally deranged.

According to O'Hare, Luther was not only mad, but morally depraved and corrupt. He makes much of Luther's strong and sometimes coarse language, but fails to notice that Luther generally uses such language in retaliation, when he feels called to administer a verbal flogging to some hypocrite or spiritual impostor. Most of the time Luther's language is singularly simple and beautiful, and in prayers and letters of spiritual counselling or addressing the bereaved or sick he often becomes almost poetical. In any case, his language never became as vulgar as that of Thomas More in *Contra Martinum Lutherum*.

O'Hare makes a great deal of Luther's words to Melanchthon, 'Sin bravely', but has not a clue to their meaning, nor does he complete the sentence: 'but *still more bravely* believe in Christ'. He refers to the bigamy of Philip of Hesse, but forgets to relate that this was normal advice of the time in such cases, advice given by the Pope himself to Henry VIII in the case of Anne Boleyn, advice that Erasmus also tendered in the same case. He states that Luther was prepared to lie his way through the scandal (casuistry that is regrettably based on fact). He asserts that Luther was not regular in his devotions, gradually lost his faith, developed into an enemy of the Church, and that in the Wartburg he was in close touch with Satan. He upbraids Luther for capturing and marrying a nun, and describes him and his wife as the Adam and Eve of the new gospel of concubinage. He argues that Luther lived indecently, decried celibacy and virginity, sanctioned adultery, dishonoured marriage, authorised prostitution and polygamy, and was a drunkard and frequenter of taverns who preached his theology in the fumes of alcohol and in the midst of his fellow revolutionaries. He attributes to Luther a fickle and cunning character, an inordinate impudence, an unbridled presumption, a titanic pride, a despotic nature, and a spirit of blasphemy; he writes, 'Luther was . . . a blasphemer, a libertine, a revolutionary, a hater of religious vows, a disgrace to the religious calling, an enemy of domestic felicity, the father of divorce, the advocate of polygamy, and the propagator of immorality and open licentiousness'.[18] (One recalls that another was called 'a gluttonous man and a wine-bibber' [Luke 7.34] with as much truth.)

O'Hare's sole purpose seems to have been to discredit Luther on the principle that if one throws enough mud, some is sure to stick. He frequently denounces Luther's inadequate theological education, his inability to reason and express himself clearly; he describes Luther as ambiguous and contradictory, saying one thing today, another tomorrow. The sad state of his soul is attributed to his attack on the Roman Catholic doctrine of good works. O'Hare accuses Luther of declaring war on the Church by composing his theses on indulgences, of inventing a new Gospel wholly opposed to Christ's, of undermining morale by his fabrication of the doctrine of justification by faith alone, of falsifying the Word of God in his translation of the Bible, and of founding his own church. He excoriates Luther as a spiritual degenerate, a heretic, an apostate, a revolutionary, a fallen priest driven by a spirit other than God's, a false hero, a false prophet, and a false reformer—in fact, not a reformer, but a deformer. O'Hare compares him with Judas and the anti-Christ, an enemy of God and of man, and denounces the Reformation as a deformation that had the direst consequences. Luther's doctrine of justification, he argues, ruined morality and encouraged libertinism.

As Stauffer has said, O'Hare did not write a volume *on* Luther but *against* Luther:[19] another batch of poison thrown into the well. Yet, as the fresh and continuous rain from heaven cleanses the most poisoned of wells in time, so the divine springs of truth will in time cleanse us of all our man-made pollutions.

H. O. Evenett, a Fellow of Trinity College, Cambridge, did much to popularise the writings of Denifle and Grisar,[20] though he

---

18. Quoted by Stauffer, *Luther as Seen by Catholics*, p. 22.

19. Ibid., p. 23.

20. See H. O. Evenett's *The Reformation*, 1937, and also his pamphlets for the Catholic Truth Society.

is much more irenic than either of them. He sees Luther as the great fighter against ecclesiastical abuses who, because he insisted on justification by faith *alone*, managed to modify the Catholic theology of salvation and thereby shut himself out of the Catholic world. He describes Luther's motives in psychological terms, portraying him as a morbid and troubled friar seeking a cure to heal his involutional despair, and dismissing his spiritual experience as a subjective experience of a typically Germanic kind. Evenett explains why this subjective and Germanic experience had such far-reaching influence and was so widely received beyond the borders of Germany throughout Europe in the following way. First, the insistence on justification by faith *alone* was much easier to accept than the traditional Catholic theology, for it lightened the moral demands and discipline of Catholicism. Second, Luther appealed to the discontent of the economic, political, and intellectual masses, who considered themselves as little more than slaves; in his powerful emphasis on the freedom of a Christian, Luther appeared to the masses as their God-sent liberator. Third—and this was the secret of his popularity—Luther seized on the traditional hostility of Germany towards Italy, which Evenett claims was based on a sense of cultural inferiority, and carried this to excess in his anti-Roman polemic. Fourth, he won over a great number of princes, for he virtually handed the Church over to the secular lords. It may be admitted that there is a grain of truth in all these specious allegations, but at the same time Evenett totally fails to see the real causes for the success of Luther.

Joseph Clayton presents essentially the same perspective in his book *Luther and His Work* (1937). Clayton's greatest failing is his total disregard for the theological issues of the Reformation. Admittedly, he tries to narrate the historical work without praise and without condemnation, but he fails to grasp the religious significance of these events, and sees them all as determined by political issues. He is no guide to the Reformation; neither is he a true interpreter of Luther. He borrows a little from Denifle, emphasizing Luther's sensuous nature and sexual activity and suggesting that Luther was a nervous and emotional character, melancholic and morbid, a doubting, depressed, sick soul, mentally deranged. He suggests that the key to Luther's lifework was this supposed psychological imbalance, that it was to meet all these terrifying psychological disorders that

Luther conceived the doctrine of salvation by means of justification by faith alone apart from works.

Although Clayton speaks of Luther as a pathological individual, he is not altogether blind to his good points: he appreciates Luther's affectionate nature, his friendliness, his warm humour, his understanding of the common people, his vivid imagination, his literary genius. Nevertheless, he dislikes Luther's self-assurance, and his conviction that he was a prophet in possession of God's truth and that his opponents were enemies of God; He also deplores his invective and strong language.

Clayton completely fails to investigate Luther's theological purpose. He makes no attempt to understand Luther's central doctrine of justification by faith alone, but speaks of it as some kind of internal arrogation whereby he found the truth in himself and not in the Gospel. He also suggests that Luther found his authority in some form of individual subjective judgment and that he was egocentric and subjective, without any objective norm or absolute criterion of authority.

Clayton takes no cognizance of the Renaissance popes, of their moral obliquity or of their theological deficiencies. He counts Luther, and Luther alone, to be responsible for the sixteenth-century schism, describing him as a man whose greatness is of the negative kind: destructive and iconoclastic. To Clayton the Reformation was just a vast desert area in which many were lost without the guidance of God; he dismisses it as a movement that was revolutionary, and antipapal.

Philip Hughes is a Roman Catholic historian who is widely read in the Anglo-Saxon world; his massive and erudite three-volume *History of the Church* (1947) has had considerable influence ever since its publication. Msgr. Hughes is aware of Luther's virtues: he recognises in him a consummate orator, artist, poet, and musician, who was endowed with a creative imagination. He recognises Luther's valiant courage and his prodigious energy for work. He even admits that Luther could be attractive and concedes his enormous stature as 'one of the Titans of history'. Nevertheless, it must be said that Hughes's understanding of Luther's doctrine of justification is quite deplorable. He, too, refuses to come to grips with the implications of the enormous popularity of the doctrine. He, too, rolls out the plea that Luther's greatness is negative. He makes of faith a psychological frame of mind, a bondage to subjectivism; he makes faith into a work. He dismisses Luther as 'a false prophet', the Reformers as 'spiritually sick rather than vicious, unfortunate rather than wicked men'. But he does lay more stress on Luther's work than on his personality. Although he describes Luther as moody and highly strung, and without any vocation for the priesthood or for the monastic life, he nevertheless firmly states that Luther's life as a monk was irreproachable.

Hughes delineates the baneful effects of Luther's theology in the areas of politics, morals, and religion. Regarding the political consequences, he argues that Luther did not give mankind religious freedom at all, but rather that he gave the State the freedom to treat the individual as it wished. In fact, Hughes goes so far as to say that Luther is the father of the police state, the creator of Pan-Germanism. This view has been echoed widely in postwar Europe and has caused much mischief, hurt, and misunderstanding. With regard to Luther's effects on morals, Hughes avers that he created a kind of religious piety that was divorced from morality and that unintentionally brought about a kind of antinomianism. He argues that the Reformation created in Germany a dissoluteness of morals that derives from Luther's doctrine of justification by faith alone apart from works and from his subjective, experiential idea of piety, which has no moral content. Regarding Luther's impact on religion, Msgr. Hughes argues that he put his 'mystical egocentrism' in the centre of man's religious experience, with the result that religion was turned anthropocentric rather than theocentric. Hughes argues that this puts the believer in a vortex of interior emotions and contradictions that must eventually drive him to despair.

Hughes sees Luther as a man who invented a doctrine of his own to solve his own inner problems, a doctrine devoid of any Christian significance and relevant to nobody else. He dismisses Luther's theology as an inversion of Christianity, and argues that he brought about no improvement in morals, no advance in learning, no social improvement, that he was a negative and destructive power. Nevertheless, Hughes does make some advance on this position in his later book *The Reformation: A Popular History* (1957), even though he continues to minimise the facts unfavourable to the Roman Church (e.g. the scandal of indulgences, the general decay of morals and faith, and the failure of the papacy and the hierarchy to answer the Reformers). He still fails to understand Luther's message (which he persists in interpreting as the private invention of a troubled monk), but he abandons the accusation that Lutheranism constitutes the negation of Christianity, and actually shows some respect for Luther himself. Furthermore, in criticising Luther he is without acrimony and avoids the bitterness of polemic.

The amelioration of Hughes's assessment of Luther that occurred between the publication of his *History of the Church* and his popular history of the Reformation is indicative of a general change in attitude that has become increasingly apparent in Roman Catholic scholarship in recent years. After a winter of disapproval as long and cold as that in which Luther was left to suffer, the thaw was neither immediate nor universal, but it has been substantial and encouraging nonetheless.

CHAPTER TWO

CATHOLIC REVALUATION OF LUTHER, 1939–1983: The Period of Respect and Interest

THE FIRST WELCOME REASSESSMENT of the traditional hostile Roman Catholic approach to Luther came in 1917 in the form of an article by F. X. Kiefl, a professor of Dogmatic Theology at Wurzburg, in *Monatschrift für alle Gebiete des Wissens*, a monthly journal. Kiefl broke with Denifle and Grisar, arguing that Luther's protest can be explained and understood only by theological causes. In that single statement he drew all the poison out of the wound, for nothing has done more to poison confessional differences than a certain obstinate denial of any religious motives to the Reformers. He saw Luther as mastered by God. It was his concept of a God who acted unilaterally that led Luther to deny free will, to affirm man's total depravity, to hold a doctrine of imputed righteousness, and finally to reject a Church that claimed to mediate salvation. Kiefl contradicted Denifle, maintaining that Luther's doctrine of justification implied works as a fruit of justification, and that Luther was no libertine seeking excuses for low morality. He made the important point that Luther never sought to replace dogma by religious feeling. He even conceded that in his debate with Erasmus, Luther showed a far deeper understanding of Christianity than his opponent.

Kiefl showed a deep knowledge of Luther's works. He appreciated Luther's profound piety, his indomitable will, and his literary genius. True, he suggests that Luther's spirituality was morbid, but he picks up the powerful phrase from Trent when Luther was reported as a powerful instrument chosen by Providence to reform the Church and purify it. Kiefl thinks Luther went too far and convulsed the

Church in internal strife, but he does bring Luther back into the religious sphere where he belongs and where he ought always to have been.

Further advance was made in Alfred von Martin's collection of essays by Roman Catholic and Protestant theologians, *Luther in Ökumenischer Sicht* (1929). Certain valuable emphases emerged in this book. The historian Sebastian Merkle courageously declared that historians must refrain from belittling and detracting from Luther, and instead must recognise him as a religious man concerned about Christian theology, see the plain evidence that he was no revolutionary or radical freethinker, and concede that he was genuinely concerned only about spiritual things.[1] Another contributor, Anton Fischer, drew attention to Luther's spirituality by describing him as a man of prayer, and showed that this is a matter of some ecumenical significance: 'The praying Luther belongs to us all. He is a truly ecumenical man. He has something to say and to give to all Christian communities.'[2] Luther's first emphasis on prayer was to meet God in his Word by the operation of the Holy Spirit, and this is common to us all, Fischer argues. He even goes on to say that the Pater Noster is at the heart of our prayer life, and that if we could use Christ's own words of prayer in the spirit of such great masters of prayer as St. Augustine, St. Francis of Assisi, and Martin Luther, the Lord's Prayer could bridge the gap that separates Roman Catholics and Protestants. That Fischer would put Luther in the company of Augustine and Francis is indicative of progress indeed.

Such men were heralds to the dawn about to break in Europe, a dawn that broke when Joseph Lortz published in Germany his mighty two-volume *Reformation in Deutschland* (1939-40).[3] In spite of the Second World War, it created great interest among Protestants and Roman Catholics alike, and blew like a Pentecostal wind through Reformation studies. He conceded that the Church of the sixteenth century needed reformation, and granted the validity of Luther's attack on it, granting him the status of historical necessity. He deplores the fact that protest and reform have no free course in the

---

1. Hubert Jedin the great historian of Trent expressed support for Merkle's views at this time.

2. Quoted by Richard Stauffer, *Luther as Seen by Catholics*, 1967, p. 55.

3. Lortz's text has been revised and translated into English by Ronald Walls and was published by Darton, Longman & Todd in 1968.

Roman Catholic Church even today, and argues the possibility of a true protest being neither an act of insubordination nor a destruction of unity. Luther was in fact a creative genius, so complex that after four hundred years scholars are still unable to arrive at any common general assessment of his real significance.

Lortz sees Luther as a religious man who can be assessed only in theological categories: the evangelist, the preacher of grace proclaiming Christ crucified and salvation in his name. He is fully aware of the deeply religious man who threw himself into the monastic life without reserve; of the Luther who immersed himself in Scripture, where he found a gracious God; of the Luther who could write on the Lord's Prayer and on the Magnificat with such tender intimacy, and uphold confession in pastoral care; of the Luther who preached faith with invincible power and warmth; of the Luther who maintained a precious estimation of the Eucharist and of the Real Presence in that sacrament; of the Luther who was always deeply concerned for the cure of souls; of the Luther who prized a powerful prayer life and the ability to teach men to pray; of the Luther whose hymns and chorals plumbed great theological depths. This recognition of Luther as *homo religiosus* marks one of the greatest advances in Catholic scholarship in four hundred years, and as such does much to overshadow the calumnies of Denifle, Grisar, and their like.

But Lortz presents some weighty criticism of Luther too. He tends to blame Luther for the schism. He refers frequently to Luther's subjectivism and individualism, his one-sidedness. Nevertheless, he does so without acrimony. Perhaps his most serious criticism is that although Luther wanted to base his theology on Scripture, he was selective: he not only neglected certain truths in his preaching and teaching, but actually simplified and reduced the Scriptural message, of which the Roman Church possessed the fulness. He attaches considerable importance to Luther's Nominalist education, which obviated his full appreciation of Thomism and rendered him insensitive to the fulness of the biblical revelation. What Luther rejected, he contends, was not true Catholicism, but rather Catholic argumentation: his intense individualism had betrayed him into a misunderstanding of true Catholicism.

Further, Lortz argues, it was Luther's radical subjectivity, his intense individualism, his awareness of being a prophet in isolation, that caused him to interpret biblical revelation in terms of his own personal needs, and thus prevented him from grasping the fulness of biblical truth. He truly sees that Luther's awareness of justification by faith did not arise from within himself, but had its objective reality in Jesus Christ, the author and finisher of his faith. Nevertheless, Lortz argues that objectivism, if it is to be truly authentic, implies an infallible Christ and an infallible Church; therefore, he sets aside Luther's genuine Christocentric faith and accuses him of subjectivism, of individualism. He was a prisoner of his own interpretations, and instead of reforming the Church, he tore it in two. This qualification—even though it may grant Luther's theological acumen, his deep spirituality and prayer life, and his powerful Christocentrism—robs all this percipient appreciation of any real significance, since Lortz comes down on the side of the accusers and opponents of Luther. His misunderstanding of Luther is in a sense insured by his presupposition that, as a good Roman Catholic, he must judge Luther solely in submission to the Church. Despite this crucial reservation, however, Lortz will ever be remembered as the man who created a scholarly basis for creative conversations between Roman Catholics and Protestants. In a sense he was a forerunner to Vatican II.

In 1943 Adolf Herte published his great work, *Das Katholische Lutherbild in Bann der Lutherkommentare des Cochlaeus*, a book that makes a more important contribution towards confessional unity than even Lortz's. Herte shows that, with few exceptions, all the Catholic biographies of Luther predating the twentieth century derive from the work of Cochlaeus. His intent is to search for the meaning of the Reformation, to calm the confessional atmosphere, and to bring healing to old wounds.

J. Hessen handled the Luther problem as a systematician in his *Luther in Katholischer Sicht* (1947). He rejected outright Lortz's theory that Luther's error sprang from subjectivism. It is true, he suggests, that Luther emphasised the *pro nobis* or *pro me*, by which he meant that every individual believer as an involved or committed believer appropriates the work of Christ and experiences it in his or her own heart and mind, but, at the same time, the content of the experience is wholly of God by the mediation of Christ and therefore completely objective: Luther was talking of a confrontation by God, rather than of some inner, subjective experience. Hessen contends that Luther was no individualist, but a *reformer* in the true sense of that word—that is to say, a *restorer* of the God-given Gospel from which the Church had strayed. He not only affirms that Luther was *homo religiosus*, but proceeds to describe him as *homo propheticus*, a man to be understood in the line of the Old Testament prophets.

Hessen proved himself highly perceptive, and elevated the debate to heights of understanding never before attained: sustained at this level, the debate will bring Catholics and Protestants into a new kingdom. Hessen showed the key significance of Luther's central doctrine of justification by faith and suggested four essential aspects of the religious life: (1) doctrine, (2) good works, or ethics, (3) the sacraments, and (4) the Church.

(1) Hessen argued that Luther's fundamental experience did not imply any break with Catholic dogma; such would be the case only if Catholic dogma were to be understood in terms of only the patristic and early medieval tradition. Luther certainly broke away from the contemporary Catholic dogma, much of which he described as novel innovation, and he certainly wanted to reform the Church's teaching of his day, as all his contemporaries saw. But in fact it could be reasonably argued that Luther's main concern was with doctrine rather than with practice or scandals.

(2) Hessen rightly argued that Luther was no antinomian. He rejected the scholastic idea that faith had to be marked by works (*fides caritate formata*) understood as a kind of contribution man puts into the bargain in justification before God, but he did so only in order to emphasize the fact that the work of salvation is all of God. He did not thereby reject good works or a high Christian morality, but taught that all good works are a fruit of faith.

(3) On the matter of the sacraments, Hessen rightly argues that Luther did not reject the sacraments as means of grace. Luther staunchly maintained the objectivity of both Baptism and the Eucharist, and all his life stressed their role and significance in the life of the Christian.

(4) According to Hessen, after Luther discovered the Pauline doctrine of justification by faith alone, he moved on to the Johannine doctrine of union with Christ. This is true in that Luther found that the Pauline emphasis yields an experience of God in Christ that is fully expressible in the Johannine idiom of the Father and the Son making their abode in the believer. When Hessen goes on to say that

this caused Luther to disregard the important reality of the Church, however, he is in error. Luther's doctrine of the hidden church is certainly devastatingly critical of the institution as such, but he had as high a doctrine of the people of God as Christ held.

All this is to say that, according to Hessen, Luther was attacking four main tendencies of his day that were tending to supplant the wholeness of the Gospel of Jesus Christ. These tendencies (or, at least, temptations) are *intellectualism, moralism, sacramentalism,* and *institutionalism.* Intellectualism tends to make faith into assent, and is content with a few formulas instead of the living and continuously disturbing creative contact of God as revealed in the biblical revelation. Moralism makes of Christ a new Moses, and subordinates the Gospel to the law by putting man's works before God's mercy. Sacramentalism has the tendency to make of religion an outward observance, to the neglect of that inner experience worked by the Word of God. Institutionalism tends to make outward observance and attendance a source of salvation. In the graphic words of Hessen, Luther only wanted to put the Gospel back on the lampstand.

Hessen says that Luther's error was in going too far, and suggests that Protestantism today should reconsider the position it has inherited from Luther in an ecumenical atmosphere. In this he is dead right. It is a sound adage of Protestantism that *ecclesia reformata semper reformanda* (the Church once reformed is in a continuous process of reformation), and it is valuable for ecumenically minded Catholics as well. Protestants should cease regarding the Reformation as absolute, and Catholics should start to understand the truth of Luther: were we all to heed it, we would all together begin to find the *una sancta,* the one holy, catholic, apostolic Church. In this context Hessen actually suggests six points of doctrine Catholics and Protestants could profitably examine together: original sin, imputed righteousness, *sola fides,* eucharistic sacrifice, the monastic life, and the power of the pope.

There followed in similar though independent vein three lectures by Karl Adam published in 1948 under the title *Una Sancta in Katholischer Sicht.* [4] He expresses a warm appreciation of Luther's personal virtues, of his faith, his religious experience, his ability, his courage, and the like, but he thinks all these are cancelled out by

---

4. The English translation is entitled *One and Holy.*

the fact that Luther was a rebel and an apostate who used his gifts not in the service of the Church but against it. His explanation of Luther's rebellion is given in psychological terms, and is thus entirely subjective. He also contends that Luther was in bondage to Occamist concepts of God and of justification — that when Luther emphasised the passive nature of God's righteousness he rightly emphasised what most medieval exegetes had already taught, but he drew from this the wrong conclusion that man was nothing but sin, and resolved his own individual problem by ruling out any justification by works.

Adam fails to grant any theological value to Luther's message. He recognises him as a man of faith, but not as a preacher of the Gospel — the only ground on which Luther would seek his own justification. Adam recognises the moral scandal of the Church in the later Middle Ages (who could defend it?), but fails to see the deficiencies and weaknesses in its theology. Had Luther been content, he maintains, to cleanse the Church of the worst abuses and to remain a faithful member, Roman Catholics would have owed him a debt of gratitude. He might have been a second Boniface, the refounder of the Church in Germany, in the company of St. Francis and of Thomas Aquinas. But he spoiled all this by moving from the area of moral reform to that of doctrinal reform, arguing that the Church was in error largely owing to false doctrine. For Adam dogma is uncorruptible. Consequently, he considers Luther to be no more than a rebel, an unhappy and erroneous theologian.

A fresh handling along historical lines followed from the pen of Ernst Walter Zeeden. His two-volume *Martin Luther und die Reformation im Urteil des deutschen Luthertums* (1950)[5] is an examination of how Protestants have understood Luther, the essential argument of which is that from 1550 to 1700 Luther was the object of dogmatic enquiry, whereas after 1700 attention shifted to Luther the man, the hero and liberator, rather than Luther's work. He does not pursue his own views on Luther, but he does indicate that he thought that Luther stressed two elements: the liberty of conscience, and justification by faith only. He makes the valuable point that these very Protestant truths have forked out within Protestantism:

---

5. The first volume has been translated into English by R. M. Bethell as *The Legacy of Luther*; the second volume (*Dokumente*) is not yet available in English.

orthodoxy has kept to the doctrine, while pietism and rationalism have stressed the personal experience of faith and the liberty of the individual respectively.

Next in importance is Friedrich Richter's study *Martin Luther und Ignatius von Loyola* (1954). A Lutheran turned Catholic, Richter shows a full sympathy with Luther, even a warm appreciation of him as a person. Nevertheless, though he considers Luther a pious believer and a man of prayer with few equals, as well as a mighty herald to repentance, in the end Richter concludes that he was but a heretic and rebel, better at demolition than at construction. His theological mistakes were that he rejected Thomas, he based his theology on personal experience, and he did not seek his guarantee of truth in the sanction of the Church. The essentially good Luther, he contends, was misled on psychological and on theological grounds: on psychological grounds because of his immoderate and self-willed nature; on theological grounds because he had never understood the Thomist doctrine of justification, and was wrong to accuse the Church of semi-Pelagianism.

In addition, Richter accuses Luther of subjectivity and of individualism, suggesting that he selected from the Bible his own truths and thus lost the fulness of biblical revelation, ending up by putting man rather than God into the centre. Richter breaks with Hessen by insisting that Luther could never be classed as a prophet, since he lacked both the objectivity and the universality required of the prophet. He concludes by calling Luther's followers to return to the Roman Church (as he did), where they will find the fulness of which they have deprived themselves.

At this time Albert Brandenburg was writing most significantly on the relationship of Luther to Catholicism, but we will come to consider his work at a later point in this discussion. We must first consider the important lectures of the Benedictine monk Thomas Sartory, *Martin Luther in Katholischer Sicht* (1961).

Sartory demonstrates an amazing effort to understand Luther in these lectures, and a striking courage in his attempt to rehabilitate his reputation. He examines Luther from four angles: psychological, historical, theological, and ecumenical. He does not see Luther as a rebel. He does not think that the Reformation happened because of sensual dissoluteness, or ethical laxity, or ambition, or hypocrisy. He will not characterise the liberty that Luther exalted as being in any way related to licence. He turns away from Denifle and Grisar. He looks at Reiter and Erikson who make Luther a manic depressive, but he cannot accept their diagnoses. If we are to understand Luther, he suggests, the religious and theological categories must take precedence over the psychological. He then turns to deal with the matter in historical categories. He deplores the influence of Cochlaeus down the centuries, but approves of the work of Herte, as well as that of Merkle and Lortz, who had rediscovered Luther's religious personality and had also sought a theological explanation of his work. He speaks of the theological confusion of the sixteenth century, and makes the Roman Catholic Church partially responsible for the events from 1517 onwards. Significantly, he emphasises Jedin's point, namely, that by failing to condemn the Reformers *by name* (in accordance with conciliar practice), the fathers at Trent had never finally closed the door on the Protestants.

As far as the theology of Luther is concerned, Sartory sees Luther as a kerugmatic rather than a systematic theologian, as interested only in the living God, and man face to face with him. There was nothing subjective about Luther, he suggests, for he bound conscience to the Word of God. He compares him in this respect to Newman: whereas Newman believed that the Church was the authoritative interpreter of Scripture, Luther granted final authority to the Bible alone, and more specifically to the Gospel he found in the Bible, namely, justification of the sinner by grace in Christ only. Sartory stresses the importance for Catholicism of the doctrine of the Word of God. He does question (with Lortz) whether Luther in his emphasis on justification had not thereby lost the fulness of the biblical revelation — whether, for instance, in his stress on the death of Jesus he had given full weight to the Resurrection.

Finally, on the significance of Luther for the ecumenical scene, Sartory maintains that Luther was a true religious personality, *homo religiosus*, and stresses the importance of seeing the religious truth he stood for. Here is a firm bridge to Catholicism. Like Brandenburg, he sees Luther as the man concerned above all else with man's Christian existence, a man who expresses powerfully his deep personal experience of God, who continually expounds holy Scripture, who proclaims the Word of God unceasingly, who expresses his adoration in the hymns he wrote and composed. The Catholic world, he suggests, should pay heed to such a pastor, such a teacher. Sartory notes, and rightly so, that when Luther speaks of God it is never in academic, abstract, philosophical terms, but always with reference to God's saving work in history. Here, too, Catholic theology has much to learn from Luther. Sartory thinks that Luther can be of assistance in this regard by virtue of the way he integrates his spiritual experience into his theology. In this context Sartory gives warm praise to Luther, by whom he has been strongly influenced. He calls his Church to regard Luther no longer as the lapsed monk, the enemy and destroyer of the Church. He deplores the fact that for centuries the Roman Church has been indoctrinated against Luther, and suggests that his Church should listen to Luther the witness to the Gospel, so that it might be inflamed with the love of God that burns in him.

If Sartory's lectures make little original advance on Lortz and Hessen, it must be said at once that they are absolutely new in Roman Catholic history. They are striking in their understanding of Luther, and courageous in their attempts at rehabilitation. Karl Rahner wholly approves of Sartory's views and thinks it high time that Catholics should speak of Luther in these terms. He reminds us of Jedin's point, that Catholicism never condemned Luther by name at Trent, and that no official judgment on Luther exists by which a loyal Catholic is bound. He says that Catholicism may reject a certain aspect of Luther's teaching, but that Roman Catholic theology has much to learn from him today nonetheless. These are heartening and hopeful words.

This welcome new trend was also explored by Albert Brandenburg, to whom we now turn. Against terrible ill health he struggled till his death to make eventually a fine and original contribution to a better understanding between Catholicism and Protestantism. In 1960 Brandenburg produced *Gericht und Evangelium*, a learned work on the theology of the Word in Luther's first commentary on the Psalms, a book warmly praised by Franz Lau in a review article in the *Luther Jahrbuch*. [6] In an earlier article in 1958, Brandenburg had called on Catholic theology to encounter Lutheran theology in the interests of Church unity. [7] In 1977, just before his death, he

---

6. Lau, "Luthers Worttheologie in Katholischer Sicht," in *Luther Jahrbuch*, no. 28 (Berlin: Lutherisches Verlagshaus, 1961), pp. 110-16.

7. Brandenburg, "Um Luthers Theologie Heute," *Rheinischer Merkur*, 28 Nov. 1958, p. 3.

published a short but highly significant book entitled *The Future of Martin Luther: Martin Luther —Gospel and Catholicity.* [8] The argument of the book is that Luther's theology will reach its essentially positive and ultimate expression within the Catholic Church, where it will find fulfilment, completion, and the expression of its own original uniqueness; by the same token, the Catholic Church will give expression to its own catholicity, comprehensiveness, openness, and future accessibility to all people by a vital and lively discussion with Martin Luther. I frankly consider this to be the most hopeful development of all, and so it is with some pain that I have noted that reviewers, both Catholic and Protestant, have been very reserved in their enthusiasm or praise.

THE ANGLO-SAXON REVALUATION

The renewal of Roman Catholic research was slower to begin in the English-speaking world. Father George Tavard took with him to America his interest in Luther and, among several works, published the significant *Holy Writ or Holy Church* (1959). While sympathetic to Luther, he nevertheless accuses him of a lack of moderation, and of having reduced the full biblical revelation to the single doctrine of justification by faith.

Father Thomas M. McDonough in his *The Law and the Gospel in Luther* (1963) shows even more sympathy with Luther. He decisively dissociates himself from Denifle, Grisar, and Maritain. He concedes that most of the medieval exegetes were saying what Luther was saying concerning the righteousness of God, and will have none of Denifle's dismissal of Luther's 'tower experience' or of his talk of Luther being a slave to sex, nor of Grisar's suggestions that he was psychologically disturbed, nor of Maritain's talk of his having been sunk in moral defeatism. He sees no evidence of Luther being tempted more than any other normal man. He sees Luther as a sensitive, highstrung monk who was more deeply aware than others of his humble creatureliness before his Creator, and who suffered more than others from the semi-Pelagian aberrations of his Nominalist masters. He considers Luther's anxiety to be not path-

---

8. Brandenburg, *Die Zukunft des Martin Luther* (Münster: Aschendorff; Kassel: Johannes-Stauda-Verlag, 1977).

ological, but born of a desire to be at peace with God, and his struggle with the Pauline justification by faith to be but the cry of a drowning man for somebody to save him. He concedes Luther's 'volcanic experience' to be an experience with God, who, of his grace and mercy alone, rescued him from being totally lost; he suggests that this should not be dismissed as an anthropocentric concern, but seen as a genuine discovery of a theocentric experience. Here was no subjectivism: his experience was the effect and fruit of God's objective, external Word.

A few significant articles that have appeared in the popular press have taken a similar line. For example, Father F. M. Quealey, who writes for a larger public, describes the evolution of Roman Catholic studies on Luther, criticising the earlier hostilities and indicating the new insight of modern Roman Catholic scholarship. This new orientation considers Luther not as some rebellious, guilt-ridden, pathological wretch who divided Christendom, but rather as a believing man, yearning for grace, whose religious assurance catalysed in the Church the desire for reform. He notes that the positive work of Lortz and his successors led Protestant theologians to reassess their position, but he also notes, with regret, that English-speaking Roman Catholics still, for the most part, follow the distasteful line of Denifle and Grisar (now long démodé) and pay little attention to the new orientation achieved by their fellow Catholics in Germany and France.[9]

Some months later Father Leonard Swidler published a popular reappraisal of the Reformation.[10] He deplores the fact that America lags so far behind Europe in Reformation studies. He summarises the history of Catholic research on Luther, and admits the historical need for the Reformation. He questions the long-standing attitude of Roman Catholic historians to be always careful to defend the Church at all costs, whether right or wrong, and thereby makes a fine plea for freedom both to seek the truth and to speak it. Both here, and in his technically more advanced studies,[11] he wants the results of Reformation research to be communicated universally to

---

9. Quealey, "The Changing Image of Luther," *The Ecumenist* 2 (1964): 3(.

10. Swidler, "Reappraising the Reformation," *Commonweal*, 81 (1964): 156.

11. For example, his "Catholic Reformation Scholarship in Germany," *Journal of Ecumenical Studies*, 2 (1965): 189-204.

the faithful without delay as the only antidote to heal the already poisoned masses. I endorse the plea.

We must also refer to the welcome studies of the Roman Catholic publisher John M. Todd.[12] An agnostic converted in middle life to Catholicism, he has developed an interest in Luther, and writes in a fair and informed way, steering clear of both praise and polemic. He does full justice to Luther's innermost religious and theological intentions, while at the same time criticizing him for having denied the sacrifice of the mass, for having repudiated the objective nature of the sacraments, for having drawn nonbiblical conclusions in his doctrine of original sin, for inaugurating a kind of irrational fideism, and for having rejected the authority of popes and councils. There is little in the book not already found elsewhere (in Rupp, for example, and in Lortz); nevertheless it is a valuable book to have at the present, issuing as it does from the pen of a sensitive and fair-minded lay historian of the Roman Catholic Church.

In fact, Todd argues, Luther was only doing what Pope John saw as the primary function of his Second Vatican Council—he was attempting to throw open the doors of the time-encrusted, cloistered Church to let in the light of new thoughts and methods, so that it could be for the modern world what the Church of the Apostles had been for theirs. Luther was defeated, Todd notes, because the dead hand was sufficiently heavy to be deadly, and there followed the tragedy of a broken Christendom. He makes a solid case in hopes of pointing both Catholics and Protestants in the right direction.

The work of Harry J. McSorley requires specific notice, not only for his numerous articles and contribution in journals and papers, but for his fine doctoral dissertation on Luther's *Bondage of the Will.*[13] The book is a scholarly and competent effort to come to grips with the heart of Luther's Reformation protest against the Church of Rome on the basis of his debate with Erasmus. He suggests that Luther's protest was not directed against the well-known abuses and laxity in the late medieval Church, but against what Luther judged to be the false doctrine taught by that Church and by its chief human

---

12. Author of *Martin Luther* (London: Burns & Oates, 1964) and *Luther: A Life* (New York: Crossroads, 1982).

13. McSorley, *Luthers Lehre vom unfreien Willen* (Munich, 1967), E.T., *Luther: Right or Wrong?* (New York: Newman Press, 1968).

pastor, the Bishop of Rome. To the question of whether Luther's central reformation protest was one such as to divide Catholic and Protestant Christianity irrevocably, McSorley answers a resounding 'No!'. All this is most encouraging.

FRENCH STUDIES

France, though it lags far behind Germany in Luther studies, nevertheless has some distinguished theologians, among the best known of which are Father Congar and Father Bouyer, who are aware of what is happening and show concern for the outcome of the Catholic/Protestant debate. In a very fine collection of essays, *Cullman, Barth and Others: Christianity Divided* (1939), by Catholic and Protestant scholars, Father Congar, writing on the causes of the Reformation, dismisses outright all talk of moral licentiousness as a motivation of the Reformers. He rejects the contention that moral abuses might be a cause as well, and instead goes to the root of the matter — deficiencies in medieval Roman Catholic theology. He sees the Reformation as a religious movement, an attempt to renew religion at its source. He considers Luther a profoundly religious man who had a deeply sensitive conscience and was obsessed by the longing to find peace of heart and a warm, living, consoling contact with God. Luther was the type who expressed the religious problem of so many of his contemporaries — how to get beyond all the human accretions of religion to the pure sources of religion, to find again peace with God. He presents Luther as a soul in quest of God who had to journey all the way back to the New Testament in his quest; the tragedy lay in the fact that he found himself in reaction to the Catholic system of the Christian life.

In 1950 Yves M.-J. Congar expanded on these views. In his *Vraie et fausse réforme dans l'Eglise* (1950) he criticises Luther's ecclesiology on the grounds of the intense dialectical opposition between the outward and visible and the inward and invisible. Luther, he argues, never appreciated the value of the external forms and visible activities of the institution, and laid too great a stress on the Word: he misunderstood church order. In fact, he suggests, Protestantism since Luther has been unable to construct an ecclesiology. It is Congar, however, who has not understood Luther here. Luther's emphasis was on the *hidden* Church known only to God, and he did not wish this to be *identified* with the institution. It was the hidden nature of the true Church, not its invisible nature, that he taught: he wanted the Church to be very visible! His emphasis on the sacraments, on preaching, and on the instruction of members in churchmanship and its responsibilities, as well as his reorganisation of parish life in Saxony all serve to refute this superficial charge and to show what a high doctrine of the Church Luther actually held.

In fact, Congar can be most reactionary (relative to Lortz and Hessen, for instance). He refers to Luther as impatient, passionate, irritable, violent, superficial, and boastful, a man incapable of grasping anything objectively — naive, unilateral, a revolutionary, an innovator. In his desire to return to the simple Gospel, Luther was no more than 'Galatian', Congar claims, a revolutionary heading a revolt rather than a reformer of the Church. [14]

On the fourth centenary of Luther's death, 1946, an article appeared from Dom T. Strotmann in the Benedictine review *Irénikon*. [15] It is not an original article, nor is it exhaustive, but it does discuss Luther's place in Catholic thought. Strotmann criticises Denifle and Maritain, and praises Lortz. He sees Luther as a genuine religious monk who was appalled by the state of the Church, and who in an intense experience of God sought to give his vision to the world. He sees Luther as a victim of the sixteenth-century unrest, but nevertheless maintains a positive revaluation.

Father Louis Bouyer took the revaluation of Luther a considerable step forward in his book *Du protestantisme à l'Eglise*. [16] Having been a Lutheran pastor before his conversion to Rome, Bouyer has retained a deep sympathy with Luther as well as a profound understanding of his significance for the Church. He does not view Luther as a revolutionary or innovator, but essentially as a truly religious churchman seeking the reform of the Church from within. He places Luther's religious principles under three heads: (1) salvation, understood as the pure grace of God, effected by and

---

14. Congar is making an analogy with Paul's white-hot defence of the Gospel against Judaisers in the epistle to the Galatians.

15. *Irénikon*, 19 (1946): 318-35.

16. *Unam Sanctam*, no. 27 (Paris, 1954), E.T., *The Spirit and Forms of Protestantism*, trans. A. V. Littledale (London: Harvill, 1956).

experienced in Christ; (2) the personal, fundamental experience of God; and (3) the sovereign authority of Scripture. [17]

Bouyer argues that the Lutheran affirmation of justification by faith alone is not a heresy, but is in perfect harmony with Catholic tradition, with the great conciliar definitions of grace and salvation, and even with Thomism. The Catholic, he suggests, may adhere without reservation to Luther's positive emphasis on grace alone. On the matter of personal experience of God, Bouyer argues that this ought not to be understood as some subjective or individualistic assertion of Luther's own insight; on the contrary, Luther experienced it as a confrontation by God the Wholly Transcendent, and what he sought to express was the positive attitude based on the believer's living experience of this relationship. He was talking of God coming in Christ to make his abode in the believer, to use Johannine language. There was nothing subjective or individualistic here at all: it was a 'Christological personalism', all of God, nothing of man. Here again Luther is completely orthodox, Bouyer argues.

Bouyer further contends that by deriving all his insights from the Bible, and therefore proclaiming the supreme and only authority of Scripture, Luther made a vital and significant spiritual discovery. He questions whether Augustine, Thomas, or Scotus, or even whether post-Tridentine Catholicism would dissent from Luther on the creative authority of Scripture. Bouyer understands the Church as subject to the Word of God, and understands the Church's magisterium as seeking to insure the constant submission of the whole Church to the Word of God.

It is important to the understanding of Bouyer's position to say that after he has stated the positive principles of Luther's reforming zeal, even claiming that these emphases belong to Catholic thinking, he also describes certain negative principles that stand alongside the positive principles but do not belong to them. It was these 'negative elements' that caused the positive and true emphases to separate the movement from the main stream of Catholicism, Bouyer contends: these elements, and not Luther's evangelical theology as such, caused the schism. He states these negative principles precisely: forensic justification, the rejection of good works, the denial of the objective

---

17. All these points, with others, are discussed in subsequent chapters of this book in the context of Luther's 'prophetic' significance for the whole Church.

value of the sacraments, the assertion of the total depravity of man, and the rejection of all ecclesiastical authority.

The question then arises, whence all these 'negative elements'? Bouyer attributes them to Luther's Occamist background, an old theme of Catholic critics. To make of Occamism, however, the scapegoat for the Reformation, and to attribute Luther's 'errors' to that source is unacceptable historically; the argument cannot be supported by hard evidence of Occamist concepts. In fact Occam belongs to the medieval world from which Luther is breaking away. True, Luther was influenced by Occam, and raised 'Occamist' questions, but his discovery of personal religion and his exposition of biblical theology belong wholly and utterly to his rediscovery of God, Christ, and the Holy Spirit—not in his personal questionings as such, but in the unilateral revelation of God and his work in Christ. Therefore, in a real sense, Luther's 'negative' principles belong to his positive principles and may not be separated from them; they are clarifications of the positive principles: the negative elements define and delimit the positive. It is at this point Catholics and Protestants diverge, and where the discussion must be pursued.

*　　*　　*　　*　　*

All that could be said against Luther has been said, full measure and running over. There is not a slur left in the murky field of slander that could be hurled against him; there is not a further epithet left to destroy his character; there is not a further error or heresy left to be levelled against him as a theologian. In these first two chapters we have briefly sketched this process through four and a half centuries, a negative process that has led nowhere: it has not enhanced the Catholic perpetrators, nor has it done the Protestant sufferers any good. It has bred intolerance, fanaticism, and hostility, and created in turn hatred, invective, and division. It has almost destroyed the Christianity both sides love, long to experience, and yearn to give to the world. To all that we turn our backs.

Had I been writing a scant fifty years ago, I would have had to end the story on that grim, sad note of failure, of betrayal, of faith bruised, of hope lost, of love destroyed. Yet, if the reader has followed the story of centuries of hostility and destructive criticism, emerging only in our own century to a Catholic revaluation of Luther expressed in terms of respect and interest, he cannot fail to discern a new and hopeful redirection. Catholic scholarship is now far, far removed from the bitter invective of Cochlaeus and his fellows of the sixteenth century, which eclipsed the sensitive and understanding theology of Staupitz, von Wied, von Gropper, Contarini, and all the other less famous, as well as those who saw Luther as 'an instrument of Providence' and 'a rod from God to the Church's back'; it is far, far removed from the odious scholarship of a Denifle or a Grisar and their fellows of the twentieth century. It has moved into a new way of reassessing Luther by the historical and theological studies of the scholars whose work I have summarised in this chapter, notably, by such men as Lortz, Herte, Merkle, Hessen, and Sartory, and not least by the lesser-known Albrecht Brandenburg.

This academic movement has had, and is having, a profound influence in our universities and theological colleges. Protestant and Catholic students sit side by side before Catholic and Protestant teachers. Similarly, at the ecumenical level, there is interchange of clergy, ministers and priests cooperating in many teaching and missionary activities of the various churches.

It is outside the scope of our considerations here to discuss these things further, but they ought nonetheless to be kept in mind in this connection as highly significant indications of the new life, new light, and new hope that I am addressing in this book. We must keep in mind the powerful influence of the compelling and authoritative leadership of a distinguished line of great popes, beginning with the universally loved and respected Pope John, who called the Second Vatican Council to bring the Church into the present era, and including Paul VI and John Paul II, all of whom together have created a new ecumenical climate and a new vision of the Church and her mission. Admittedly, there is no evidence that John Paul II has any significant knowledge of or sympathy with the evangelical, biblical theology of Luther, but regardless of this, there seems to be no chance that either he or the Roman Catholic Church will ever forsake the gains of Vatican II; this being the case, there is great promise that the authoritative relevance of Luther will continue to be heard.

We turn then from the past to the future, from the analytical study of earlier centuries to the constructive reassessment of what Luther has to say to the Church in the present century that constitutes Part Two of this book. We will explore the resonances of Luther's prophetic voice to the Church of God and reevaluate his constructive and creative relevance. Luther himself as a person has nothing whatever to say to the Church, but the Gospel tones of his prophetic voice will ring down all the ages.

PART TWO

LUTHER'S SIGNIFICANCE FOR THE WHOLE CHURCH

CHAPTER THREE

LUTHER AS THE PROPHETIC REFORMER

WHEN GOD ADDRESSES a human being, and when that person hears and obeys, it is a shattering and terrifying experience. The experience authenticates itself in the truth so given, and the person experiences an almost cataclysmic new birth and a burst of power and energy to declare the fresh truth and make it effective. What is more (and this thesis is central to this book, since it is God who is involved in this experience), God, who has shown his hand, as it were, in both the event and to some extent in the word issuing from the confrontation, gives the historic occasion a significance, even a permanence, for all men for all time. It may be said that the historic occasion has a "cardinal" significance, in the strict sense of *cardo* as a hinge—a hinge round which history turns.

So was it with Martin Luther, as it was with the biblical prophets before him and has been with religious leaders and saints after him. There are no other terms on which Luther may be properly and fully understood and assessed. Of course, a genius of such stature, who committed the medieval world to its grave and who at the same time was midwife to the modern world, has significance for the historian, the linguist, the sociologist, the politician, the musician, and almost every researcher and student. Nevertheless, it must be firmly stated that Luther saw himself only as a theologian, a theologian called by God to bring the Church back from its secularism and materialism to the role God had intended for it in Christ, to restore its original charter and message, to offer *re-formatio* to that which had suffered *de-formatio*. So Luther understood himself: so I understand and interpret him.

God called Luther from a chosen and planned career in law to the life of a religious. Such an unexpected step staggered his family, his friends, his fellow students. What staggered Luther, however, was that when he was expecting a sequestered life of peace and prayer, God harried him and harassed him with doubts, despair, and dreams until he physically collapsed, so fearsome and awesome were the divine disturbances. He did not realise at the time that these experiences were all of God, and all of the love of God. He did not then understand that his darkness was but the shadow of the hand of God as it reached out in love to touch him and bring him to the vocation and mission known only to God himself. As Paul spent years in the Arabian desert before he was fully prepared for the mission for which God had laid his hand upon him, so the young monk Luther was to spend some years yet in the deserts of monasticism before he was ready for the task and mission set him by God.

It may not be too much to claim that to no man since St. Paul had God revealed with such clarity the terrifying and stark otherness of the Gospel in its warm and vital totality; and with that revelation came God's loving and unresting care to win lost man to himself and thereby redeem and restore his Church as the people of God. Here indeed in Luther was the totality of biblical theology given again, opened up once more for the common man to see. Here was all that God intended for mankind, God's Word addressed to man — nothing added, nothing removed; catholicism, pure and complete. There is nothing about this to encourage any kind of Luther cult or Lutheran theology. Luther used to say that he himself was nothing, and that he himself had nothing to offer. He joked of himself that his name was mud (literally true when Luther's name is Latinised — *lutrum*), that he was only 'a bag of worms'. He begged his students never to consider his books and commentaries to be substitutes for the Bible, and to burn them all at his death, lest a Luther cult should ever develop into a kind of Lutheran school of theology and the Word of God fall to the ground once again. 'Let him who boasts, ˙boast of the Lord' (1 Cor. 1.31), warned Paul, and Luther echoed him. He described himself simply as a pointer to Christ.[1]

---

1. There have been greater saints than Luther, and perhaps greater preachers, writers, doctors and theologians: God has never left himself without witness. One could think of the warm, liberal Clement and Origen; of the great evangelical genius Augustine; of the mighty Cappadocian Fathers; of the saintly, though fiery, ascetic Chrysostom; of the many Celtic saints, scholars and missionaries; of the medieval saints and scholars, Francis and Thomas, Anselm and Abelard. But comparisons are odious. What I am arguing here is that to no man was the Gospel

In this rediscovery of the pure Gospel, Luther experienced what he called the "very certainty of life" (*vita certior*), which gave him that compelling and infectious certainty of conviction, the certainty of a man to whom had been revealed the truth from God about man—and with this, *a fortiori*, the truth about God. This may seem to claim too much, to commit the unforgiveable sin of *hubris*, so hated by the gods, so dreaded by the ancient sages, but before the modern reader levels such an accusation, he may be reminded that this is exactly what Christ meant when he spoke of being 'born of God' and 'taught of God', and of 'the truth heard of God' (John 1.13; 6.45; 8.45, et al.). The modern reader may be at a loss to know what Christ meant by these words, but I would ask you to keep an open mind at this point. What is clear is that if we reject Luther at this point, we are rejecting not Luther, but Christ: we are rejecting the Gospel. One is at perfect liberty to reject both Christ and his Gospel, but it is important to understand the implications of such an act. It is to stand with Judas, Caiaphas, and Pilate; with Porphyry and Celsus; with Voltaire and Gibbon; with all our contemporary secularists and atheists, and with all who rejected and reject Christ.

Luther's significance for the twentieth century, indeed for any century, is the same now as it was in the sixteenth: to show the significance of Christ and to open up every age to a living *re-formatio* of what perpetually suffers *de-formatio*. Every church in every age needs cleansing and renewal under God. Luther is poison as much to Protestantism as he is to Catholicism. But he is that curative, beneficent, therapeutic poison that kills not the patient but the Adamic pathogen within the system of the patient that is itself lethal for both the individual and his church. To change the metaphor, we might say that Luther is the salt that alone can preserve the meat of Catholicism.

Yet Catholicism in the form of the papal church rejected its

---

vouchsafed in its totality and immediacy more clearly, more poignantly than it was to Luther. My concern is not to praise Luther but to make clear what he was concerned to say. He has a great deal to say for the healing of the nations and for the mending of the churches. As there is more of the Gospel in Paul than in the Gospels in that it is so incisively expressed, so there is more Gospel in Luther (the second Paul) than in any other Church Father or doctor. And just as Paul divided men into Judaisers and believers, and yet has the secret to unite them (Rom. 9-11), so Luther, who divided Christendom, will yet prove the ground of its unity.

God-given doctor, as Israel rejected Jeremiah (and all the prophets), as Jerusalem would have none of Christ. The dismal pattern repeats itself in every generation. The children put up memorials to the prophets their fathers rejected (Matt. 23.29-38). The important thing is to take heed of these errors, for the future lies with those who do. Hubert Jedin,[2] the great Catholic scholar of the Reformation, concedes that the rejection of Luther by the papacy was an unmitigated tragedy, a position taken up nowadays by a large and telling number of Catholic scholars throughout the world. When the papacy rejected Luther and his teachings, Catholicism then transmuted itself to *Roman* Catholicism, and has not been truly catholic since. Luther belongs to the Catholic Church even though it reject him, exactly as Christ belongs to Judaism, even though Judaism reject him. A further consequence was that those who sought reformation were forced into confessional positions, with a grotesque situation of a church now called 'Lutheran', a most lamentable matter, which Luther never wanted and continually disclaimed. Roman Catholic scholars have further conceded that the Lutheran confessional statement known as the Augsburg Confession of 1530 (written not by Luther but by Melanchthon) is, as was said at the time, 'a pious and true catholic confession.'

A new situation is before us today, and it was brought into being by the Vatican, the last place in the world where one might have expected a new look to begin and a rapprochement to Protestantism to be made. When John XXIII called a council, he expressed the hope that the separated brethren of Protestantism would be brought into Catholicism. Many have taken this to mean that the Protestants would have to return to the fold, and many still take his words in this way. But his words and hopes were more profound than this. He envisaged a renewed and reformed Catholicism that could incorporate evangelical theology into itself and thereby allow the Luther protest finally to fulfil itself by restoring the Roman Catholic Church to one truly holy catholic Church. It cannot become this until and unless it takes to itself the total witness of Luther for the Gospel, as well as his entire evangelical theology.

The refusal by the Curia in the sixteenth century to allow the

---

2. For a significant assessment of the influence of Jedin on Catholic research into the Reformation, see John O'Malley's essay "Catholic Reform" in *Reformation Europe*, ed. Steven Ozment (St. Louis, 1982), pp. 297-319.

Luther protest to reach its full head *within* Catholicism impoverished Catholicism by that amount, a fact affirmed today by a growing
body of Catholic scholars (and humble priests and laity, for that
matter). A further effect of such refusal was the outbreak of a confessionalism in all Protestant areas — Switzerland, Germany, Holland,
Denmark, Norway, Sweden, Finland, England, and Scotland. This
confessional movement should not be considered sectarianism or
heretical. It arose only as a second stage within the Lutheran movement, and then only when Catholicism had rejected outright Luther's theological insights, excommunicated him, and put him under
the imperial ban along with all those who followed him (even anybody who might offer him shelter, food, or drink). Yet Luther was
in no sense a heretic, though admittedly there are certain emphases
in Luther's theology (e.g., the special office of a priest, the nature
of penance, and the doctrine of the Eucharist) that Catholicism
found (and still finds) unacceptable. Nevertheless, Luther's theology
was biblical and catholic and should never have been the cause of
a divided Christendom.

The later confessional movement (carried through by Lutherans
rather than by Luther) was still a movement to preserve the full
catholic faith on a basis of Scripture, patristic tradition, and com-
monsense reason directed all too often against what is now the *Roman* Catholic position. It was actually a Catholic movement in the
true sense of that word, a position agreed upon by many catholic
scholars since the Lutheran/Catholic conferences of 1980 celebrat-
ing the 450th anniversary of the Augsburg Confession of 1530.

If Luther is brought to a new appreciation within Catholicism,
as is happening today, a radical question is thereby set for Protestantism, a question already put time and again particularly by those
Protestant theologians engaged in the ecumenical movement. These
men have always seen that confessional statements make frontiers,
and that such definitions tend to take on the nature of a static and
authoritative statement, often conceptualised, to which people are
expected to subscribe and give assent. Further, these confessional
positions all too easily became identified with a particular nation,
an establishment, a culture, or a monarch. Many of the distinctive
features are cultural or accidental, and are nearly always nontheological. Can Luther be brought out of such confessionalism? If he
is so delivered, he will fulfil his destiny in effecting the Reformation
today, and the renewed Catholicism will thereby be made truly cath-

olic and placed in a position to offer the total Gospel to the whole world.

It is worth reflecting for a moment on the role of the ecumenical movement in all this. More than seventy years have passed since Christian men and women began to search for a truly worldwide catholicism, which they approached in the establishment of the World Council of Churches. Yet this movement has forked out into two lines of activity. The one has conceptualised Christianity and goes on endlessly discussing various denominational concepts as theological ideas. The other has branched out into activism, in which Christianity is politicised and socialised and made into an ideology. The first is running out into arid theological discussions, the other into de-theologised social activity, such as the financial support of guerilla activities in Zimbabwe and the self-styled 'freedom fighters' in South and Central America and elsewhere. Neither movement will get Christendom anywhere beyond its present position. The true ecumenical movement has been initiated by Vatican II, which has given the preexisting ecumenical movement a new orientation. If present-day Roman Catholicism will meet Luther in his emphasis on the Gospel and in his total range of evangelical theology, it will once again become true catholicism, and the Protestant confessional emphases will become the framework of a totally new evangelical catholic Church: Luther is the only ecumenical hope, and the only future for Protestantism, or Catholicism.

Luther's significance is not a matter of his own personal qualities any more than Paul's was a matter of his. It is true that Luther was a religious genius, a theological giant with a superb mastery of language and of languages, a preacher who towers over all other preachers, but these virtues are not to the point. His real significance derives from the fact that no man since Paul had been so seized by the power of the Gospel, and with that the total grasp of the biblical theology of God's unfailing grace in Christ. This was given him by God. This he offered to his Church. This his Church rejected. One consequence of that rejection was a lamed Catholicism, self-styled (and rightly so) as *Roman* Catholicism, and thereby no longer truly catholic. The other consequence was a confessional Lutheranism, regionalised, Germanicised, nationalised. God has clearly shown us (or, if that is too strong a statement for some, then we might at least say that time has shown us) that these were disastrous consequences, not only for the Church as a whole, but for both Lutheranism and

Catholicism separately. The whole Church of today, Protestant as well as Catholic, must go forward to Luther to find again the Gospel and to offer this to a world growing ever more worldly, a world not knowing where it is going, a world fearing the future. Here is a matter we should all look into together on this five hundredth anniversary of Luther's birth.

In this book I am attempting to clarify the true concerns of Luther, attempting to show that in some unique way, not on account of his person, but on account of God, he is ever present in the Church of God. Above the altar in the town church of Wittenberg, where Luther for twenty-five years preached the Gospel in a way never done since Paul, Cranach painted Luther standing in a pulpit, his outstretched finger pointing to Christ. That picture stands there today, a kind of haunting and foreboding presence in that dark church. That is the significance of Luther for the Church: a perpetual reminder of what God did in Christ. He often described himself as a *Wegweiser*, a pathfinder. Luther will make Roman Catholicism truly catholic once more, and thereby bring all the emphases of the Protestant confessional statements within the totality of Christendom.

I am not speaking here merely of the restoration of unity to Christendom though that would be a source of incalculable blessings, since it would empower Christianity to speak the big language of national and international unity to a humanity torn and divided against itself on every political, economic, and sociological difference. But unity would be little more than an added blessing issuing from true relationships, from the strength of which Christianity could offer to humanity a true explanation of peace and unity, and the reason for the discord and disunity in which we are all daily compelled to live. The real point at issue for both Catholicism and Protestantism is the shared recovery of the total Gospel with the entire evangelical theology which is the experience of the Gospel expressed in communicable terms that would result from such a restoration of unity.

The historian, the humanist, the politician, the sociologist, the linguist (even the psychologist now) all show an interest in Luther— naturally, since his birth saw the death of the old world, and his death the birth of the new, the world we now live in, and more than any other person, his life contributed to that change. He restored to Christianity its native biblical theology, an experience that Christendom found so cataclysmic that half of it shrank back and sank into its old ways. Sovereign states arose, a new capitalist economy emerged, a new society struggled to be born; all of these occurrences were inextricably bound up with Luther's new ideas of religion, his ideas of freedom and independence. He gave the German people a new German language, and translated for them the Bible into an incomparable German they quickly learned to call their own. Men will naturally and legitimately examine all these matters and write their books on these aspects of Luther and his influence.

Luther's only concern was (as my concern in this book is) to tell his Church about Christ and the power of the Gospel. But the great pain of such a divine commission is that though it is the ultimate wisdom, the truth supreme over all truths, the world in its wisdom is unable to discern such truth, and naturally rejects it for appearing to conflict with its own wisdom. This situation was faced by Paul within twenty years of the death of Jesus (see 1 Cor.), and will be with us to the end of time. Christians think and see not in the spirit of this world, which spirit every person has, but in the spirit that is of God, so that they might know the things that are freely given us of God (1 Cor. 2.12), yet a spirit given only by God and never found by our own strivings. Luther argued that the natural man must be converted before he can see and know. Man had to be freed from himself and his own interests, from his own prejudices and presuppositions, before he could know the truth in itself, the truth *as it comes to him in Christ* and *makes itself known to him*, the truth as God sees it and expresses it, the truth that shall set men free, the truth as it is in Christ. This is what Christ meant when he said that if anybody was to be his follower or disciple, he must first 'deny himself'. The natural man cannot receive the things given by the Spirit of God, for in his own light and wisdom, true enough in themselves, they seem foolishness to him. He cannot even understand them, for they are discerned and differentiated only in the light of the gift of faith by God. This is what Luther offers to the churches, Catholic and Protestant alike.

The researches of historians, sociologists, linguists, and political scientists into Luther and his significance (i.e. the academic research of the natural man) are all valid enough, valid as interesting cross-lights on the picture. The true Luther, however, the real Luther, *the one he would recognise for himself* were he to return to the twentieth-century scene, is the Luther of the theologians, not he of the social scientists. It is this Luther, the religious Luther, who now addresses the Church both in its Catholic and its Protestant forms, the *Lutherus Praesens*, the Luther ever-present. Like Paul, he can be discerned and understood not by the natural man in the light of his own wisdom, but only by the spiritual man, the man moved by the Holy Spirit of God. (1 Cor. 2.12-14).

May I be permitted a brief excursus into the Bible to throw a considerable light on this argument of Luther's role?

When God called Abraham to leave country and kindred for the Promised Land and he responded in faith, a new beginning was made in history. The people of God were established. Similarly with Moses when he was called from following the sheep: he brought the faithful back to the Promised Land and gave his people the Law — not simply *laws*, which other nations such as the Egyptians, the Assyrians and Persians, and other civilisations wrote for themselves and are now one with Nineveh and Tyre, but *the Law* that came from God and is significant for all humanity and for all time. Similarly with the prophets, of whom Jeremiah may be taken as the best example. Ordained by God Himself (Jer. 1.5) as a prophet to the nations, he called faithless Israel back to its true habitation, where God's Law would be not simply obeyed but written on their hearts. And similar, too, was the work of Christ: he fulfilled the Law in the Gospel by showing that in the eyes of God no man could keep God's Law, and that the only relationship to God was evangelical (i.e., based on the Gospel), wherein a man was opened to the grace of God in forgiveness. In the interests of the God-given Law, Paul furiously resisted this Gospel, but God resisted him in a shattering and blinding experience. It took him some years to come to terms with this experience, in which he was given 'the gospel of Jesus Christ, the Son of God' (Mark 1.1), but when he had, he emerged as Christ's own apostle, who established God's people in faith, where there was neither Jew nor Greek, male nor female, bond nor free.

These men are selected as examples: Abraham, the founder of all the people of God — Jews, Muslims, Christians, all men eventually — taken by God to give us this truth, round which the history of the world turns as on a hinge; Moses, actually confronted by God face to face, to give his people the Law and a land; Jeremiah, prophet of all prophets, recalling men to a true reformation, of theology and ethics, issuing neither from king nor clergy, but from God alone;

and Paul, who showed the total content of the Gospel in fulfilment of the Law.

The one important point to see in these examples is that these men had a terrifying confrontation by God himself, described in unique terms: a bush that burned without being consumed, voices and visions other than of human dimensions, awareness terrifying and awesome, beyond man's usual vocabulary. The significance of these meetings of God with man is that God, unknown and hidden, is addressing his creation in and through a person he has chosen, and that what God does and says in such meetings belongs not simply to the historical events per se, nor to that person per se, but to all time and all humanity. In general terms it can be argued that God is responsible for all history, but what is said here is that in these particular events, the hidden and unknown God shows his hand and speaks his mind. To use German terms, it is to show the *geschichtliche* in the *historische*. It is to discern the significant event in all the rich confusion of historical actuality, to detect, amid all that just happens, those events that give meaning to history.

Abraham is the father of all spiritual men. Moses the permanent moral guide. The prophets teach us all, and show all of us the abyss of institutionalism, legalism, spiritual pride, and religious rationalism and fanaticism. Christ is God's final Word to his creation; 'Hear Him!', God says in a 'voice from heaven'. Paul clarified all this, and was made 'the Apostle to the nations'. These events are historical, but also more than historical, for they interpret the meaning of all history for all time for all men.

Luther stands in this line of the significant men chosen by God to speak to his contemporaries, and on the grounds of that call, to be significant to all subsequent generations. In no sense does he derive his significance from his abilities and powers, awesome though they were, but simply from the fact that God chose him to give again to the Church and world of his day the God-given Gospel; furthermore, it is only on this ground that men of the Spirit see and understand this significance. It is in this sense that Luther may be described as a prophet to the whole state of Christ's Church. He offered to a Church that had suffered *de*-formation a *re*-formation under the power of the Holy Ghost, and inspired them to see that this would be a continuing process alike for those who accepted reformation and for those who rejected it.

Those readers who will grant this one presupposition will not only find that all the historical facts of the Reformation yield a meaning and begin to cohere, but they will also begin to discern that it offers positive principles and joyous hope in interpreting the events of today. They will experience the joy of a scientist, of an Archimedes or a Galileo, who will cry out to the world, 'This is the way things really are! Just look at the evidence!'

WHAT RESPONSIBLE REFORMATION MEANS

The Reformation should be seen in terms of a *Christological corrective*: a movement seeking to reform the Church along the lines of Christ's original teaching and purposes by submitting all the Church's thinking and doing to the light of the Gospel. The Reformers were never innovators, but renovators, as the scholarly John Jewel, bishop of Salisbury (1522-71), expressed it. They sought to re-form what had been de-formed.

Historians are bound to describe the Reformation in terms the Reformers used, particuarly in terms of the later confessional statements, but it should never be forgotten that these confessional statements arose only because the actual live movement of reform was rejected and banned. The confessional statements represent a hardening out of the original movement and are expressed in defensive or polemical terms. By far the most serious result of the Protestant movement was that it was largely conceptualised, made into a defined dogmatic position, to which one can give assent or not as one chooses. This is a far cry from the original work of Luther, as it is a far cry from the New Testament. Luther never offered the Church anything new; he only showed it what it already possessed, the Gospel, which the Church he now reluctantly opposed had nevertheless still preserved and given him. He brought the Church back to the living reality of Christ: this is what it means to see the Reformation as a *Christological corrective*. To find a true idea of the Reformation, to know what the Reformation is concerned to maintain, one must look behind the confessional statements in which later it was to express itself in controversy, to those early years when Luther saw the light and believed all men would welcome it, even the Jews. Contemporary, confessional Protestantism bears about as much relation to Luther's Protestantism as the Christianity of the Borgia popes and their court bears to Christ teaching his disciples on the shores of Galilee.

Thoughtful men will realise that genuine revival, renewal, and reformation is never fanatical, revolutionary, or destructive, but restorative and creative. It is done in love, never in hate. Man has never made proper religious advance by turning his back on the past. No genuine religious revival has ever been a wholly new departure. True religious revivalists open men's minds to what they already have. Though men tend to crave for what is modern or novel or fashionable, responsible reformers offer what is abiding and eternal. Old Testament prophets recalled men to the promises and hope of that which God in his grace and mercy had already given them in the Law, and implored them to turn aside from the corrupt idolatry that passed for worship and religion among them in order to return to a true relationship with the living God.

'Is it not even thus, O ye children of Israel?' (Amos 2.11) Amos asked Israel when they rejected the prophets sent by God. Isaiah likewise addressed himself to a people who had forsaken God and gone backward (Isa. 1.4), yet were the seed of Abraham, God's friend (Isa. 41.8). Jeremiah said to his people, 'The prophets prophesy falsely, and the priests bear rule by their means; and my people love to have it so; and what will ye do in the end thereof?' (Jer. 5.31). He saw their only hope as the fresh writing of the old covenant in their hearts (Jer. 31.33). He saw his people as those who had rejected God and were but sheep lost on the mountains (Jer. 50.6), a people who had forsaken the fountain of living waters and had hewed out for themselves cisterns, broken cisterns unable to hold the water. He finally offered the hope that they would once again ask their way homeward (Jer. 50.5), be restored to the habitation where they belonged (Jer. 30.18), and join themselves 'to the Lord in a perpetual covenant that shall not be forgotten' (Jer. 50.5). 'Ask for the old paths and the good way' (Jer. 6.16), he besought lost and confused Israel on the eve of their humiliation and mass deportation.

Christ himself identified his mission and message with God's divine activity in history. He came not to destroy the Law or the prophets, but to fulfil them (Matt. 5.17), and every disciple was like a wise householder bringing out things new and old (Matt. 13.52). The apostles, most notably John and Paul, saw the clear divine fulfilment of the Law in the Gospel. So did Luther, who simply pointed men to what was already there, and in doing so made possible the disposal of all manner of worthless spiritual trinkets and ecclesiastical bric-a-brac. He sought only to redeem the Church by restoring to it the totality and freshness of the Gospel. It was this that awakened those who would listen. He called them back to the pattern of grace clearly visible from Abraham onwards, alerting them to God's mercy and love when he finally showed his hand in Christ. He called them back to be the true Church and to fulfil in the world the mission demanded of it by God.

In every age *God is the Reformer* who calls his church to reform. Any conception of the Reformation must capture this divine dimension of God's undying love for his Creation, this positive winning drive of the Gospel and of evangelical theology, the truth of Christ's words, 'Fear not, my little ones, it is your Father's good pleasure to give you the Kingdom' (Luke 12.32). We should think less of abuses and scandals (the all-too-human feature of all churches, Protestant no less than Catholic), and more of the winning truth of the Gospel, of joy in believing, of love in action. Only a man who loves the Church may dare to reform it, and then only under God. All the men God called to the fray were in the first instance reluctant to come forward, but when they heard the awesome and unmistakable voice of God and obeyed, victory was assured, for it was God's cause, not theirs. As Paul perfectly expressed it, 'Faithful is he that calleth, who will also perform it' (1 Thess. 5.24).

We must at all costs preserve this divine drive of the Reformation, understanding it to be a kind of reform that is categorically different from that which a new headmaster might institute in a school, or a new librarian in an old and neglected library, or a new rector in a moribund parish. There is quite a religious ferment today: new translations of the Bible, new liturgies and prayer books, new synodical government, new liberations in sexual mores, new initiatives from the Vatican following the Council and inspired by a series of great popes deeply concerned about the Gospel.[3] So im-

---

3. I am all too intensely aware of contemporary economic and political crises as well, not to mention cultural and philosophical upheaval, movements that most people would describe as more serious than any crisis in theology. I make no comparisons; it is simply the case that I have limited my area of enquiry to theology, which is itself no insignificant part of the larger reality, and indeed provides a unique perspective upon the whole.

portant are these movements that they have been of interest to even the secular press. Loud calls have been issued in recent years for a New Reformation. Yet it is important to distinguish between the Reformation inspired by Luther, which has yet to reach its fulfilment, and all the reforming schemes afoot today.

Many of the current reform movements seek a fresh theology in terms of contemporary ideologies, expressed in a way contemporary man can understand and is prepared to accept. The motive for reaching de-Christianised secular man is laudable, but they seek to modify the approach of traditional Christianity: they begin with man rather than with God, and seek truth in the depth of man's own being rather than in the God who addresses man. This may well end in a faith without foundations, in a kind of existentialist commitment. Such was never Luther's concern. He offered a Reformation seeking a greater and deeper fulness of the traditional faith: he offered more, not less. He never questioned that reformation must proceed within the framework of Christendom's historical development. He was humbly aware that Christian truth is infinitely greater than the pronouncement of any church council, of any pope, of any church doctor, of any reformer. Like Paul, he counted himself as having not yet apprehended; he simply pressed on, under God, to God, for God. He rejected the heteronomy of Rome, as well as the autonomy of learning, and accepted the theonomy of the Gospel. He would concede infallibility to no authority other than the objective revelation of God in his Word.

Catholic scholars never make a greater mistake than when they condemn Luther for his 'subjectivity': he never referred to his own private judgment; neither has authentic Protestantism made this error. He does not talk about himself, but about God. He is not like Erasmus, spinning edifying and witty tales, nor like Thomas More, writing about an impossible Utopia. There is a profound earnestness and seriousness about Luther. He knew he had a divine commission and only a few years within which to fulfil it. He knew nothing save Christ. Even at table he shared the most devastating theological sallies and the wittiest and tenderest perceptions of the Gospel. Students and professors alike waited on him, notebooks in hand, to catch for all time those precious pearls of theological insight so freely scattered in joyous spontaneity.

Torrance[4] draws some parallels between Athanasius[5] and Luther; that he is correct in doing so would seem to be substantiated by Luther's powerful interest in and close knowledge of the Greek Fathers.[6] The early church, however, stopped short of Luther's propositional formulation of truth, conceived as a kind of safeguard of truth revealed; it did not (perhaps it saw no cause to) carry through its Christological work into the whole realm of the Church's thinking, and living, and worshipping. This is exactly what Luther undertook. He argued that in Christ God had done all that he could, that in Christ God in his entirety was at work. This theology galvanised current doctrines of grace.

For too long—since Ignatius[7] in fact—the Church had been too ready to conceive grace in terms of a 'thing', a commodity—as, for example, in the terms 'the medicine of immortality' or 'the bread of life'. These terms are lovely in themselves, but their actual imagery and poetry can serve to distance men from the living Christ, the consuming reality who gives them their meaning.

Luther stepped beyond Athanasius. He took seriously his *homoousion* language (i.e., of Christ being incarnate yet one with God) and carried it through into the realm of grace. He argued that grace was not *something* God communicated, like milk poured into a jug, but was none other than the living, active, working Christ, no less than *God communicating himself to us.*[8] It was this insight that effected the transition from static, conceptual, propositional, intellectual theology to a theology that was dynamic, personal, biblical— a theology that in its real objectivity stood over against the Church as a challenge, a challenge felt by many to be a threat. This aware-

---

4. Thomas F. Torrance, *Theology in Reconstruction* (London: SCM Press, 1965), pp. 259-83.

5. The Greek Father who maintained orthodoxy at the Council of Nicea 325, defeated the heretics, and gave Christendom the Nicene Creed.

6. Adolf Harnack makes the colourful and discerning comment that Luther joined hands with Athanasius across the centuries (*Lehrbuch der Dogmengeschichte* [Frieburg i. B.: J. C. B. Mohr, 1890-94], 3:814.

7. Saint Ignatius (35?-107?), Bishop of Antioch, who, on his way to martyrdom in Rome, wrote several significant letters to the churches of Asia Minor, giving unique information on Church order and doctrine.

8. It was his close study of Augustine that gave Luther this evangelical insight, almost lost in the medieval church. See Augustine, *Patrologia Latina*, ed. J. Migne (Paris, 1884ff.), and Erich Przywara's *An Augustinian Synthesis* (London, 1936).

ness of God as a God who intervenes in history as its Creator, Preserver, and Redeemer appeared as a disturbing challenge both to Renaissance man in his intellectual self-sufficiency and to Catholic man, who was taught to identify truth with the Church. It is a tragedy of history that Lutheran orthodoxy was soon to put the liberated Lutheran into a straitjacket just as confining as that from which Luther had freed him, as we shall come to see.

The effect of Luther's thinking was to shift the centre of gravity away from the priority of *thought* to the priority of *being* — that is, to truth not so much *known* and conceptualised, but objectively *experienced* in history and life.[9] Rome sought the certainty and security of identifying truth on terms that it dictated. Luther argued that the unredeemed man must be converted before he can see and know; man has to be freed from himself and his own interests, from his own prejudices and presuppositions before he can know the truth in itself, as it comes to him and makes itself known to him. True knowledge of this kind requires obedience to God and total submission to the ways he has revealed himself to us in history. Luther's theology was shattering to the Church precisely because he carried through his theological perceptions into the sphere of church practice and everyday living. He set Christ in the centre in the theological schools, Christ in the centre of our everyday life. Had his theology remained a debate among academics, Luther would have had no more significance than any other of the many learned German professors of theology of his day. By pursuing it to its proper end, he lifted Christianity off its hinges and rehung it. There lies his permanence, his abiding significance for all time and for the whole Church.

---

9. Jesus used the phrase '*doing* the truth' (John 3.21).

CHAPTER FOUR

THE CATHOLIC LUTHER AND CONFESSIONAL LUTHERANISM

THOMAS CRANMER UNDERTOOK the reformation of the Church of God in Britain until that favourable time when God would grant a universal reform and renewal of the Church in its entirety (i.e., true catholic reform). To him, as to all the principal continental Reformers (Anabaptist and left-wing revolutionaries excepted), Protestantism was a quest for true catholicism, for solidarity with the catholic Church that Jesus founded. With a view to calling a general council in Britain in order to establish a true and peaceful Reformation on biblical, traditional, and catholic principles, he wrote to virtually every Reformer—to Vadian, à Lasco, Hardenberg, Bucer, Melanchthon, Bullinger, and Calvin—some several times.[1] For this, he had the support of both Henry VIII and Edward VI, but, most regrettably for the true cause of reformation as well as for ecumenical theology, the accession of Mary put a violent end to such hopes. Cranmer further made his purposes clear in his appeal at his degradation in Oxford, where he argued that reformation would never come from the Bishop of Rome, and therefore called for 'a free general council' to which he might freely and safely appeal.[2]

Would one be too bold in prophecying that future historians will see in the calling of the Second Vatican Council of 1962-63 the arrival—or the dawn, at least—of Cranmer's longed-for catholic reformation? It might at least be said that at the Second Vatican

---

1. See John Edmund Cox, ed., *The Works of Thomas Cranmer, Archbishop of Canterbury*, Parker Society Edition (Cambridge: At the University Press, 1886), 2:240ff.

2. Ibid., 2:224-28; see especially p. 227.

Council, for the first time since the death of Luther, Rome had finally left behind over four centuries of discreditable history and come to terms with reality. In the sixteenth century Rome had simply anathematised Luther. In the eighteenth century, when the *Aufklaerung* shed its light across Europe, Roman Catholic leaders and thinkers received a new and second threat in the form of the questions modern thought was putting to all Christian theologians, Catholic and Protestant alike. The nineteenth century sharpened these questions — questions concerning the origin of man and his evolution and the nature of man and society in the light of what Marx and Freud were saying, questions of simple historical enquiry and evidence, questions about the authorship and historicity of the books of the Bible. For a century Rome had faced this threat in the same authoritarian way it had answered Luther, with condemnation and anathematisation. Official apologists of the Church had either ignored the problems or provided final and authoritative answers that no genuinely informed person could regard as satisfactory. A worse aspect of this mentality, manifested more markedly in the attitude to Luther and the Protestants than to modernist thinkers, was to pursue with special hostility those Roman Catholics who offered criticism, showed doubt, or attempted to take a different line from the official. Rome still claimed to be the infallible source of all truth.

When the much-loved and universally respected Pope John XXIII called the Second Vatican Council, two far-reaching changes were inaugurated. First, it was decided that the Church would no longer attempt to keep out or avoid the questions that the outside world was putting to it; and second, it was decided that the Protestants, hitherto anathematised as heretics, would henceforth be referred to as 'separated brethren', as still somehow belonging to the Church, though now separated from it. This was a far cry from the days when the Pope demanded the charismatic monk of Wittenberg be delivered to him at Rome in chains, when the Dominicans demanded fire and faggot, when the monk stood before the Emperor to be rejected and banned. This change of attitude may indeed turn out to be the most significant event since the birth of Luther five hundred years ago. Such a statement must be justified and examined, but it needs stating categorically and without qualification.

Many of the old fathers summoned to the Second Vatican

Council were eagerly anticipating some further pronouncement on Mary, but they were to find a very different spirit abroad. Too many had become convinced that the Church could no longer refuse to deal with the questions that the outside world was raising. Too many Roman Catholic scholars knew that the questions had to be faced and could no longer be avoided. Too many of these good and godly men were all too aware that the questions Luther had put to the Church had yet to be answered. Since that day the great majority of Roman Catholic Christians have become aware that modern thought presents grave questions to the Christian faith, not just to Roman Catholicism, and that if that challenge is to be met properly, the traditional faith will need to undergo considerable reassessment. This had been realised by Protestants since Luther, but until Vatican II the Roman Catholic Church had officially regarded the efforts of other Christian scholars as simply heretical.

Most Roman Catholic scholars freely admit that the faith needs to find fresh forms of expression to meet the questions put to it by the advances in thought in recent centuries. The evidence is clear. There are books and articles published by Roman Catholic scholars today that fifty years ago would have been censored, but that today meet with no disapproval from the Vatican. Virtually all of today's gatherings of theological scholars will contain a significant complement of much-loved and respected Roman Catholic scholars, whereas only twenty-five years ago a Roman Catholic scholar had to ask his bishop's permission to attend such theological meetings (and the permission was generally withheld). Even senior nuns had to seek permission to attend a university extension lecture. And in fact I recall that at this time Catholic students attending the University of Sheffield were not permitted to read Biblical Studies. All this is past. It is generally admitted among thinking Roman Catholics and Protestants that they have a great deal to learn from one another, particularly in the field of critical biblical scholarship and contemporary theology. In fact, joint research and study over a wide field, along with joint teaching at university, have become commonplace for Roman Catholic and Protestant scholars; Protestant students attend Roman Catholic seminary lectures and vice versa.

What this all means — and it is important to emphasise it — is that informed and responsible Roman Catholics and Protestants alike freely admit that we all face the same problems, are up against the same difficulties, and undergo the same crises. Protestant and Catholic are on the same side; both have surrendered the smug assumption that they have an absolute guarantee of a final authoritative answer to all questions. We all wrestle with the same problems, and it is high time we realised that only together will we find more penetrating and creative answers to the questions all theologians are facing, Catholic and Protestant alike.

These facts are staggering enough in themselves. Twenty years ago no one would have thought them possible. Yet they have come to pass. The most staggering fact of all, however, is that virtually the whole Roman Catholic community has gone along with this movement. True, there have been, and still are, pockets of resistance in certain conservative areas (Ireland, parts of France, and Mexico, for instance), but this is scarcely surprising. After all, if people have been taught for generations that Protestants are heretics and schismatics, and that it is a sin worthy of the confessional even to enter a Protestant building, it is hard for them to have to see these people overnight as 'brethren separated by the accidents of history'. All they need is time. Yet it cannot be denied that many have hearkened to the new voice and obeyed. It means that the old policy of triumphalism and exclusivism is behind us, as far behind as the scandals of the Borgias.

The span of a generation has seen unprecedented changes in the Roman Catholic Church. In the first place, no pope may ever again rely on the automatic submission and obedience of every Catholic on his own authoritative statement. This was shown by the publication of the encyclical *Humanae Vitae* in 1967, for instance, wherein the Pope gave express commands to the faithful in the matter of contraception: I have carefully consulted with many Catholic women, all of whom are committed, even devout Catholics, and they confidently advise me that perhaps only one half of their number in Western Europe and America follow the Pope's ruling, though in the less developed countries it is more generally obeyed. This would seem to suggest that henceforth a papal statement is not likely to command obedience merely by virtue of its source, but only if it convinces the individual believer by the pure weight and self-evident authoritativeness of its content. People who disregard papal direction nevertheless continue to consider themselves loyal Catholics, notwithstanding their disobedience.

A second major change to have been recently introduced is that the Roman Catholic Church may no longer claim to have the final and authoritative answer to all problems. Examples of the error of this claim may be seen in this century in, for example, the papal encyclical on modernism, or Marxism, but a more flagrant one can be seen in the Biblical Commission instituted by Leo XIII in 1902 for the dual purpose of furthering biblical studies in conformity with the demands of modern scholarship and safeguarding the authority of the Bible against uncontrolled criticism. Some of its notable decisions concern the Mosaic authorship of the Pentateuch (1906), the authenticity and historicity of the Fourth Gospel (1907), and the Synoptic Problem (1912). The decisions of the Commission do not claim infallibility but are binding in conscience under pain of grave fault, which means they command both the exterior and interior assent of the clergy and the faithful. The Commission provided the prompt and precise answers expected of it to all the questions set before it, but almost everybody with any critical biblical expertise considers the answers to be largely in error. In a manner parallel to the modification of the authority of the pope, the position now is that guidance on biblical and theological matters will have to be seen to be true by the faithful themselves, and may no longer be asserted by authority.

A third momentous change is that the Roman Catholic Church will no longer assume the proud and magisterial role of being the only true Church, and thereby deny the churchly status of all other Christians. It is ceasing to be the triumphal Church and playing more the role of the servant church: no longer *domina* but *ancilla*, not mistress but handmaid. It is still true that it does not recognise other churches as full and proper churches, as parts of the catholic Church, but it is manifest to all that the old exclusive spirit is fast disappearing. Cooperation and friendliness prevail everywhere — in universities, in parishes, in pastoral and social concerns, at all levels.

Now this movement, inaugurated by Pope John XXIII some short twenty years ago, was called by him the *aggiornamento*, a bringing up of Catholicism into present-day realities. One of the points I wish to make in this book is that this movement has an implication for the whole of Christendom and is not a merely Roman Catholic activity. A remarkable feature of this movement is that the four-century-old antithesis between Catholicism and Protestantism is virtually at an end, or is at least totally transformed. Catholics are becoming more like Protestants: they are now keen students of the Bible, their priests preach the Word of God in a way known only in Protestantism hitherto, and they are concerned about the charismatic movement, even holding prayer meetings at home in a way only zealous Protestants were wont to do. Similarly, Protestants are becoming more like Catholics, particularly in the area of liturgy and worship, as well as in spirituality and in the religious life. Protestant men and women listen carefully to radio and television broadcasts of Roman Catholic services and talks nowadays, and pay as close attention to the statements of the Pope and his cardinals as they do to their own church leaders. They read Catholic books on spirituality and on theology. Other movements have brought them nearer, too, such as the rise of a militant, aggressively totalitarian and atheistic Communism; the earlier growth of Nazism and its tyrannical domination in Europe; the persecution of intellectuals and Christian characteristic of these totalitarian regimes; the rise of a materialist consumer society and the concomitant impoverishment of the Third World; the development of a permissive society with its decadent morality; a growing concern for the environment; a more tender conscience for the welfare of the aged, the handicapped, the defenceless, the little children. All these movements have contributed to convincing Catholics and Protestants not only that they have far more to unite than to divide them, but that they both stand together over against a secularised world, and together have a great deal to offer to a lost society.

It is precisely at this point that Luther's significance comes into its own. The Church of his day could not carry or accommodate such a prophet, but Luther now has a provisional place at least in the Catholic Church again. This is not seen by everybody in the Catholic Church. It is in fact a secret known only to the few. There must again be a place for the rejected monk, the suffering preacher of sin, grace, and God's work on the Cross. Now is the moment for the Church to receive Luther. His preaching is truly valid and fully real only in the ecumenical discussion now opening up before us. No Church is complete if it does not hold in its view the other. Such is the totality of those who confess Christ: such is the new catholicity.

How would Luther restore that full catholicity? What is his

significance for Christendom? If Roman Catholicism finds it too much to take in Luther all at once, let it begin in stages, and let all the other churches hear again that prophetic reforming voice. Let us all hear together — the entire Church in its totality.

It is manifest from all the evidence that Luther protested as a Catholic within the Catholic Church: he sought *re-formation* of that which had suffered *de-formation.* He wanted his Church to be truly and fully catholic and to take within itself again the pure Gospel. This the Church of his day rejected. If today, in the wake of Vatican II, Luther were to be received by the Church and his teaching fully integrated into it, there would be a conclusion and culmination of Luther's protest: the Church would be truly catholic and evangelical. All down the centuries Luther has been interpreted in many different ways, most often from a confessional point of view, but never from an ecumenical perspective that seeks to set him where he belonged, namely in the Church in its totality. It is my plea here that we might *understand him in this total setting,* rather than in the narrower confessional setting; it is only now, in the new era following Vatican II that this has been possible. It is my wish not so much to present you with a survey of the essential evangelical teaching of Luther, but to lead you in an exercise of trying to understand that teaching in its true natural setting and in relation to catholicity. I steadfastly maintain that a final, valid, legitimate, complete, and unique interpretation of Luther emerges only when all he thought, said, wrote, and did is set in its relation to a total catholicity. This is how it all happened in the sixteenth century, but when it was rejected, the earnest and devout monk was compelled to continue to express it all as a protest against the Church he loved and that had given him birth. Only now, only since 1963, can Luther's thinking be brought into a living and creative relationship with catholicity. If Luther be seen and studied in this context, he comes into his own with respect to his calling as a prophetic theologian of the whole Church. It further explains why Luther actually happened, as it were, and what the whole nature of his religious experience actually amounts to.

Let us seek to justify this claim. When Luther's teaching is discussed in the circle of Catholic scholars in sympathy with the new Catholic interpretation that has followed Vatican II, a quite astonishing convergence begins to take place. Consider, for example, the old divisive argument about Scripture and tradition that has so deeply separated Catholics from Protestants, in which the latter claimed *sola scriptura* while rejecting tradition as less authoritative. Yet, such a polarised view falsifies the true position today, for, on closer analysis it is found not to be the case that the authority of Scripture is the prerogative of Protestantism. Catholics equally hold the unique authority of Scripture, and see tradition as comment or clarification of Scripture. They do not now put tradition *above* Scripture; rather, they see the Word of God at work in the ongoing life of the Church. Other matters that have been problems between the two churches are now looked at in quite a different light as well. Luther theology is in fact much closer to the theology of the new Catholicism than is generally understood. This convergence is most striking and most stimulating to those engaged in such enquiry.

But for real proximity, almost harmonisation, between Lutheran thinking and post-conciliar Catholic theology, one should look less at the distinctively Lutheran doctrines (i.e., at Luther's way of understanding the Christian faith) than beyond them to the *actualisation* of the faith in the believer's life—for instance, to his buoyant, infectious, confident belief in God and his Gospel revealed in Christ, to the unique dynamic of this theology of the Cross, to his teaching on repentance, and to his preaching on the hiddenness of God. We need only to listen to his sensitive handling of sin and its forgiveness and the quieting of the troubled conscience, his joyous awareness of the grace of God, his distinction between Christianity as security (*securitas*) and as certainty (*certitudo*), his brave facing of death with the message of hope and future glory.

Luther does not impose heavy doctrinal interpretations of Scripture in these areas, but rather speaks in soft, new, simple accents, offering fresh impulses to the ministry of preaching, giving new ground for hope, allowing us to experience afresh the Gospel of God's joy and gladness. In the Roman Catholic Church today, nobody would be heard more gladly than the rejected monk of Wittenberg. His revolutionary preaching and biblical exposition ought and could find an unimaginable response. It is not a matter of both churches getting together and simply drawing nearer to one another; it is a matter of establishing and of furthering in an open ecumenical context what has happened historically and what is yet to come. Luther belongs to the whole Church.

How could such a thing happen? How could Luther, a banned and excommunicated monk, a one-time 'notorious heretic', be heard within Catholicism? Quite simply. It could happen as an act of reconciliation, a quite simple Christian act. There is no need of any spectacular act of lifting the ban and removing the excommunication; without pomp or fuss, the once-rejected monk might be given his due within the fellowship of the Church, in accordance with Pope Paul VI's declaration of forgiveness, as well as in accordance with the decision of the Council. Some sort of reception might take place within the Church. It would overcome all stiffness and formalism, for it would prove to be an act of life-giving. Christians must act with energy and conviction, and act in concert. Such a reception would reveal at once the genuine catholicity of the Church. Churches must be strong enough to contain contrasting positions within themselves, strong enough to hold difficult men within the fellowship, even when they are revolutionary, rebellious, and contrary, difficult and prickly men, lonely and tragic men.

If this were to happen, the Church would experience a certain suppleness and freedom from rigidity, a kind of easy competence to deal with the situation that would stand it in good stead in the ministry of preaching. The secret of the all-powerful strength of Luther's theology lies in the dialectic of his thinking. The Protestant tendency to narrow theology down — its principle of faith *alone*, grace *alone*, Scripture *alone* — could remain valid, but, it would come into its full worth in the dialectical emphasis of a real and effective relation to God: this is clearly seen in the past as the hand of God at work in history, and in the present when grasped in faith. It is perfectly true that the *sola* principle was a key principle of Luther's approach; nevertheless, it is no less true to say that the principle of dialectic is clearly there too, and, further, that it belongs to the human predicament. It even makes the *sola* principle sharper. For instance, how frequently the important word '*et*' (and) occurs in Luther: *simul justus* et *peccator*, at one and the same time justified by faith, yet a sinner; the Wrath *and* the Grace of God, when Luther spoke of the deep 'Yes!' of God through the 'No!' of the Wrath; of God being 'hidden' under a contrary form; of life through death in his theology of the Cross. Examples could be quoted in numbers that would fill volumes. The important thing to see is that though Protestantism is thought of in exclusive and restrictive terms (with respect, for instance, to the *sola* principle), and rightly so; nevertheless, at the heart of Luther was the principle of dialectic, and in the maintenance of the dialectic tension, the *sola* principle is not lost, but actually sharpened.

The question is bound to be raised concerning whether Luther as he is described in these pages can really be accepted by Catholicism or even the other Protestant churches. Well, it is a striking fact of Luther research that every generation draws up its own picture of the man, and almost every study begins by rejecting its predecessors. One can only respond by providing solid evidence of the claim that Luther belongs to the whole Church and inviting the Church to heed his perennial call to hear again the Gospel. That is all Luther asked of the Church. How often he quoted the words of Gamaliel, given to the first men to resist the Gospel: 'If this counsel or this work be of men, it will come to nought: but if it be of God, ye cannot overthrow it; lest haply ye be found even to fight against God' (Acts 5: 38-39). Luther asked only for the Gospel to be heard and to be given free course: all the rest would follow. If he were wrong, the whole movement would perish naturally. For himself, he was not going to fight God.

But even if Protestant churches might generally accommodate Luther, it might nevertheless be asked whether it is realistic to suppose that the Catholic Church, that structured, disciplined, ordered, visible Church, in which Luther did not believe, and against which he spoke so strongly and which excommunicated him, could ever accept him once more within its ranks. The answer may be given that Luther never thought of an 'invisible' Church; he spoke of a 'hidden' Church — quite a different thing. The Church to Luther was always 'visible', but could only be understood in the full sense of that word by men of faith within the Church. The Church was not to be seen as a crowd of cardinals' caps. There is a 'false' Church, and a 'true' Church, the latter being known only to God: Catholics are in that 'true' Church as well as Protestants, and Protestants, too, may stand in the ranks of the 'false' Church.

Luther's views begin to be appreciated only when the Church collectively says 'Yes!' to him: it is only then that he comes into his own. The Church cannot *exclude* a man of such apparent charisma, a man on whom the hand of the Lord had been laid, and who preached the Gospel more boldly and effectively than any other man. His word may come as seemingly destructive, hurting, threatening, or even offensive; it may appear in all-too-human expressions of a culture hemmed in by its own limitations and spiritually blinded by contemporary concerns. All this may be true, but it is equally true that in no other way can God through the Holy Spirit act upon his Church to cleanse it and redeem it except in, by, and through such people. We are called to hold a kind of principle of balance or compensation, but *never exclusion* — and all this in a fellowship of love. Here is an element of Catholicism we rarely see: the embracing Church, the reflection of God's embracing love.

As I was working on this book, discussing its thesis with theologians on the continent during 1980 and 1981, it was not only Catholic scholars, but also evangelical scholars who were suspicious of this kind of suggestion in the various shapes and forms it had so far appeared, particularly as it had emanated from the more advanced Roman Catholic theologians eager to forward the work of Vatican II. In any event, the latter were not being very well received in their own communion! To meet these valid objections, I would say at once that I am fully aware of the differences between the world of the sixteenth century and the late twentieth century; you may rest assured that I have studied each sufficiently to be able to distinguish between them. The thought forms of the two periods are totally different, their characteristic concerns and responsibilities wholly other. I do not advocate restoring Luther's teaching and theology to the Church, nor engaging in the disputes and controversies of the sixteenth century. I do not ask that we bring Luther's theology into relations with the contemporary climate. I am interested in a wholly different kind of approach, a fresh driving force, an openness to new stimuli, to new charismatic demands. I ask that we be open. That is all.

Therefore, let us freely admit that Luther's attack on the Roman Catholic Church is indisputable: it cannot be denied. It is a fact of history, and such attacks are bound to occur throughout history, for the Church is in varying degress a 'fallen' Church, or at least a Church made up of 'fallen' men and women, and it is only in attacks such as Luther's that God can speak to his Church the redeeming and saving word.

Further, Luther is no *authority* in the Church that (wrongly) bears his name. The average Lutheran pastor may know no more about Luther than any schoolboy facing History O-level. It would be as wrong to introduce him to non-Lutherans as an 'authority' in the Church as it was for the Catholics to label him as a heretic and to exclude him from the Church. In any event, scholars vary quite widely in their interpretation of Luther, and as long as this is the case, he may not be cited as authoritative. He described himself as merely a teacher, or a pathfinder to Christ, or as a preacher of the Gospel. Let us keep Luther where he understood himself to be. Therefore, if and when he is taken into the Church, it will be *the collective mind of the whole Church* that will begin truly to assess his significance, less in the area of academic assessments of his theology and more in the religious experience of God in Christ that he offered to the Church of his day. Admittedly, Luther made some criticisms of the Pope likely to hurt or offend any Catholic, but one must recall the popes of his day from the Borgia on, against whom he animad-verted. There was no John Paul II sitting in Rome in his study, praying for the Church and the world, giving the Word of faith and hope and love. Luther's concern was for the purity of the Gospel and the protection of the Church (and the world) from a line of base, irreligious, worldly, secularised, *unbelieving* popes. That is another fact of history. Luther had no objection to a good, godly, pastoral Holy Father caring for Christendom; he simply called the other kind what they really were. Had the sycophants listened to Luther, we would have had a reformed Catholicism instead of a divided Christendom.

Our concern is not to justify Luther, but only to consider the factual outworkings of his protest that actually took place in history, and to see that as the significant fact in the ecumenical situation we face today after Vatican II. It is a matter of opening ourselves up to Luther's basic concerns — his experience of God, his knowledge of Christ in the Gospel, his emphasis on justification by faith alone, his new understanding of the relationship between Scripture and tradition, and the like. Luther always agreed that all the truths nec-essary for salvation are contained in Scripture, and it is precisely here, on the meaning and authority of the Bible, that Vatican II made its most astounding breakthrough. Further, it should be re-called always and always, that though Luther was an academic and an intellectual of considerable proportions, he nevertheless main-tained the priority of faith over knowledge and intellect. He was also crucially concerned with the theology of grace and the freedom of a Christian man. These points are less doctrines to be understood by the intellect than relationships, understandings, experiences a person has with God, open to child or peasant, to scholar or saint, to king or serf. It is at the level of such concerns that Luther begins to take on his reality. In fact it could be argued that, to the extent these truths of Luther's theological battle are received and taken over by the Church, to that same extent Luther steps in to the contemporary picture with his doctrine. If done in this manner, the sting that a Catholics feel in Luther's doctrine would be drawn, and they might conceivably be strongly drawn towards Luther and even feel called to integrate him into the whole Church.

If Luther is considered in these terms, the entire relationship between Catholicism and Protestantism takes on the nature of an almost ideal possibility of convergence on a basis of historic truth and contemporary reality. In this way the *entire* Church can take a new look at him and see him as he truly is, can learn to recognise him and know him for what he was. If the whole Church in its catholicity would recognise him anew, that would in itself be the re-creative act in its whole life. The danger of seemingly aggressive and hostile manifestations would thereby be bent back in to the fellowship, not least those named in history and banned by the Church: they would thenceforth be not destructive but constructive. Nothing is further from this hermeneutical method than to prettify ugly facts, to conceal truths, to smooth away rough places. On the contrary, we seek to bring within the orbit of the Church's life the full weight of Luther's Pauline-dialectical utterances about God, the power of his Gospel preaching, and the liberating strength of the Word of God.

This must be the basic model of all ecumenical confrontation. The churches are seeking models for ecumenical advance, but here is more than a model. It is a meeting on a personal level of fellowship to create deeper fellowship. Certainly the Luther movement in all its completeness, in all its unique once-for-all quality, must be taken and received on its own personal level as a model for all future patterns of fresh orientations in ecumenical relations. What must be avoided is any kind of neutral, noncommittal, objective model; what is recommended is a meeting of persons, which in the last analysis is something of a mystery after all. It is in this meeting, which it is our responsibility to face and to fulfil, that God will reveal something of the fulness of his Truth.

How can we better characterise this ecumenical meeting of Luther with catholicity? To put the same question another way, what would Luther's place be in the coming Church? This question is not answered by referring to Luther's description of himself as a humble penitent, a mere beggar before God, for it is bigger than Luther's person and now concerns the entire Lutheran Church. That Church will have to face the disturbing fact that Luther's teaching is not being proclaimed as the Reformation preaching of justification by faith only, but rather that it is a given within the Catholic corpus where it belongs, and that it is expressed in different terms. That would not disturb Luther, nor should it disturb Lutherans either, for Luther's concern was the Gospel, not formulae to preserve it when resisted. The truth contained within the doctrine of justification by faith may be expressed in simple terms of the grace of sovereign God, free and unmerited. Our concern is with truth and fact, not formulae or slogans.

If Luther were brought to a new appreciation within Catholicism, a deeply radical question would thereby be put to the reformed confessions. This question has long been pondered by Lutheran theologians who have been engaged in ecumenical conversations. Professor K. E. Skydsgaard of Copenhagen, in his book on *Tradition and Traditions* (1972), for instance, reminds us that to call a Church 'Lutheran' was to Luther himself an absolute abomination. Luther permitted the adjective 'papist' in reference to the Catholic Church because its members acknowledged the pope as their infallible head, whereas the Church is Christ's, and ought to have no other appellation. There can only be one Church, the holy, catholic or apostolic Church, the true Christian Church, the *regnum dei*, which is always under attack from the false church, the *regnum diaboli*. Skydsgaard goes on to say that the break with Rome did not happen all at once, but transpired in stages, until there existed various confessions, which stood as more or less finished and final statements. What are confessions? he asks. *Confession* means 'a church defined and delimited'. It means a collection of variously formulated opinions and doctrinal statements, whereby a Church knows how to distinguish itself from other churches. A confession can then assume the character of a static and authoritative final statement, closed for all time. Churches of a confession can take on the nature of structures now final and closed, and be lordly masters of their own doctrines. The danger here is that such a church moves round one spot. In this sense a confession takes on rather a gloomy role, and if understood in this way, makes it quite impossible to accept in any Christian sense. Skydsgaard argues that that is exactly what the West European and American confessional churches have suffered and indeed still suffer. Many of the factors that come into play in the making of a confession are thoroughly nontheological. Confessional statements may become identified with a city or a particular culture at a particular time.

To free Luther from confessionalism, at least from a confessionalism that sees itself as mistress in its own house, would mean to set him in the centre of a new catholicity, where he once belonged and still belongs. Christianity is more than any confessional statement and must certainly grow in its response to the world in which it is set. Christendom should not be confined to such structures as are implicit in confessionalism: it could disappear with them. It is with these thoughts we view the significance for Christendom of Luther, that Christendom will renew itself with his continuing power of the Gospel. It is this Luther, who preaches the living voice of the Gospel, who is our common hope.

CHAPTER FIVE

THE FUNDAMENTAL
RELIGIOUS EXPERIENCE

IF THE ARGUMENT of Chapter 4 be accepted, namely, that the rejected monk of Wittenberg belongs to the Church catholic, then the first thing to emphasise is Luther's overwhelming experience of God reconciling man to himself through the Gospel of Christ. In this experience Luther found peace with God, and in that peace, a total explanation of this life and the certainty of joyous life with God forever. Luther wagered his all on God, and would not be silenced unless proved wrong. If modern man could but begin to understand Luther's faith, a faith that throws itself upon God in life and in death, he would begin to understand Luther's significance for Christendom.

Luther never argued this; neither did he seek to prove it on intellectual grounds: he simply proclaimed it. This is the way of all such charismatic leaders. They all have the prophetic gift of spiritual insight and vision, by which they see and experience God, as well as the gift of warm, compelling speech to communicate what they have seen, felt, heard, and known. In some faint and far-off way they all possess the insight and manner of Jesus.

This way of knowing is not unrelated to the new approach of the scientist in the post-Einstein period. Newton and Descartes were analytical; they *separated* themselves from the phenomena they examined, and observed, described, and related these materials that they had separated out for closer study. This process seemed necessary, and yielded valid conclusions. Since Einstein, however, it is becoming clearer that reality must be seen as a whole, and all of it organically related, not static but always dynamic: it must be integrated. In other words, the scientist is no longer an *observer*, but rather *participant* in the phenomena he observes and seeks to interpret. This is very close to what Luther meant when he spoke of the experience of faith, and still closer to what St. John meant when he spoke of revelation.

When Luther spoke of faith he was not explaining Christian doctrine in some objective terms, or giving a reasonable and impartial account of Christian faith and morals. He could do so well enough when the occasion demanded it, but he chose not to. No, he had been taken hold of by God, and his life was now hid with Christ in God. What he was now talking about was not doctrine or morals along the lines of a medieval schoolman observing such phenomena: he was now a partaker in God and a participant in the life that God intended for man, which he had revealed in Jesus Christ and was now sustaining by the Spirit of Truth. This was the way things were: this was the explanation of the mystery of existence. In some small way Luther was experiencing a glimpse of the mind of God, if that is not too much to say. Faith was the compelling power of God, given by God, and enabling him to see the divine meaning and purpose of life, as it had been revealed in Christ. He saw all phenomena of time and space under God as a whole, himself a partaker and prophetic exponent. In other words, as St. John explains it, it is the gift of the Holy Spirit, who comes and makes his abode with a man and who guides him into all truth. It was such an experience, the very gift of God himself, that Luther meant by faith. This is no confessional or Lutheran emphasis: it is the very heartbeat of Christianity.

Melanchthon, in a preface to Luther's works, noted that Luther had always insisted on the distinction 'between philosophy and the Gospel, something which is not in fact present in Scotus, Thomas and their fellows'. By 'philosophy' Melanchthon meant logical ratiocination, purely speculative thinking, carried through in a detached, objective frame of mind: to study with disinterest, as if the conclusions did not affect us. 'Gospel', on the other hand, *being an activity of God*, is inaccessible to human reason, often contrary thereto, and requires personal involvement and commitment of the kind Luther exemplifies if it is to be understood. One of Luther's objections to his scholarly medieval predecessors — 'Sophists' as he was wont to call them — was what he called a lack of 'sincerity', in that they treated 'rationally' those truths that are revealed to passion alone (i.e., to one committed, to one involved). Luther always contended that Erasmus embodied this very 'superficiality' or 'insincerity', which 'thinks of the Christian religion as a comedy or tragedy. That it contains no real events, but fictions conceived to teach good behaviour.'[1] Luther simply said, 'He is not committed.' He asked, 'How can you deal with people who have no firm belief to which you might appeal? You cannot refute them by scripture for it does not mean anything to them.'[2]

It is important to my argument here to recall that what Luther called 'sincerity' is precisely that quality of his mind that separated him from many churchmen of his day, and that continues to be unacceptable to contemporary Catholics who may admire him and who freely recognise the abuses of the Church that he opposed and corrected. Those abuses needed to be reformed. They were in fact reformed; they are all dead and gone. It has been my experience that the modern, educated, ecumenically minded Catholic agrees with the Catholic moderates like Cardinal Contarini, and is generally of the opinion that the schism was both unfortunate and unnecessary. Luther, on the other hand, said repeatedly that the issue was not about scandals and abuses, but about doctrine, 'propter Deum'. The distinguished Catholic church historian Joseph Lortz, who more than any other man brought Luther out of the ghetto to which the Catholics had banished him, and reintroduced him to the light of open and free examination in the Catholic world of today—even he described this as Luther's 'subjectivism'.

Lortz could not reconcile subjectivism with the Catholic Church. He argued that Luther was subconsciously arguing on the *false* assumption that the transformation in us, whereby we are justified, must be experienced with such immediacy and emotion as to produce absolute certainty. Here is a fundamental disagreement, a disagreement that can be expressed in terms that twentieth century man can understand and accept. Shall priority be given to intellectual understanding, or to subjective experience? I do not mean to suggest that these should be seen as alternatives or mutually exclusive, but rather that when a man is taken hold of by God, he then learns the truth of his real nature as a man and his place in the world in

---

1. *D. Martin Luthers Werke: Tischreden* (Weimar, 1930-), 2, 346, 17-19.
2. Ibid., 5, 183, 27.

God's plan and purpose; this experience, described as 'being taken hold of by God', refers to a divine activity, and is not (or rather, is much more than) an intellectual conviction that has been arrived at by normal approved intellectual procedures. A person who has undergone such an experience arrives at a perfectly sound intellectual position, in that it provides an explanation of his state of being that gives a satisfactory and complete interpretation of the mystery of his human existence. It is an intellectual position as much as the agnostic or even the atheist occupies, open to all the criticisms such people make, and with the intellectual responsibility not only of meeting the objections of such, but of expressing its ultimate position in terms they understand. It is my contention that the man of faith may hold a sound intellectual position, but that that position cannot be arrived at by intellect alone, in the way one proves a theorem of Euclid or works out the distance of a star. In other words, *it is created by God, not fashioned by man*. With respect to Lortz and the many Christian scholars who share his view, Luther's concern ought not to be described as 'individualism' or 'subjectivism', but in terms of divine activity (see 1 Cor. 2.5, 12-13). This point is worth pursuing further.

The experience Jesus underwent, through the long years of testing in the wilderness and wrestling with God, is the paradigm of what is being discussed here. Lesser men, such as the apostles, all shared this experience in some way. They describe it having 'been with Jesus'. Charismatic leaders, such as St. Francis and Luther, also share in some small way this kind of experience and the authority that goes with it.[3] It would cast a great deal of light on our understanding of Luther to take a brief look at this experience as portrayed by Jesus Christ.

In the Gospel narratives, Jesus comes before men with complete assurance and resolute authority. He is not a trained rabbi, and yet he challenges the scribes to combat as if he did not need the support of either institutional training or public position. He speaks with authority, and silences all opposition on its own grounds. He appears as sovereign over all authorities that stand in his way. This invincible

---

3. It is not only of charismatic leaders of the past that I speak. Contemporary leaders such as Pope John Paul II and Metropolitan Anthony also share this spiritual experience and carry about themselves this spiritual authority.

lordship over every person and situation is the expression of his mysterious nature and power; it evokes astonishment and awe, enthusiasm or terror, as appropriate in each situation, but in every case a deep emotion and agitation in face of this new and unwanted and unheard-of thing that confronted them in his person.[4] It should not go unobserved that this authority was claimed over 'demons' and natural forces; it is also authority over sin and even over death.[5]

His greatest authority, however, is a preacher and teacher,[6] the roles he was sent to fill, and not as a worker of miracles. His call to conversion extends to *all* — to learned Pharisee, disgraced prostitute, tax extortioner, and devout disciple alike; note particularly the rejected transgressors of the Law, the utterly lost, the sinners. Sin is stripped of its consequence, decisively by his own Word and his own deed. He eats with sinners and declares the forgiveness of sins. This is the ultimate point beyond which a decision about Jesus can no longer be postponed. For by forgiving sins, Jesus not only sets himself against the Law that teaches that sinners should be punished, but steps right into the place where only God can stand: who can forgive sins but God only?[7] As St. John succinctly expressed it, he made himself equal with God.[8] 'What things soever the Father doeth, these also doeth the Son likewise'.[9] 'I and my Father are one'.[10] 'Whom makest thou thyself?' the Jews asked of Jesus as He taught in the temple.[11] There is no ready-made category under which Christ can be subsumed. Both friend and enemy puzzled over the enigma of his person;[12] only St. John, who lay on Jesus' bosom, could resolve this.[13] It was the Resurrection, and earlier the Transfiguration, that enabled the disciples to transcend this situation. First, the riddle of his person was solved: he was God's own Son, Messiah, Saviour, Redeemer, Lord of this world and the world to

---

4. See Matt. 22.46; Mark 9.32 and 12.34; and Luke 20.40. Above all, St. John's Gospel expresses this authority of Jesus as no other Gospel does.

5. Matt. 10.1; Mark 1.27; Luke 10.19.

6. Luke 4.43.

7. Mark 2.7; Luke 7.49.

8. John 5.18.

9. John 5.19.

10. John 10.30.

11. John 8.53.

12. Matt. 11.3 and 12.23; Mark 6.2f, 6.14-16, and 8.27f; and Luke 4.41 and 5.21.

13. St. John both states the enigma and offers the solution.

come. And this implied a new dimension to the authority of Jesus as well, in that it now continued as a present reality.

When Christ strode across the stage of history, claiming to be far more than prophet or sage, showing that he was God's last Word in the redemption of man, saying that all men had need of him and that he alone could save and redeem, he set forth his claims in a manner unique among all founders of religions. In fact, Christianity is not properly regarded when it is seen as a religion: it is a revelation. He made his claims calmly and deliberately, as a matter of course. He never explained himself. He never reasoned his position. He simply announced it, and let conviction steal into the hearts and minds of his followers as they heard his unique words and witnessed his unique deeds. 'He that hath ears to hear, let him hear.' This was always his manner. 'Take heed how ye hear.' He never deigned to explain mysteries the curiosity of his disciples would fain penetrate. He simply took for granted many things modern men would long to discuss. His sayings proceeded from One who is in perpetual communion with God, and therefore were uttered with a breathtaking authority, quietly and assuredly, nothing doubting, completely confident that they carried their own self-authenticating power and conviction.

No one comprehended the character of Christ more clearly than did St. John: Christ did nothing of himself (5.19, et al.); all was of God, word and work alike (5.19, 5.30, 14.10, et al.); it was God who gave faith to believe and understand Christ (6.44, 6.45, 8.47, et al.); only he knows God (8.55) to see him is to see God (14.7, 9-11); Christ, with the Father, would send the Spirit of Truth to abide with believers forever (14.16, 26, et al.). Never in recorded history has any other person made such claims; never in any religion has any founder assumed such authority, and yet always delivered with the self-assurance of one confident that his words and deeds carried their own self-authenticating authority, their own compelling power, for such is the nature of Truth. The world cannot receive this Spirit of Truth: it cannot see it, and it cannot understand it. The disciples will know, for the Spirit shall dwell with them and be in them (John 14.17). Flesh and blood cannot perceive this; only God can reveal it to man (1 Cor. 2).

It is important at this point to distinguish sharply between what the New Testament describes as the work of the Holy Spirit and what generally might be called *illuminism* or *inspiration*. Luther in his biblical exegesis distinguished between the spirit and the letter, but to draw this distinction clearly the guidance of the Holy Spirit himself was necessary.

> for nobody understands these precepts unless it is given him from above. . . . Therefore, they most sadly err who presume to interpret the Holy Scriptures and the law of God by taking hold of them by their own understanding and study. [14]

The words, ideas, and phrases of Scripture will not of themselves bring enlightenment and inward comprehension, for what is uttered *vocaliter* needs to be understood *vitaliter*, in the heart and conscience. Luther argued that the Holy Spirit is hidden in the letter of Scripture, since the letter itself may proclaim only the Law, or the wrath of God, whereas the Holy Spirit conveys the word of grace, the gospel. This means — and this is a most happy and creative consequence — that the interpretation of Scripture is not something that is settled once for all, as a fixed body of belief or a received tradition. On the contrary, it is a task that each and every man must assume for himself if the knowledge of the Word is not to sink once again to the level of a dogmatic literalism. The true reading of the Bible is a continuous process of perpetually bringing faith to birth: it is a constant renewal and re-creation of the spiritual understanding. 'The natural man receiveth not the things of the Spirit of God: for they are foolishness unto him: neither can he know them, because they are spiritually discerned' (1 Cor. 2.14). Such things are hidden from the wise; only Christ reveals them (Matt. 11.28, 2 Tim. 3.15).

Nevertheless, in stressing that such truth comes only from the Holy Spirit, Luther was acutely aware of the dangers of the kind of illuminism that the radicals and enthusiasts were energetically seeking to foist on to the Reformation. He vigorously repudiated such claims for failing to acknowledge the direct operation of the Holy Spirit; in his view, they led to pride, fanaticism, intolerance, and division. He emphasised the historical, objective witness of the divine revelation: it was the Holy Spirit who unfolded its meaning to the penitent and believing heart.

St. Paul had a similar experience and carried a similar power

---

14. *D. Martin Luthers Werke: Kritische Gesamtausgabe* (Weimar, 1883 ff.), 57, 185, 21. Hereafter abbreviated WA (Weimar Ausgabe).

of authority. His writings carry more theology than all the writings of all the Fathers, but such authority lay in that it pleased God who had separated him from the womb (cf. Jeremiah) to call him by grace, to reveal his Son in him, that he might preach him among the heathen. His authoritative theology derived from his religious experience. Such a calling, such authority he deigned not to confirm by any human authority. [15] He lived unto God, yet it was no longer Paul who lived but Christ who lived in him, and the new life he now lived was by faith in the Son of God. [16] He more than denied himself; he was crucified with Christ. He was a wholly new creation in Christ. [17] He knew nothing but Christ crucified. [18] His position was not authenticated by men's wisdom, but only by the power of God. [19] Neither wrath nor Law, neither sin nor death, nor the tyrants who destroyed men would ever separate him from the love of God in Christ. [20] He began from his personal experience when he was called by the resurrected Christ.

So it was with Athanasius. The place of Athanasius as a great religious leader has been overshadowed by his immense theological and biblical learning, which ousted Arianism and paganism. It is as a theologian that he is remembered, in his fight for the Nicene orthodoxy, quite rightly; but first and foremost he was a man of the profoundest religious experience of Christ. The theology is the outcrop of his religion. His inner fortress was his spiritual intuition: he *knew* that *his* Saviour and Redeemer was the God who made heaven and earth. It was less his intellect than his unflinching and invincible faith that convinced his generation. We should ever recall that it was his spiritual strength that gave that powerful personality such moral and mental vigour, loved and respected even among the heathen. Loyal to friends, generous to foes, he won everybody over with his irrepressible humour. In all his long years of exile and banishment, hounded by the state police, he was never once betrayed. Gregory and Epiphanius, Augustine and Cyril, Luther and Hooker, not to mention moderns, all pay tribute to this saint. Even

---

15. Gal. 1.15f.
16. Gal. 2.20.
17. 2 Cor. 5.17.
18. 1 Cor. 2.2.
19. 1 Cor. 2.5.
20. Rom. 8.39.

Gibbon laid aside his 'solemn sneer' to do homage to Athanasius the Great. But it was his spiritual experience of the living Christ that was the fountainhead of that brilliant and irrefutable theology. As proof of this, his single letter to Dracontius in 354/5 urging him to accept office is eloquent testimony.

So it was with Augustine, Bernard, and Francis; with Bunyan and Wesley; and indeed with every great leader of the Christian people. Their strength, whether of knowledge, or conviction, or sympathy, has always come from a direct communion with Christ, an experience they have felt and known individually and communicated to others in language grasped by them and in deeds recognised by them as having the authentic touch of Christ. All such men have experienced that strange warming of the heart, that penetration of the mists of doubt and uncertainty; and all who knew them and experienced their ministry knew that it had pleased God to reveal Christ in them; all who knew them echo the words of the blind man healed by Christ, 'One thing I know, that, whereas I was blind, now I see' (John 9.25).

It was not otherwise with Luther and with the Reformation of which he was the leader. The power behind Luther was his shattering spiritual experience that reshaped him entirely. When Luther felt the touch of God, when he realised that there was no thought he could create, no prayer he could offer, no deed he could perform that could bridge the painful gap between himself and God, but that God himself had come all the way in Christ, he said,

> When I had realised this I felt myself absolutely born again. The gates of paradise had been flung open and I had entered. There and then the whole of scripture took on another look to me. . . .[21]

It was the old experience of all the saints, and yet it was new, for in it was the creative power of God. There was nothing new in Luther's experience, but as it was of God, it made everything new. He *knew* that his life was hid with Christ in God in spite of all evil, in spite of sin, in spite of guilt. All his old dread of God, all his fears and anxieties, all his doubts and uncertainties vanished like the morning mist, and in their place arose a buoyant and glad-hearted love of

---

21. WA, 54, 186 (for the Introduction to the Latin edition, Wittenberg, 1545).

God in answer to the love that was kindled by the experience of what God had revealed in Christ. This Luther experienced with a compelling certainty, and this he proclaimed from pulpit, lectern, and desk. It had pleased God to reveal his Son in him, and this experience, and its proclamation in spoken and written word, was the sole foundation on which the Reformation was built. From this experience in Christ all of Luther's theolgoy derived: one could even have the religious experience without the theology to explain it.[22]

The beginnings of the Reformation were experiential, not doctrinal. In fact it could be argued that it was Luther's experience that opened up to him the Bible, Church history, and doctrine. He now saw what the Bible was about and what God had done of pure love in Christ for us men and our salvation. This vision opened up the whole field of Church history to him like a panorama from a mountaintop. It was this experience that made him acutely aware of all the innovations and accretions that had grown up over the centuries—transubstantiation, infallibility, monasticism, indulgences, Mariolatry. It was this experience that made him see that the theology of his day, the scholastic philosophy, was but an intellectual speculation on the nature of God and his attributes, and was no theology at all; it certainly was not about the God and Father of our Lord Jesus Christ. The outcome of such intellectualism, apart from its benefits as mental gymnastics, was to create an idol, a figment of the human mind.

Doctrines and their formal expression in theology are not the beginnings of things. They are formulations, even warehouses, where centuries-old experience of the one thing needful is stored. There is always at the basis of knowledge, whether of men or things, some sensitive and delicate relationship of personality with personality. Logic and reason help to keep us from making errors, but vision, growth, development, and insight are fired when soul meets soul and shares the truth of experiences. This is true of scientific enquiry and aesthetic and artistic growth; how much more true it is of re-

---

22. I have met it in a Fraserburgh fisherman resting on the quayside at Whitby and in a plumber come to mend a burst pipe. Not many wise, not many mighty, not many noble are called (1 Cor. 1.26). For 'the natural man receiveth not the things of the Spirit of God: for they are foolishness to him: neither can he know them, because they are spiritually discerned' (1 Cor. 2:14). That is why it is as foolish to try to argue a person into faith as it is to try to torture him into it.

ligion. We must be in touch with God to know him in the true sense of knowledge.

At the beginning of any real advance in religion there must be a personal encounter, an intimate vision of God impressed upon us as a religious experience that we know to be true because we have felt it. The vision and experience of the one is caught by the other: it is *caught* rather than *taught*. The revival under Francis of Assisi spread in the way it did because the fire burning in his heart kindled a flame in the heart of every man, woman, and child who met him. Luther headed the greatest reformation and revival of all time, because men felt and knew that he had found a gracious God by a total trust in the grace of God revealed to him in Christ Jesus. It was neither the Augsburg Confession nor the Lutheran theology that gave us the Reformation; it was the benificent contagion of the religious experience Luther found in Christ. The expansion of that experience finds inadequate expression in any confession or creed. Let us study that experience a little more closely.

It is not to intellectual difficulties or doctrinal uncertainties that the beginnings of Luther's pilgrimage can be traced, though it is true that when his religious experience fulfilled itself, it resulted (in those areas where it was accepted) in the collapse of the Catholic culture, the breakdown of the Catholic hierarchical structure, civil and ecclesiastical, from the local convent to the authority of Rome, and the revision and reconstruction of the Catholic doctrinal system. But the cause of that upheaval lay elsewhere.

There is an old proverb that it is doubt that makes a monk. This was not true of Luther: there was not the slightest trace of intellectual difficulties about doctrine during Luther's great crisis. He had a brilliant university career in the Faculty of Law, was lively, witty, happy, gifted musically, and well set for a fine career in what we would call the civil service. But he gave the world up, he gave his career up, to find the one thing he did not possess — peace with God. [23] Luther did the only thing he could do in his plight, and that

---

23. As a university professor in close contact with students, I have found countless students, not necessarily theological students, nor even religious students, horribly disillusioned with politics which they think are getting them nowhere, dreading to be caught up in the world of work with the selfish and senseless aim of 'getting on', sorely tempted to drop out of the daily round, the daily grind, simply longing, even aching, for a life of decency, dignity, and meaning. This

was to go into a monastery, the one place on earth where he could give his whole life to save his soul. Almost everybody of Luther's day would agree that that was the one and only course open to him — save, of course, men such as his commonsensical father, or the witty and brilliant Erasmus, who had long been disillusioned with monkery, having been through it all himself.

As Calvin was later to show, the very anthropocentric manner in which Luther expressed his *cri de coeur* showed how wrongly he had diagnosed his malady, how hopeless was his quest. He wondered when he would ever do enough, ever make himself good enough, to reach a gracious God and be found worthy of acceptance. God heard his prayer, but Luther was yet to learn the difference between God *hearing* prayer and God *answering* prayer. The Psalmist wrote, 'In my distress I cried unto the Lord and he heard me' (Ps. 120), and yet in woe God left him to sojourn in Mesech, and to dwell in the tents of Kedar; yet he was to learn what it was to be heard and to be *answered*: 'In the day when I cried thou answeredst me, and strengthenedst me with strength in my soul' (Ps. 138.3). God revived the Psalmist, saved him, and in his mercy perfected the work he had begun by his Word. Luther was not yet ready for such profound spiritual truth.

Inside the monastery, Luther devoted all his ability with the utmost fervour to use to the uttermost the penitential system in order to make himself fit to be the receptacle of the grace of God. His obedience to his supervisor was absolute and rigorous. He sought the confessional to find peace of mind. He did not doubt the place of the confessional, but when he could not experience the reality of it in his heart, he thought that there must be something wrong with him, some inadequacy in his confession. He made full use of the sacraments, and waited in vain for the mysterious, inexplicable experience of the grace he expected to flow from them. He turned to all the other established means: private chastisements, fastings, vigils, prayer. He sought not only to propitiate God by doing extra works, but to compel him to remove from his soul the consciousness of guilt. He failed. But it was himself he blamed, not the methods.

concern is widespread, and if unresolved, leads to disillusionment or disruptiveness. The secularised world and permissive society are causing countless numbers of our most sensitive young people to put (*mutatis mutandis*) the very questions that Luther put to Church and society. Certainly without peace with God there is nothing worth the wear of winning.

He persevered, in spite of the feeling of continuous failure. He later said, 'If ever a monk could have got to heaven by monkery, I could!'

One might reasonably ask whether Luther had never heard of the grace of God. We must remember that his spiritual and academic teachers alike all taught that a man had to earn grace by doing everything that was in him — 'all that in him lay' was the technical expression. This only sharpened Luther's anguish, for how could he ever know that he had done 'all that in him lay'? Luther felt an overpowering sense of God's presence, but as a mortal sinner he found it an oppressive and portentous experience indeed. He was like the moth longing for the candle flame about to destroy it. He said of this experience that 'When I looked for Christ it seemed to me I saw the Devil.'

Two long years of such anguish dragged on. His superiors believed him to be a young saint; his fellow monks thought him the perfect monk. In his heart, Luther knew otherwise. He thought that he was wrestling with his own sin; what he was really struggling with was the religion of his times and of his Church. He was probing it, testing it, examining it in all its depths, wrestling with the whole Church's understanding of grace. What he expected to be sources of comfort, strength, and joy turned out to be the wellsprings of terror. Luther was too brilliant, too percipient, too spiritual, and above all too deadly earnest to overlook the fact that none of these things was leading him to any solid ground on which he could base his confidence and hopes for this world and for eternity. He was much too honest to allow himself to be persuaded otherwise. When his father confessor told him that God was not angry with him, *he* became angry with God: 'My confessor once told me after I had submitted foolish things as sins (*stulta peccata*): "You are foolish; God does not bear you a grudge; you bear Him a grudge. God is not angry with you; you are angry with God." '[24]

It was his work on the Bible that saved him, in particular the discovery of the meaning of justification by faith as recorded in his exposition of Romans 1.17, in which he says that he felt born again, the gates of paradise were flung open to him and the whole of Scripture began to take on another look.

It was this perspective, this entrance into Paradise, that gave Luther not only the insight to interpret his own desperate spiritual

---

24. *D. Martin Luthers Werke: Tischreden* (Weimar, 1930-), 1, 122.

struggle, but also the immediate and total awareness of the nature of the Gospel: to be set right with God, to live at peace with him not by virtue of one's own righteousness, but by the sovereign grace of God in Christ reconciling his world to himself—to be justified by faith.

By faith, he says. What then did Luther mean by faith? To understand this term is not only to grasp the whole significance of the Bible and what God's purpose in Christ is and was, but it is to have the key to the Reformation. To apprehend Luther's experience of faith, to understand Luther's religious experience, is to know in essence the theology of the Reformation, for the theology is but the doctrinal and intellectual formulation of that experience. To know the theology is not the same thing as to have the experience—one can know the theology and know nothing of the experience—but to know the experience is to know both. That is why it is so important to understand what Luther meant by faith. As Luther himself put it,

> It should be noted that there are two ways of believing. One way is to believe *about* God, as I do when I believe that what is said of God is true; just as I do when I believe what is said about the Turk, the devil or hell. This faith is knowledge or observation rather than faith. The other way is to believe *in* God, as I do when I not only believe that what is said *about* Him is true, but put my trust *in* Him, surrender myself to Him and make bold to deal with Him, believing without doubt that He will be to me and do to me just what is said of Him . . .
>
> This faith, which ventures its all on God, and dares to believe, in life or death, that God is what He is said to be, is the only faith that makes a man a Christian and obtains from God whatever it will. This faith no false or evil heart can have, for it is a living faith; and this faith is commanded in the First Commandment, which says, 'I am the Lord thy God, thou shalt have no other gods'. Wherefore the word 'in' is rightly used; and it is carefully to be noted that we may not say, 'I believe God the Father', or 'about the Father', but '*in* God the Father', '*in* Jesus Christ', '*in* the Holy Ghost'. This faith we should render to no man but to God. Therefore, we confess the divinity of Jesus Christ and of the Holy Ghost, when we believe in them even as we believe in the Father. . . .[25]

---

25. 'A Brief Explanation of the Creed' (1520), in WA, 7, 215.

Faith is the 'Yes' of the heart, a conviction on which one wagers one's life, but it does not arise in or from us, it is wholly the gift of God. Faith is the 'Yes' of the heart, a conviction on which one stakes one's life. On what does faith rest? On Christ, born of a woman, made under the Law, who died etc. as the children pray. To this confession I say 'Yes!', with the full confidence of my heart. Christ came for my sake, in order to free me from the Law, not only from the guilt of sin but also from the power of the Law. If you are able to say 'Yes!' to this, you have what is called faith; and this faith does everything. . . . But this faith does not grow by our own powers. On the contrary, the Holy Spirit is present and writes it on the heart. [26]

Peter explains it, and correctly so: Grow in the knowledge of our Lord Jesus Christ (2 Pet. 3.18). . . . This knowledge is faith itself, not only an historical faith, which the Devil also has and with which he confesses God, just in the way heretics do. It is rather a knowledge which rests on experience, and on faith. This word 'know' is what is meant when, according to Gen. 4.1. 'Adam *knew* his wife; it means that he 'knew' her by the sense of feeling, he found her to be his wife, not in any speculative way or historical fashion, but by experience. . . . A merely historical faith does not act in this way. It does not add the experience of feeling and the knowledge that is a personal experience. To bë sure, it says, 'I believe that Christ died and that He died also for me'; but it does not come to this personal feeling, this experimental knowledge. [27]

In a disputation of 1536 Luther writes:

Therefore this 'for me' or 'for us', when believed, constitutes true faith and differentiates this faith from every other faith which merely hears the facts of history. [28]

And in a sermon of 1523 he says that faith and unbelief determine the real and basic character of a man's life:

Sin cannot remain in the presence of faith, so good works cannot exist where unbelief dwells. That is why nothing more than faith is required in order to do good works, and nothing more than unbelief to do bad works and sin. Hence it follows that he who believes has no sin and does nothing but good works; conversely, he who does not believe really does not perform any good work, but whatever he does is sin. [29]

---

26. WA, 49, 9.
27. WA, 40, 3, 737f.
28. WA, 39, 1, 46.
29. WA, 12, 558f.

In his 'Babylonian Captivity' (1520) he writes,

> do not think lightly of faith, which is a work, and of all works
> the most excellent and the most difficult to do. Through it
> alone you will be saved, even if you should be compelled to
> do without any other works. For it is a work of God, not of
> man, as Paul teaches. The other works He works through us
> and with our help, but this one He works in us and without
> our help (*sine nobis*).[30]

The faith that he prized above all else, and about which he
sang such raptures, is that religious faculty which throws itself upon
God and wagers its life upon him. From the outset Luther realised
that this was not something we achieved, like learning to speak a
language or play a musical instrument; it was wholly and directly
a gift from God. Having it, we have everything; without it, we have
nothing: *Wer glaubt, der hat.* Here we have something entirely new,
or at least hitherto unexpressed, so far as medieval theology was
concerned. Medieval theologians had recognised faith, but faith of
this kind Luther called *fides historica*, historical faith, or *frigida
opinio*, nothing more than cold, neutral opinion, that had as much
effect on one's life as the knowledge that the sun is 93,000,000 miles
distant from the earth. It is difficult to imagine that they did not
somehow see that to put one's whole trust in God, to believe in
God, is very different from simply believing that there is a God;
nevertheless, faith for the schoolmen was simply one among many
human efforts all of which were considered to be equally necessary
in order to see and know God. Faith of this kind is little more than
assent, and does not change human nature.

In his exposition of 1 Peter 1.5 (1523), Luther argues that both
the producing and the sustaining of faith in man call for the power
of God:

> When God creates faith in a man, it is certainly as great a
> work as if He were creating heaven and earth anew. . . . [Peo-
> ple who do not understand such thinking] imagine their own
> vain fancy is faith, and that faith may exist without good works.
> But we say, just as Peter does, that faith is a divine power.
> When God produces faith man must be born again and be-
> come a new creature. Thereupon good works must naturally
> follow faith. Consequently, it is unnecessary to say to a Chris-

---

30. WA, 6, 530.

tian, who has faith: Do this or that work. For he does pure
good works of himself, and unbidden.[31]

The real faith, the faith that is total trust, the unique and
precious divine gift that impels us to throw ourselves upon God,
gives us the vibrant assurance of a living God who has revealed
himself, and makes us see his loving fatherly heart in Christ Jesus.
Luther emphasised that in Christ, God has done ALL he could for
man, his Creation lost in its own self-centredness; God could do no
more:

> Here God pours out not sun or moon, nor heaven and earth,
> but *His own heart and His dearest Son*, and even suffers Him
> to shed His blood and die the most shameful of all deaths for
> us shameful, wicked, ungrateful people.[32]

This is the Christian religion in its very core and centre; this is
Luther's faith. The sum total of Christianity is (1) the God of grace,
manifest in the flesh in Christ Jesus, and accessible by every man
and woman, and (2) unwavering trust in him who in his love for
us has given himself to us in Christ Jesus — *unwavering*, not because
our faith is strong, but because Christ with his word has undertaken
our cause and made it his: we can no more lose out than Christ lost
out. 'Faithful is he that calleth you, who also will do it' (1 Thess.
5.24).

The God we know in this experience, the God we trust because
we have thrown ourselves upon him, and who has come and made
his abode with us and sustains us by his Presence, is no metaphysical
or philosophical abstraction described in creeds, argued about in
syllogisms in the lecture room. The most our creeds and confessions
can do, the highest peak our philosophies and theologies can achieve,
is to preserve this truth and safeguard it from erosion. God is seen
and known because we see and know Christ Jesus. 'He that hath
seen me, hath seen the Father.' With Luther, and indeed all the
Reformers, Christ fills the whole sphere of God: they do not recognise any theology that is not a Christology.

When we speak of a faith that throws itself upon God, that
wagers its all upon him, we are not speaking of mere mystical aban-
donment; certainly Luther never meant this. Faith is the sum total

---

31. WA, 12, 270.
32. WA, 36, 426, 34ff.

of our very life, as Luther never tired of saying. It actually is *God within us*, welling up in all kinds of activities. Faith receives all from God, and is moved by him to give its all to its neighbour in love. Faith in God and love towards my neighbour together constitute the great hinge round which all religion and all ethics truly turn:

> Surely, there is no faith where not love but its opposite appears and shows itself. Although the works of love do not justify and save, yet they must follow as fruits and tokens of faith.[33]

This is what came to Luther and ended his long and terrible struggle. He is tireless in describing it: whether in lecture room or pulpit, in book or letter, even in conversation at table. The descriptions are expressed in a great variety of ways — sometimes in medieval scholastic propositional form at a disputation; sometimes with texts from Psalms, prophets or New Testament, sometimes phrases from the medieval mystics; sometimes phrases of startling rugged beauty and originality; sometimes he would draw his illustrations from the feeding of his little robin on his windowsill with the breakfast crumbs, or from his little dog Rascal as he stroked him and rubbed his ears. Always and always whether to pope or prince, priest or people, the meaning is always the same and always clear.

This conception of what Christianity means, what Christ intended, what the true flavour of the authentic religious experience really is, is the religious soul of the Reformation. It contains within it, in that they naturally issue from it, all the religious principles that inspired it. We should not think of it as a dogma, or as Reformation theology, or even as evangelical theology; it is an experience, it is the one thing needful, and that is why it is of prime importance to see it first in these terms. Nobody knew more theology than the young monk Luther; nobody knew more or practised more devotedly and devoutly his religion, and yet he did not know God.

Luther's experience, the way he expressed it, the way he thought through and beyond the theology and practise of his day to be confronted by the stark simplicity and finality of Christ, is what made him relevant to all men of his day, and gives him his abiding significance. Grant this thesis, and it will be seen how relevant are the religious principles that issue from that experience, and how disturbing they always are to the religious establishment, Protestant and

---

33. 'Sermon on John 15.14', WA, 45, 691.

Catholic alike. But first and foremost, it is an experience, and the phrases that set it forth are the descriptions of an experience a soul has gone through. The thing itself is beyond description, as all deep experiences are. It must be felt and gone through to be known. The Reformation started from this personal experience of the believing Christian, which it declared to be the one elemental fact in Christianity that could never be proved by argument or dissolved by criticism. It proclaimed the great truth (which had been universally neglected throughout the whole period of medieval theology by everyone except the saintly Mystics) that in order to know God, or speak one word of truth and sense about him, man must be in living touch with God himself, and God must first have spoken to him. Therein lay all its freshness and appeal, all its originality and power.

Luther made Christ the Redeemer the centre of his writings just as he found him to be the centre of Scripture. Unless we understand who and what Christ is, we will not be able to properly appreciate either Luther or Scripture. Luther and Scripture are both foreign ground to all who do not recognise Christ as their Redeemer:

> Note that this is the judgment and punishment which God permits to come upon those who do not see this light, that is, do not accept and believe God's Word concerning Christ and then go about steeped in utter darkness and blindness and no longer know anything whatever of matter divine. They now understand no article of Christian teaching: what sin is, what man's ability is, how one gets rid of sin and becomes righteous, what Law or Gospel is, what faith is, what good works are, what the Christian estates are. And since they do not know Christ, they cannot really know and see a Christian but must condemn and persecute the true Church and Christians, who teach the word of Christ.[34]

Luther rediscovered religion when he declared that the truly Christian man must cling directly and with a living faith to the God who speaks to him in Christ, saying, 'I am thy salvation'. The earlier Reformers never forgot this. Luther proclaimed his discovery, and though a masterly disputant, never attempted to prove it by argument: it was something self-evident—seen and known when experienced. Like his master, Christ, Luther had the prophetic vision and the magnetic speech to proclaim to others what he saw, felt,

---

34. WA, 46, 28.

and knew. And, like the man in the parable, when he found the one pearl of great price, he went and sold all that he had, and bought it.

Not even Joseph Lortz managed to plumb the depths of Luther's experience, what Luther described as 'this personal feeling,' 'this *experimental knowledge*'. Many Catholics still see it as Lortz described it—namely, as 'subjectivism', 'individualism', or 'private judgment', and turn to the Catholic Church for authoritative judgments on all matters of faith and morals. Nevertheless, it was the fine Catholic scholar Albert Brandenburg who, wrestling with a crippling illness and within sight of death, wrote a small book (or, more accurately, *dictated* it, for he could no longer hold a pen) in which he appealed to his Church to see Luther afresh.[35] His plea is not that we study the different theologies of Catholicism and Protestantism, and by comparison and contrast to seek to relate them; rather, he would have us see Luther as a true Catholic protester for the truth, and further, to apprehend and comprehend him within the Catholic structure.

With a similar end in mind, I have made Luther's religious experience, Luther's confrontation by God, the first step towards seeing Luther as the prophet to the Church catholic. This experience is as old as man: it was experienced by Adam, cherished by the goodly fellowship of the prophets, made incarnate in Christ to perfection, given permanent expression in the New Testament by the apostolic witnesses, and captured (all too rarely) by the saints and doctors of the Church, among whom Luther must be eternally numbered and remembered.

I would extend an invitation to debate, not for Church unity, but for truth's sake. We are not concerned about Luther doctrines or Luther teachings as such, but about Luther's prophetic insights into God, Christ, the Holy Spirit; sin, grace, and salvation; and the holy people of God, their call to life in Christ, and their mission to the world. These are the biblical insights that Luther offered and offers to the whole state of Christ's Church; such was his significance for the sixteenth century, as it remains his significance for ours.

---

35. Brandenburg, *Die Zukunft des Martin Luther* (Münster: Aschendorff; Kassel: Johannes-Stauda-Verlag, 1977).

CHAPTER SIX

THE GENERAL PRIESTHOOD OF BELIEVERS

THE SIGNIFICANCE OF Luther's overwhelming experience of God is manifestly a real and living understanding and appropriation of the Gospel, and *in itself* is catholic, universal, clear to all men and open to all men. There is no reason for a Catholic or anyone else not to find it wholly acceptable. Had Luther been a missioner of the first century, or even a Father of the Early Church, his interpretation of the Gospel would have been seen as authentic and generally received. It was when his Gospel was articulated in the sixteenth century that it was found to disturb, even discredit, much medieval theology and religious usage.

During the period from about the twelfth to the sixteenth century, the clergy had developed into a separate and powerful caste and, by virtue of the so-called Benefit of Clergy, were by that time above the law and outside its reach. It was who found the new biblical theology not a liberation but a threat to their position and role. Luther's opponents were essentially papists rather than Catholic theologians; many of the latter, along with bishops and monks, welcomed Luther's fresh theological insights. There was nothing in Luther's fundamental religious experience that necessarily conflicted with the contents of the old ecclesiastical doctrines, nor even with the common usages of the religious life. He introduced a change in attitude towards both, and an entirely new estimate of their religious value, but nothing that called for their immediate criticism, still less for their destruction. The difference now was that faith could be no longer *based* upon them. They were not the essential things they had been believed to be. There was no harm in their being aids or adjuncts to the spiritual life, but they certainly were not the springs and sources of the Christian life.

The idea that the entire sum of Christian living consists in an unwavering trust of the heart in Christ (a trust that grants the personal assurance of faith because Christ with his work undertakes our cause) simplified religion marvellously, and made many things hitherto regarded as essential to the faith mere auxiliaries. Nevertheless, the new theology did not necessarily sweep them away. Certain things were now no longer seen as essential to the Christian life — such as the acceptance of certain forms of doctrines, auricular confession, the monastic life, communion by the laity with bread only and no wine, fasting, going on pilgrimages, forgoing meat on Fridays, and the like. Nevertheless, it was not necessary to insist that one never forgo meat on Fridays, never fast, never go on a pilgrimage, never become a monk, never receive Communion in one kind. The only thing that mattered was the spirit in which such actions were done or left undone. The fundamental religious experience had shown the liberty of the Christian to trust courageously in God and count all things of little moment compared with the one thing needful. Vatican II has placed a stamp of approval on this new attitude. Many good Catholics now feel free to consider such issues a matter of conscience — and yet this does not in any sense diminish the vitality of their faith; if anything, it makes them better Catholics. They have found a 'simpler' view of Christianity, much less cluttered. This is exactly what Luther created. According to Harnack, he saw the Christian religion as 'the living assurance of the living God who has revealed Himself and opened His heart in Christ — nothing more.'[1]

It was vital to this simplification that this living God who had shown his hand in Christ was accessible to every man, woman and child. Quoting Harnack again, we might note that,

> Rising above all anxieties and terrors, above all ascetic devices, above all directions of theology, above all interventions of hierarchy and Sacraments, Luther ventured to lay hold of God Himself in Christ, and in this act of faith, which he recognised as God's Work, his whole being obtained stability and firmness, nay, even a personal joy and certainty, which no medieval Christian had ever possessed.[2]

God Himself gave the believer the power to throw himself di-

---

1. Harnack, *Lehrbuch der Dogmengeschichte* (Freiburg i. B.: J.C.B. Mohr, 1890-94). E.T., *History of Dogma* (Boston, 1907), 7:183.
2. Ibid., p. 184

rectly on God. True as this is, it contradicts one of the most widely diffused and most strongly held religious beliefs of the medieval Church, and was bound to come into collision with it whenever the two were confronted with each other. More than once in these pages I have made reference to Luther's constant emphasis that faith is a gift of God and not a product of our own works and efforts (Eph. 2.8-9), and yet it was the unquestioned and universal belief of medieval piety that the mediatorial work of a priest was necessary for salvation.

Medieval Christians believed that the life of the soul was *created*, nourished, and perfected through the sacraments, and that the priests who administered them possessed, by virtue of their ordination, powers whereby they daily offered the true sacrifice of Jesus Christ and realised his presence in the Host, power to forgive sins, divine authority to teach the truths of salvation. It was this universally accepted power of a mediatorial priesthood that had enslaved Europe and rendered the freedom of a Christian man an impossible thing. Everywhere the priesthood was presumed able to bar the way to God. The Church, which ought to have shown to all men the glorious openness of God, his pure and immediate accessibility to the believer, had fenced off his presence with a triple wall of defence, through which no man could gain entrance unless admitted by a priest. Those who were troubled about their sin were instructed to go not to God, but to a man, often of known moral obliquity, to confess their sins before him because he was a priest. When they wished to hear the comforting words of pardon, it was not from God, but from a priest that the assurance was supposed to come. God's grace, to help men to live and to prepare them to die, was given in a series of sacraments, sacraments that a priest could grant or withhold. Man was born again in baptism; he came of age spiritually at confirmation; his marriage was cleansed from lust by the sacrament of matrimony; penance brought him back to grace and to spiritual life; the Mass gave him the necessary spiritual nourishment during his life's pilgrimage; deathbed grace and the guarantee to ultimate eternal life with God were imparted in extreme unction. They were, in fact, operations of jealously guarded professional powers, which the priests held as of right, sometimes withheld by priestly fiat, and often granted grudgingly for money. These ceremonies were hardly the signs and promises of God's free grace and mercy under which Luther meant men to live.

Even Vatican II, for all its progressive thinking, preserved the clear gap between the priesthood and the laity, precisely expressed in the *De Ecclesia* as well as in the 'Decree on the Priestly Ministry and Life'. 'There is an essential difference between the faithful's priesthood in common and the priesthood of the ministry or hierarchy, and not just a difference of degree' (*De Ecclesia*). Priests, defined in a Levitical sense, are 'given the power of sacred Order to offer sacrifice, forgive sin, and in the name of Christ, publicly exercise the office of priesthood'. By 'a special sacrament . . . they are signed with a specific character and portray Christ the priest.' 'They reconcile sinners to God and the Church through the sacrament of penance. . . . They sacramentally offer the Sacrifice of Christ in a special way when they celebrate Mass' ('Decree on Priestly Ministry'). They 'share, at their own level of the ministry, the office of Christ, the sole mediator' (*De Ecclesia*). It is not possible to reconcile Luther's evangelical and New Testament views on the ministry with those of Roman Catholicism; in fact, it is perhaps at this point that we see the deepest cleavage between them, perhaps even the fundamental cause of the great divide of the sixteenth century. Certainly it is the one most marked today, for it is at this point that both the Church and the world sense the difference between the two communions. It is neither in contemporary Roman Catholic theology nor in Roman Catholic preaching today that one is likely to experience a pure, living, and evangelical theology on the doctrine of the priesthood or the priesthood of the laity.

Nevertheless, Protestants should remind themselves that even when the doctrine is expressed in such exclusive and sacerdotal language, it remains effective as a scheme of salvation. It could be argued that the system worked (and still works) for countless numbers of simple unquestioning people in a quite positive way, and it would have been better left alone. Yet, apart from its errors, it contained a malevolent hidden negative principle, visible not when the sacraments were being offered to people (the normal custom), but when they were being withheld. The popes had given many an object lesson on this, even in Britain under the vassal King John.

If a town or a country had been a source of offence to the pope or the papal curia, the place was put under an interdict, which meant that the priests were to withhold the sacraments from the people. They withheld from the newborn babe the grace of baptism, without which it was supposed none could attain heaven. They refused the dying their deathbed grace that was supposed to certify their eventual passage into heaven. They refused to unite the young people in holy matrimony. They removed the daily office and withheld the grace of the Mass. The God of grace could not be approached, the blessings of pardon and the strength from prayer for daily living could not be procured, because a king or councillor had crossed the pope's path in some matter of worldly policy. The Church—that is to say in this context, the clergy—barred all access to God by refusing to communicate the grace of God in our Lord Jesus Christ. The pope, by a mere stroke of his pen, could prevent a whole nation, it was believed, from approaching God, because he could prohibit all his priests from performing the sacramental acts that the people believed brought him near. An interdict meant spiritual death to a place, and to a typical believer was a worse death than any plague could bring.

Everybody shuddered at the awful and mysterious powers that a mediatorial priesthood was supposed to possess. These powers were enhanced at the ordinary level of daily existence, for nobody was permitted to buy from, sell to, give to, support, help, or have any dealings with a town or country under interdict. It meant not only spiritual but economic death, and could bring the proudest to their knees. It was the most closed of 'closed shops', if such language may be permitted.

Luther's theology was wholly other: if the characteristic of Catholic teaching was 'closedness', the characteristic of Luther's teaching was 'openness'; if the Catholic key was meant to keep the door locked, Luther's key was meant to open it. I have argued that the fundamental religious experience of Luther meant that God the Father who had revealed himself in Christ is directly accessible to every humble penitent and faithful seeker. The first tenet of that theology was the principle of the universal priesthood of believers, or, as it is generally translated, the priesthood of all believers. Luther presented it already in that most effective of his books, *The Freedom of a Christian Man* (1520); he described it in a covering letter to Pope Leo X, to whom he sent the book, as 'the whole of Christian living in a brief form', and an example of the kind of studies he would rather engage in, if the Pope's godless flatterers would allow him. Subsequent critics have endorsed this view and described it as his most beautiful book, far above all the controversies of the day, and in 'full possession of the positive truth and peace of the religion of Christ.'[3] It certainly is a pearl among Luther's writings.

He begins by speaking of faith as the living fountain of Christ ever springing up in the heart (John 4.14), and proceeds to draw upon 1 Corinthians 9.19 ('For though I be free from all men, yet have I made myself servant unto all'), establishing his famous antithesis, 'A Christian man is the most free lord of all, and subject to none: a Christian man is the most dutiful servant of all, and subject to everyone.' He then explains what it is to be free:

> No external thing, whatsoever it be, has any influence whatever in producing Christian righteousness or liberty, nor in producing unrighteousness or bondage. A simple argument will furnish the proof. What can it profit the soul if the body fare well, be free and active, eat, drink and do as it pleases? For in these things even the most godless slaves of all the vices fare well. On the other hand, how will ill health or imprisonment or hunger or thirst or any other external misfortune hurt the soul? With these things even the most godly men are afflicted, and those who because of a clear conscience are most free. None of these things touch either the liberty or the bondage of the soul. The soul receives no benefit if the body is adorned with the sacred robes of the priesthood, or dwells in sacred places, or is occupied with sacred duties, or prays, fasts, abstains from certain kinds of food or does any work whatsoever that can be done by the body and in the body. The righteousness and the freedom of the soul demand something far different, since the things which have been mentioned could be done by any wicked man, and such works produce nothing but hypocrites. On the other hand, it will not hurt the soul if the body is clothed in secular dress, dwells in unconsecrated places, eats and drinks as others do, does not pray aloud, and neglects to do all the things mentioned above, which hypocrites can do.[4]

Luther argued that all manner of works, even contemplation, meditation, and all that the soul can do, avail nothing. 'If the Son therefore shall make you free, ye shall be free indeed' (John 8.36). The soul can do without all things except the Word of God, but

---

3. Philip Schaff, *Modern Christianity: The German Reformation*, vol. 7 of *History of the Christian Church*, rev. ed. (New York: Scribner's, 1910; Grand Rapids, Mich.: Eerdmans, 1980), p. 224.

4. *Treatise on Christian Liberty* (1520), in *The Works of Martin Luther*, ed. Henry Eyster Jacobs (Philadelphia: Muhlenberg, 1943), 2:313f. Hereafter abbreviated *WML*.

where that is missing, there is no help for the soul in anything whatsoever. This Word is the Gospel of God concerning his Son, who was made flesh, suffered, rose from the dead, and was glorified through the Spirit who sanctifies. To preach Christ means to feed the soul, to make it righteous, to set it free and save it, if it believe the preaching. For faith alone is the saving and efficacious use of the Word of God. . . . The end of the Law is Christ, unto righteousness to every one that believeth. . . . This Word of the Gospel cannot be received or cherished by any works whatever, but only by faith. . . . This, then, is how through faith alone without works the soul is justified by the Word of God, sanctified, made true and peaceful and free, filled with every blessing and made truly a child of God (John 1.12). In the soul only faith and Word hold sway. As the Word is, so it makes the soul, as heated iron glows like fire because of its union with fire. Faith further honours and reveres Christ in whom it trusts, cleaves to his promises, fulfils his commands. Faith also unites the soul to Christ, and Christ and the soul become one flesh. Luther speaks of the wedding ring of faith. Thus the believing soul by the pledge of its faith is free from all sins, secure against death and hell, and endowed with eternal righteousness, life, and salvation by Christ, its bridegroom.

Christ imparts his all and shares his all with everyone that believes: the believer is one with Christ. No danger can hurt his soul, no sorrow utterly overwhelm him; he can never be alienated from Christ, in life or in death. Hence we are all kings and priests, as many as believe on Christ (1 Pet. 2.9):

> The power of which we speak is spiritual; it rules in the midst of enemies, and is mighty in the midst of oppression, which means nothing else than that strength is made perfect in weakness, and that in all things I can find profit unto salvation, so that the cross and death itself are compelled to serve me and to work together with me for my salvation. This is a splendid prerogative and hard to attain, and a true omnipotent power, a spiritual dominion, in which there is nothing so good and nothing so evil, but that it shall work together for good to me, if only I believe. And yet, since faith alone suffices for salvation, I have need of nothing, except that faith exercise the power and dominion of its own liberty. Lo, this is the inestimable power and liberty of Christians. [5]

---

5. WML, 2:324.

He goes on to say,

> Not only are we the freest of kings, we are also priests for ever, which is far more excellent than being kings, because as priests we are worthy to appear before God to pray for others and to teach one another things of God. For these are the functions of priests, and cannot be granted to any unbeliever. Thus Christ has obtained for us, if we believe on Him, that we are not only His brethren, co-heirs and fellow-kings with Him, but also fellow-priests with Him, who may boldly come into the presence of God in the spirit of faith and cry, 'Abba, Father!' pray for one another and do all things which we see done and prefigured in the outward and visible works of priests. . . .
>
> You will ask, 'If all who are in the Church are priests, how do those whom we now call priests differ from laymen?' I answer, 'Injustice is done those words, "priest", "cleric", "spiritual", "ecclesiastic", when they are transferred from all other Christians to those few who are now by a mischievous usage called "ecclesiastics". For Holy Scripture makes no distinction between them, except that it gives the name "ministers", "servants", "stewards", to those who are now proudly called popes, bishops, and lords and who should by the Ministry of the Word serve others and teach them the faith of Christ and the liberty of believers. For although we are all equally priests, yet we cannot all publicly minister and teach, nor ought we if we could. Thus Paul writes in I Cor. iv, 'Let a man so account of us, as of the ministers of Christ, and stewards of the mysteries of God.' . . . Rather ought Christ to be preached to the end that faith in Him may be established, that He may not only be Christ, but be Christ for thee and for me, and that what is said of Him and what His name denotes may be effectual in us. . . . For [the faithful heart] believes that the righteousness of Christ is its own, and that its sin is not its own, but Christ's; and that all sin is swallowed up by the righteousness of Christ is, as has been said above, a necessary consequence of faith in Christ. So the heart learns to scoff at death and sin. . . . For death is swallowed up not only in the victory of Christ, but also by our victory, because through faith His victory has become ours, and in that faith we also are conquerors.[6]

In the first part of the treatise, Luther argues that everything a man has derives from his faith. If a man has faith, he has everything; if a man has no faith, nothing else suffices him. *Wer glaubt, der*

---

6. *WML*, 2:324-27.

hat. In a parallel way, he argues in the second part that everything a Christian does must issue from that faith. It may be necessary to fast and exercise discipline: it may be necessary to do good works. The important thing to remember is that these are not good works in themselves, in the sense that they make a man good; rather, they are signs of his faith, to be done in joy, as God's true works. Like Adam before the Fall, he works freely to please God, and therein is his joy:

> We do not, therefore, reject good works; on the contrary, we cherish and teach them as much as possible. We do not condemn them for their own sake, but because of this godless addition to them and the perverse idea that righteousness is to be sought through them. . . . Therefore, in all his works he should be guided by this thought and look to this one thing alone, that he may serve and benefit others in all that he does, having regard to nothing except the need and advantage of his neighbor. . . . Faith is truly effectual through love; that is, it issues in works of the freest service cheerfully and lovingly done, with which a man willingly serves another without hope of reward, and for himself is satisfied with the fullness and wealth of his faith. . . . I will therefore give myself as a Christ to my neighbor, just as Christ offered Himself to me; I will do nothing in this life except what I see is necessary, profitable and salutary to my neighbor, since through faith I have an abundance of all good things in Christ.[7]

In this sense, as far as spiritual position, privileges, and responsibility go, the laity and the clergy are on the same level: they both have immediate access to God through faith, and they are both equally obliged to do all that is in them for their fellowmen. Luther asserted that men and women living their lives in the home and on the farm, in workshop or civic office, had equally a vocation to that work, and fulfilled God's will for them in secular work as much as any religious in his vocation. The difference between clergy and laity was not that clergy had a 'higher', 'spiritual' vocation, and laity a 'lower', 'secular' vocation. All alike were on the same footing, justified by faith. The clergy were simply men called out of the community, trained and appointed to fulfil pastoral and spiritual duties; their function did not make them holier than, say, the farmer or the merchant. Should the priest fail to perform his proper duties,

---

7. WML, 2:333-38.

there would be no reason why the people should not compel him to mend his ways or even remove him from office and put him back into the fellowship to fulfil a lay role — to put him back into the pew where he might once again learn to be a Christian.

This great principle is present in all the *Reformation* Writings of 1520. One finds it in the *Babylonian Captivity*:

> Let every one, therefore, who knows himself to be a Christian be assured of this and apply it to himself, — that we are all priests, and there is no difference between us; that is to say, we have the same power in respect to the Word and all the sacraments. However, no one may make use of this power except by the consent of the community or by the call of a superior. For what is the common property of all, no individual may arrogate to himself, unless he be called. And therefore, this sacrament of ordination, if it have any meaning at all, is nothing else than a certain rite whereby one is called to the ministry of the Church. Furthermore, the priesthood is properly nothing but the ministry of the Word, mark you, of the Word — not of the Law, but of the Gospel. . . . Whoever, therefore, does not know or preach the Gospel, is not only not a priest or bishop, but he is a plague of the Church, who under the false title of priest or bishop — in sheep's clothing, forsooth — oppresses the Gospel and plays the wolf in the Church. [8]

And again one finds it strongly emphasized in the *Answer to Emser*:

> The Scriptures make us all priests alike, as I have said, but the churchy priesthood which is now universally distinguished from the laity and alone called a priesthood, in the Scriptures is called *ministerium, servitus, dispensatio, episcopatus, presbyterium*, and at no place *sacerdotium* or *spiritualis*. I must translate that. The Scriptures, I say, call the spiritual estate and priestly office a ministry, a service, an office, an eldership, a fostering, a guardianship, a preaching office, shepherds. . . . [The terms] 'priest' and 'bishop' are used interchangeably in the Scriptures [Tit. 1.5, and 1.7f]. . . . That we now have bishops, rectors, priests, chaplains, canons, monks, and other similar titles signifying a difference in office, should not surprise us; it has all come from our habit of so interpreting Scripture that not a word of it retains its true meaning. Therefore God and His Scriptures know nothing of bishops as we now have them. These things are all a result of man-made laws and ordinances, and through long usage have taken such

---

8. *The Babylonian Captivity* (1520), WML, 2:282-83.

hold on us that we imagine the spiritual estate is founded on the Scriptures, although it is twice as worldly as the world itself, because it calls itself and pretends to be spiritual, but there is no truth in its claim.

I called this priesthood churchy because it grows out of the Church's organisation and is not founded in the Scriptures. For it was the custom years ago, and ought to be yet, that in every Christian community, since all were spiritual priests, one, the eldest or most learned, and most pious, was elected to be their servant, officer, guardian, watchman, in the Gospel and the sacraments, even as the mayor of a city is elected from the whole body of its citizens. If tonsures, consecrations, ointments, vestments made priests and bishops, then Christ and His apostles were never priests or bishops. [9]

It was this principle of the *priesthood of all believers* that delivered men from the vague fear of the clergy and certainly was the greatest threat to the power and authority of the priest. This deliverance spurred men on to take in hand the reformation of the Church that was so badly needed. It could be argued that it is the one great religious principle that lies at the basis of the whole Reformation movement. [10] It could be further argued that it is Luther's profoundest challenge to Roman Catholicism: it was certainly felt as such by the clergy at the time, and is still seen as such today. In the light of the decrees and constitutions of Vatican II, it must still be regarded as the one outstanding difference between Catholics and Protestants. It derives directly from Luther's profound evangelical experience of Christ.

Some will doubtless say that it is absolutely impossible for the worldwide organised Catholic Church to take such theology into its system. Nevertheless, before that conclusion is drawn, certain most important points must be heeded. First, Protestants must admit that even when the Roman doctrine is expressed and practised in the most sacerdotal and exclusive terms, it remains effective as a scheme of salvation: it brings the faithful to Christ, maintains them there, and in the matter of moral witness enables the faithful to give a clearer and nobler account of themselves to the world than many Protestants do. Under persecution and fire, they stand firm; in home,

---

9. *Answer to Emser* (1521), WML, 3:321-24.

10. In a conversation I had some years ago with Ernst Käsemann, he expressed the view that in his opinion it was the central principle of the Reformation.

in school, and in work they maintain Christian principles (and, of course, since Vatican II, now live and think happily with other Christians). Some validity must be granted to the Catholic practice, in that it works and has withstood the test of time. Further, it is certainly part of the tradition and can be shown to have some basis in the New Testament.

Is it not possible for Protestants to grant the pragmatic truth that resides in pastoral Catholic practice? In vast areas of the world, Protestant doctrine, though biblically based and undeniably true, is spiritually and intellectually beyond the range of millions of simple believers and true practitioners. Can we not 'let both grow together till the harvest', without describing one as wheat, the other as tares? Protestant theology, open always to argument, criticism, and fresh evidence, can freely live and breathe within Catholicity, as Vatican II has shown; Catholic theology, with Catholic pastoral care and practice, may just as freely live and breathe. Both could emerge stronger, if allowed to re-create each other within the one fellowship of the Holy Spirit, which is what the Church truly is.

A second point is equally important: Luther and Lutheranism have a very high regard for the doctrine of the ministry. It was in the earlier years (1519-23) that he maintained his doctrine of the universal priesthood of all baptised believers, but he never modified his views on the centrality of ministry and oversight. He believed theological knowledge, special training, and precise personal qualities to be the foremost requirements for the clergy. He thought that the ministry was the concern of the whole congregation, and that no man dare presume to take on the role of minister before the congregation had verified his call from God, and in their turn, had called him to serve in that place. The idea of a universal priesthood certainly never meant that everybody was a priest and could take on the ministry of preaching and the cure of souls. To use Luther's own language, the congregation was not to be like a pack of women in the marketplace, everyone wanting to speak, no one to listen.

Nevertheless, it was not merely on grounds of order and decency that he maintained these views. Beneath Luther's theology were the deep theological concerns of a call from God with the commission to preach his Word and care for the souls of men as Christ cared. His concern at this point was to clarify the doctrine of the priesthood of all believers, because, resisting this theology, true in itself, there stood the monopoly of the consecrated priest, seeking to demolish it on grounds of self-interest, certainly not for theological reasons. 'It is true', he said, 'we are all priests—but we are not all parsons [*Pfarrherr*].' He never dropped altogether the old distinctions between 'clergy' and 'laity': Protestant theology has preserved the distinction. What Luther shows is that Christianity may carry a high doctrine of the ministry and at the same time maintain an effectual doctrine of the priesthood of all believers.

After Luther had made his biblical point, and particularly when the Enthusiasts and radicals and revolutionaries sought to abolish ministry and church, claiming divine inspiration and the possession of the Holy Ghost, he emphasised the other side, the Catholic side, in seeking to maintain a better balance. God instituted the ministry and continues to call men to that office, and normally only the lawful minister, duly called and publicly instituted, has the right to exercise that office. It may be different for folk shipwrecked on a desert island, but Luther was not speaking to that situation.

His view was aptly expressed by way of the analogy of the citizens and the mayor: all citizens have equal civic rights, but this does not mean that every citizen may seize for himself the office of mayor. All the citizens together elect one of their number to fulfil the work of the mayor, who, in the name of all, has to administer the common rights of the city. He does not *become* a citizen by this election; he *is* already a citizen, and brings his rights as a citizen with him into the office of mayor. In the same way, all Christians have equal rights as priests, but they may not arbitrarily take upon themselves the priest's functions. They must elect one of their kind 'to the highest office in Christendom':[11] to him is delegated the power to administer the common rights of a Christian community. The Christian does not become a priest by election to the ministry or by ordination. He was already a priest by virtue of his baptism. 'We are all equally priests in so far as we have been baptised.'[12] His election as a minister bestows on him the right to exercise all priestly functions. It is the will of God that these functions be reserved for the ministry only. The older Luther grew, the more he sought to

---

11. *D. Martin Luthers Werke: Kritische Gesamtausgabe* (Weimar, 1883 ff.), 11, 415, 30.

12. Ibid., 6, 564, 6.

strengthen the authority of the ministry, but never, of course, to abrogate his earlier emphasis on the priesthood of all believers.

I mean to suggest that (for the ecumenical situation that now exists since Vatican II), the high doctrine of the priestly office associated with Catholicism might, on the simple pragmatic basis that it works well, be supposed to have the potential to work creatively and in harmony with the disturbing doctrine of the priesthood of all believers, so dearly and rightly treasured by Protestants. Is it not of some significance that at the Diet of Augsburg in 1530, where Melanchthon and the Protestants with Luther behind them were seeking a *modus vivendi* with Rome, no mention was made of this principle? Yet it has been held these 450 years as strongly as it was in the first century and in the sixteenth. Is catholicity not comprehensive enough to hold them in mutually creative tension? Luther changed his emphasis without retrenching his theology.

Strong support for this argument has come from the *Final Report* of the Anglican/Roman Catholic International Commission, which gives a special and complete section on Ministry and Ordination, (pp. 29-45). This comprises the *Agreed Statement* (1973), followed by *Elucidations* (1982). The *Agreed Statement* is manifestly clerical, obviously drawn up by bishops and clerics of both communions, and further, relates the ministry in very priestly categories to the sacrificial language of the Eucharist. The statement does not start from the basic biblical exposition of the Church as the called people of God and take the reader from there; it defines the Church in relation to the clergy, instead of the clergy in relation to the Church. It further states that the ministry of the ordained priest is 'not an extension of the common Christian priesthood but belongs to another realm of the gifts of the Spirit' (whatever 'another realm' means).

Nevertheless, it does admit that there are a 'diversity of forms of ministerial service' and that the New Testament churches enjoyed 'a considerable diversity in the structure of pastoral ministry'. The *Statement* records the wide variety of images that the New Testament uses to describe a minister's functions — 'servant', 'herald', 'ambassador', 'teacher', 'shepherd', 'steward', and 'example'. More important, it affirms a 'priesthood of all the faithful'. Still more significant, it stresses that ministers are ministers of the Gospel, that they must preach the Word of God according to the New Testament, and that therein lies the source and ground of their preaching and authority. It calls attention to a teaching ministry and to the Church's responsibility of mission to the outsider. Such statements represent far-reaching developments on the whole period from Trent of the sixteenth century to the *Mystici Corporis* of the twentieth (1943), and bear eloquent though late testimony to the prophetic insights of Luther. If Luther were included in these conversations instead of excluded, as he was at Trent and since, they would complete their work within our lifetime.

CHAPTER SEVEN

JUSTIFICATION BY FAITH

ANOTHER CENTRAL CONCERN OF Luther that needs consideration within the wider framework of catholicity is justification by faith. I have argued that Luther, after leaving the university, entered the rather superior and well-disciplined Augustinian monastery at Erfurt to find his soul and to learn to know the God of grace who would yield him that compelling certainty of pardon of sin and peace. He took in with him (and inside met at its finest) traditional religion, which contended that the penitent must work hard and prepare himself to experience the grace of God. Luther entered that monastery as the ideal monk, in total dedication, highly sensitive spiritually, with a fine mind, seeking one thing and one thing only — God. The essential thing for the twentieth-century reader to understand and appropriate before he can begin to know what Luther meant by the phrase 'justification by faith only' is that it was not until God lifted that awful weight from his mind and freed him from that dreadful sense of oppression that Luther broke through (we say advisedly 'until *God* lifted', not 'until *Luther* found'). He then experienced the pardon he sought, then began to learn the authentic Christian experience. The phrase 'justification by faith only' describes the experience; the experience matters, not the phrase. God delivered Luther from his anthropocentric attempts to find how *he* could find grace and directed him to the theocentric deliverance available through Christ and all that *God* had done for us men and our salvation. This practical experience of Luther must be borne in mind when we come to investigate his understanding of justification by faith, rather than any later sense of a Protestant party cry nor of Catholic/Protestant polemic.

The first distinction to be borne in mind is Luther's distinction between mere historic faith (*fides historica*) and true faith (*fides vera*). A man may have no questions to raise, give assent to the creeds and various doctrines, believe that there is a God, and even believe the Incarnation, but yet have no faith. As Luther once quaintly expressed it, even the Devil believes that! The faith Luther so strongly taught and so effectively preached was true faith, *fides vera*. This kind of faith is another thing altogether. It is the faith kindled and created by God (Eph. 2.8-9). When Luther spoke of justification by faith, it was this latter kind of faith he meant. Even Protestants sometimes forget this and make of faith some kind of work, something we put into the bargain.

This true faith has its beginnings in God, not in man; it entails God working in us and on us. As we keep ourselves open to his activity, we find this newly kindled divine life fed and kept strong by his Word addressing us, calling us; he himself makes effectual that to which he is calling us. 'Faithful is he that calleth you, who also will do it' (1 Thess. 5.24). The promise of God on God's side and faith on man's side relate and create new spiritual life of the divine kind. Luther brings this out in many passages, such as the following:

> When faith is of the kind that God awakens and creates in the heart, then a man trusts in Christ. He is then so securely founded on Christ that he can hurl defiance at sin, death, hell, the Devil and all God's enemies. He fears no ill, however hard and cruel it may prove to be. Such is the nature of true faith, which is utterly different from the faith of the Schoolmen, Jews and Turks. Their faith, produced by their thoughts, simply lights upon a thing, accepts it, believes that it is this or that. God has no dealings with such delusion; it is the work of man, and comes from nature, from the free will of man; and men possessing it can say, repeating what others have said: I believe that there is a God. I believe that Christ was born, died, rose again for me. But what the real faith is, and how powerful a thing it is, of this they know nothing. . . .
>
> Wherefore, beware of that faith which is manufactured or imagined; for the true faith is not the work of man, and therefore the faith which is manufactured or imagined will not avail in death, but will be overcome and utterly overthrown by sin, by the devil, and by the pains of Hell. The true faith is the heart's utter trust in Christ, and God alone wakens that in us. He who has it is blessed, he who has it not is cursed.[1]

---

1. *D. Martin Luthers Werke: Kritische Gesamtausgabe* (Weimar, 1883ff.), 10, 3, 352-61. Hereafter abbreviated WA (Weimar Ausgabe).

All this is perhaps most simply expressed in Luther's 'Sermon on the Twofold Righteousness' (1519), and is later expressed at greater length in his commentary on Galatians.

The first kind of righteousness Luther calls 'alien righteousness' (i.e., that which Christ himself offered, without our works, by grace alone). The second kind of righteousness is what Luther calls 'good works' (e.g., love to neighbour, meekness and fear towards God, etc.); this righteousness he sees as a consequence of the first. Luther respects this righteousness highly, but ascribes salvation to the first, and *only* to the first. To express this in technical terms, he is differentiating justification from sanctification (or to put it in other terms, gospel from law). This distinction was vital to Luther, (and is vital to Protestantism). As he puts it in his commentary on Galatians,

> Christian righteousness . . . is the imputation of God for righteousness or unto righteousness, because of our faith in Christ, or for Christ's sake. When the popish schoolmen hear this strange and wonderful definition, which is unknown to reason, they laugh at it. For they imagine that righteousness is a certain quality poured into the soul, and afterwards spread in to all the parts of man. They cannot put away the imaginations of reason, which teacheth that a right judgment, and a good will, or a good intent is true righteousness. This unspeakable gift therefore excelleth all reason, that God doth account and acknowledge him for righteous without any works, which embraceth his Son by faith alone, who was sent into the world, was born, suffered, and was crucified etc. for us.
>
> This matter, as touching the words, is easy (to wit, that righteousness is not essentially [*formaliter*] in us, as the Papists reason out of Aristotle, but without us in the grace of God only and in his imputation; and that there is no essential substance of righteousness [*nihil formae seu iustitiae*] in us besides that weak faith or first-fruits of faith, whereby we have begun to apprehend Christ, and yet sin in the meantime remaineth verily in us); but in very deed it is no small or light matter, but very weighty and of great importance. [2]

When Luther identifies this alien righteousness with Christ, and calls it a passive righteousness to distinguish it from any that we may already possess, he declares it in many places to be a whole—an

2. *A Commentary on St. Paul's Epistle to the Galatians* (1557; London: James Clarke, 1957), p. 227.

eternal and an infinite righteousness that is freely given to the believer not by measure, but instantaneously, wholly, entire, and without reserve.

Luther called the second kind of righteousness active righteousness, the righteousness of the law. It is a gift of God, the gift of the Holy Spirit to enable a man to do the works of God. This active righteousness, in contrast to passive righteousness, cannot atone for sin, satisfy justice, or appease the conscience. As Christians, we must be diligent to do good works, but equally diligent never to trust in them for our salvation. To trust in active righteousness, even though it is a gift from God in that he is giving us strength to obey, is to fall from grace. Active righteousness is the fruit of passive righteousness, or in other words, sanctification is the fruit of righteousness by faith:

> When I have this righteousness reigning in my heart, I descend from heaven as the rain making fruitful the earth: that is to say, I come forth into another kingdom and I do good works, how and whensoever occasion is offered. If I be a minister of the Word, I preach, I comfort the broken-hearted, I administer the Sacraments. If I be an householder, I govern my house and my family, I bring up my children in the knowledge and fear of God. If I be a magistrate, the charge that is given me from above I diligently execute. If I be a servant, I do my master's business faithfully. To conclude: whosoever he be that is assuredly persuaded that Christ is his righteousness, doth not only cheerfully and gladly work well in his vocation, but also submitteth himself through love to the magistrates and to their laws, yea though they be severe, sharp and cruel, and (if necessity do so require) to all manners of burdens and dangers of this present life, because he knoweth that this is the will of God, and that this obedience pleaseth him. . . .
>
> When we have thus taught faith in Christ, then do we teach also good works. Because thou hast laid hold of Christ by faith, through whom thou art made righteous, begin now to work well. Love God and thy neighbour, call upon God, give thanks unto him, praise him, confess him. Do good to thy neighbour and serve him, fulfil thine office. These are good works indeed, which flow out of this faith and this cheerfulness conceived in the heart for that we have remission of sins freely in Christ. . . .

> When sin is pardoned, and the conscience delivered from the burden and sting of sin, then may the Christian bear all things easily. . . .[3]

This distinction between the righteousness of faith and the righteousness of the law, between justification and sanctification, was the foundation of Luther's doctrine. He insisted on this distinction for two main reasons — 'for the glory of Christ and for the comfort of troubled conscience'. He contended that salvation is based solely on the righteousness of faith, on the righteousness of Christ, by grace alone, by faith alone. If we bring into this relationship, or associate with it, sanctification (active righteousness), we obscure the glory of Christ, because we fail to ascribe our salvation to his doing and dying alone. Nothing we do or say or are can mitigate the annihilating wrath of a holy God that we as sinners earn except Christ who loved man and gave himself for man. Compared with Christ's work of infinite righteousness, the active righteousness of all men, the sufferings of all the martyrs and the good works of the saints, are nothing. And yet God grants them a conditioned value nonetheless:

> This is our divinity, whereby we teach how to put a difference between these two kinds of righteousness, active and passive. . . . Both are necessary, but both must be kept within their bounds. . . . I am indeed a sinner as touching this present life and the righteousness thereof. . . . But I have another righteousness and life above this life, which is Christ the Son of God, who knoweth no sin, no death, but is righteousness and life eternal. . . .
>
> Therefore do we so earnestly set forth and so often repeat this doctrine of faith or Christian righteousness, that by this means it may be kept in continual exercise, and may be plainly discerned from the active righteousness of the law. (For by this only doctrine the Church is built, and in this it consisteth.) Otherwise we shall never be able to hold the true divinity, but by and by we shall either become canonists, observers of ceremonies, observers of the law, or Papists, and Christ so darkened that none in the Church shall be either rightly taught or comforted. Wherefore, if we will be teachers and leaders of

---

3. Ibid., pp. 28, 138.

others, it behoveth us to have great care of these matters, and to mark well this distinction between the righteousness of the law and the righteousness of Christ. And this distinction is easy to be uttered in words, but in use and experience it is very hard, although it be never so diligently exercised and practised; for in the hour of death, or in other agonies of the conscience, these two sorts of righteousness do encounter more near together than thou wouldest wish or desire.

Wherefore I do admonish you, especially such as shall become instructors and guiders of consciences, and also every one apart, that ye exercise yourselves continually by study, by reading, by meditation of the Word and by prayer, that in the time of temptation ye may be able to instruct and comfort both your own conscience and others, and to bring them from the law to grace, from active and working righteousness to the passive and received righteousness, and, to conclude from Moses to Christ. For the devil is wont, in affliction and in the conflict of conscience, by the law to make us afraid, and to lay against us the guilt of sin, our wicked life past, the wrath and judgment of God, hell and eternal death, that by this means he may drive us to desperation, make us bond-slaves to himself, and pluck us from Christ. Furthermore, he is wont to set against us those places of the Gospel, wherein Christ himself requireth works of us, and with plain words threatenth damnation to those who do them not. Now, if here we be not able to judge between these two kinds of righteousness, if we take not by faith hold of Christ sitting at the right hand of God, who maketh intercession unto the Father for us wretched sinners [Heb. 7:25], then are we under the law and not under grace, and Christ is no more a saviour, but a lawgiver. Then can there remain no more salvation, but a certain desperation and everlasting death must needs follow.[4]

The Formula of Concord (1556) reiterated these basic Luther insights on the twofold righteousness. The righteousness of faith is declared to be our only righteousness before God. This righteousness consists in the obedience of the divine-human Christ in both life and death, by which he fulfilled and satisfied the law on behalf of poor, condemned sinners. God imputes this righteousness to all who believe the Gospel, and by it they are justified and saved. Justification is a declaration or verdict *of God* that the sinner is acquitted and counted as righteous for the sake of the obedience and death of Jesus Christ.

---

4. Ibid., pp. 24-25, 27.

Renewal, sanctification, and the life of new obedience 'succeed the righteousness of faith'. This is called 'incipient righteousness' because it is never complete in this life owing to the corruption of original sin that inheres in the flesh of all saints. This righteousness consists in a life of active obedience to the law of God, which becomes the rule of life for the believer. No one can 'retain' justification if he despises God's law and the necessity of good works. The Holy Ghost indwells believers and enables them to live this life of new obedience. Nevertheless,

> this indwelling of God is not the righteousness of faith which St. Paul calls the *iustitiam Dei*, that is, the righteousness of God, for the sake of which we are declared righteous before God; but it follows the preceding righteousness of faith, which is nothing else than the forgiveness of sins and the gracious adoption of the poor sinner, for the sake of Christ's obedience and merit alone. [5]

The Formula of Concord declares there must be no confusion of the two kinds of righteousness:

> neither renewal, sanctification, virtues nor good works are . . . our righteousness before God, nor are they to be constituted or set up as a part or cause of our righteousness, or otherwise under any pretext, title or name whatever in the article of justification as necessary and belonging thereto; but the righteousness of faith consists alone in the forgiveness of sins out of pure grace, for the sake of Christ's merit alone; which blessings are offered us in the promise of the Gospel, and are received, accepted, applied, and appropriated by faith alone. [6]

THE HISTORICAL AND OBJECTIVE OTHERNESS OF CHRIST

I spoke earlier of Luther's deliverance from his own self-centred preoccupation to find God to that glorious liberty of faith that God awakens and creates in the heart, from which a total trust in Christ arises. This faith had a firm and unshakeable basis to rest upon, namely, the historic Christ. Such faith (and noboby knows this better

---

5. *Die Bekenntnisschriften der evangelisch-lutherischen Kirche*, ed. E. Wolf (Göttingen: Vandenhoeck and Ruprecht, 1967), p. 927.

6. Ibid., p. 933.

than an academic who has taught Theology and Biblical Studies) is neither helped nor hindered by a detailed knowledge of the person and work of Christ or a mastery of the biblical languages or a command of his earthly ministry. A man who has the faith described by Luther, the *fides vera*, may learn a great deal about the doctrine of Christ and much about his ministry, and such knowledge will do his true faith no harm, provided he does not make the mistake of thinking that doctrines about Christ, the ways in which the human understanding of Christ are expressed in every age, constitute either the fact of Christ themselves or something better than the fact; but the doctrine and the language have only a *referral* significance: they *refer* to the *fact* of Christ. It is in the fact of Christ that there lies the original, objective, ultimate truth, the reality outside us, to which we all, theologians and professors, saints and sinners, Protestant and Catholic alike, recognise, expressed as it is in all the splendour of the evangelists and the Apostles in the New Testament. It stands over against us in its objective otherness.

The faith that is the gift of this objective otherness causes us to see the practical significance of the historic Christ: it is the objective reality of Christ standing before us, the manifestation of the fatherly love of God, revealing and offering to us our own forgiveness, and with that the possibilities of the Kingdom of Heaven and our place therein. Christ is there as a fact, for all the world to see, believers and nonbelievers alike. The difference is that God stirs the heart and mind of a man, and in that divine kindling of faith, the power of God lying in that faith makes him see with compelling certainty the meaning of the fact of the historic Christ for us men and for our salvation. All that man offers is an openness to the truth. When the truth of God grips a man, he is a new man indeed: he begins to see, feel, think, and understand as Christ. 'If any man is in Christ, he is a new creation' (2 Cor. 5.17). The experience cannot be dissimilar to that of an Archimedes as he discovered the laws of flotation, of a Galileo studying the heavens, of Newton studying gravity, of Lavoisier examining chemical structure—or indeed of any person seeking to understand reality, *the way things are*.

The vision of truth has within it a strange quality of a desire to communicate it: all discoverers are missionaries. So it is with religious truth. When once one has this deepest of all personal experiences, one immediately seeks to offer it abroad, to find oneself in the fellowship of the Holy Spirit. In that fellowship the faithful offer further faith and love, one to the other, not dissimilar to the faith God first kindled in us, out of which faith spring works of love.

What we now call 'justification by faith' may be better thought of as a description of a religious experience within the believer of the kind Jesus preached, which the Apostles nailed down for all time, and which the saints, the fathers, and the doctors of the Church experienced and expressed, which they understood, and to which they related. It amounts to this: the believer who has that faith which is the gift of God, is regenerate, and a member of the Christian fellowship. In the strength of that faith he is called to do good works, and actually does those works of love. His relationship to God is not made by these good works, nor do the good works give him his righteousness, assurance of pardon and salvation, or peace with God. When he has done all, at his finest hour, he is still but an unprofitable servant. His salvation lies only in the mediatorial power of Christ's most perfectly righteous work, a power he has begun to appreciate in faith. His good works may be really good, and be a blessing to his home, his church, his community, and yet they are necessarily imperfect. In the religious experience we call justification by faith (or rather justification by grace through faith in Christ), the believer is aware that his own works, however good they may be, cannot compare with Christ's perfect work; he recognises that his pardon and salvation depend on that alone — on Christ alone.

This comparison offers a strange strength to sensitive and tender souls. The sense of free forgiveness, undeserved and unmerited, that flows into the human soul is always experienced as a revelation of wonderful love. It is the work of God, the act of God. Being a divine act, it is never over and done with; it is continuous. Luther always taught that the divine pronouncement of forgiveness is continuous because it is God who makes it: it is not the act of a single moment in contrast to the priestly absolution, which was the work of a moment, and in the nature of the case had to be pronounced over and over again. In an Easter sermon on Luke 24.36-47, Luther expressed this in the simplest terms:

> A Christian is at once a sinner and a saint; he is wicked and pious at the same time. For as far as our persons are concerned, we are in sins and are sinners in our own name. But Christ brings us another name, in which there is the forgiveness of

sins, that for His sake sins are remitted and pardoned. So both statements are true: there are sins, for the old Adam is not entirely dead as yet; yet, the sins are *not* there. The explanation is this: for Christ's sake God does not want to see them. As far as I am concerned I have my eyes on them: I feel and see them only too well. But as far as Christ is concerned, He stands there commanding that I be told I should repent, that is, confess myself a sinner and believe the forgiveness of sins in His name. For repentance, remorse, and knowledge of sin, though necessary, are not enough; faith in the forgiveness of sins in the name of Christ must be added. But where there is such a faith, God no longer sees any sins; for then you stand before God, not in your own name but in Christ's name. He adorns you with grace and righteousness, although in your own eyes, and in actual fact, you are personally a poor sinner, full of weakness and unbelief.[7]

Sometimes in Protestant polemic with Roman Catholic doctrines the conception of justification by faith is contrasted with justification by works. This is misleading for this argument belongs to the New Testament—for example, in the matter of Christ's conflict with rabbinism in St. John's Gospel, or in the still sharper argument of Paul with the Judaisers in Galatians and Romans—rather than in the Reformation dispute with Rome. It is also unfair, for Roman Catholics are not Judaisers, and generally have a very high awareness of the doctrine of grace. Examined closely, the word *justification* carries a different meaning in each phrase. *Justification by works* suggests the performance of meritorious works sufficient to make one acceptable to God. This is not, and never was, Christianity: it is Judaism. Justification by faith means that God, holy and righteous as he is, has accepted the sinner, unholy and unrighteous as the sinner is, solely on the grounds of his free forgiveness and grace in Christ.

Certainly in Roman Catholic usage the direct counterpart to the Reformation thinking on justification by faith is the absolution pronounced by a priest. Here the two systems are poles apart, and belong to two wholly disparate spheres of thought. The medieval man was thinking of spiritual powers working through Christ in the well-worn institutional channels of ecclesiastical institutions, priestly consecration, the confessional, and meritorious works, all within the

---

7. WA, 52, 264f.

supernatural and ecclesiastical organisation in which he had been born. Luther thought otherwise. Justification by faith, a God-centred and self-authenticating mastering experience within his soul, set Luther in the continuous line of the Christian fellowship. He knew the reassuring strength of God in his exercise of faith — an experience that comes from laying himself open to the work of Christ, which he is able to do by the faith that is the gift of God.

According to the Protestant, justification is a direct, divinely created, personal experience. It is complete in itself. It needs neither priest nor external ecclesiastical machinery. According to the Medieval, it is a prolonged action of a combination of usages, sacraments, priests, buildings, and all kinds of external machinery, which together are supposed to change a sinner gradually into a saint, so that he becomes righteous and acceptable to God. For the Protestant, the process is continuous, because it is of God, who is ever active. For the Medieval, it tends in the nature of the case to be intermittent, for the external means are used occasionally, being by times laid aside.

Further light can be cast on this subject from two directions, the first being a discussion of the teaching of the schools, and the second being a discussion of the idea as it is presented in the New Testament.

MEDIEVAL THEOLOGY

Although St. Augustine (354–430) stands within the ancient *imperium romanum*, he is nevertheless the father of Scholasticism. The medieval Church never accepted the Augustinian theology in its entirety, and yet Augustine's great intellect and profound Pauline theology of grace, effectualized by powerful spiritual perception and deep religious experience, sustained a marked influence for a thousand years. Medieval theology, for all its creative developments under Aquinas, Anselm, and Abelard, had never repudiated the Augustinian theology; in theory at least, it admitted that man's salvation — and justification as part of it — depended in the final analysis on the prevenient grace of God. The introduction of the works of Aristotle into Europe in the thirteenth century displaced the Platonic/Augustinian world view when Aquinas made a synthesis of

Aristotle and Augustine, thereby emphasising the action of the free will of man as a pure capacity of choice between two alternatives.

Scotus (1264– 1308) was a vigorous critic of Thomas. 'There is no rational argument for those things that belong to faith', he categorically laid down. He sought to clear up the confusion that existed between the *gratia operans* and the *gratia cooperans* of Augustine (i.e., *grace as operation* and *grace as cooperation*) by speaking of the grace of God that lay at the basis of man's justification as a *gratia habitualis*—an operation of the grace of God that gave to man's will a *habitus* (habitual tendency) in the direction of love towards God and man. Scotus conceived of God in terms of will and purpose and act rather than in terms of the mind and its concepts—a good biblical emphasis. In this connection he argued that when conduct is considered, an act of the will is far more important than any habitual tendency, for it is the act that is making use of the habit and apart from the act the habit is a mere inert passivity. It was his view, therefore, that the chief consideration in meritorious conduct is less the habit that has been caused by God's grace than the act of will that makes use of the habit. In this way the grace of God appears to be the general basis of meritorious conduct, whereas the decisive and all-important factor is the human act of will, which can make active and put to good effect the habit of mind that in the nature of the case is passive.

Recalling that the Schoolmen thought of justification as a process by which a sinner was gradually made into a righteous man, thoroughly and substantially changed by a righteousness *imparted*, we can understand why they thought of it as an infusion of divine grace that creates a habit of the will towards love to God and love to man; they supposed that acts of the will embrace this habit and produce positive acts of love towards God and man that are meritorious and that gradually change a sinner into a righteous person. This is the theory, but this theory had to be related in practice to the technique or machinery devised by the Church, provided to aid men to appropriate the grace of God, which is the basis and foundation of it all, and so it came to be supposed that the sacraments infuse grace.

The first sacrament is baptism. If a man were baptised, it was supposed that he would have sufficient grace to start with; extra injections or infusions would be granted from time to time in the

Mass. That would be all that would be needed to set a man on the path of meritorious conduct. That is the ideal path of justification according to medieval thought; yet this life is never ideal, for the new life begun in baptism can be destroyed by mortal sin. It is the sacrament of penance, which is presumed to renew this life slain by deadly sins, that is the most important; it is in the sacrament of penance, the 'second plank' of Jerome which rescues the drowning sinner, that one can observe the medieval teaching on justification. The good will of the sinner towards God is inferred from his disposition to go to confession. This movement of the spirit towards God reaches its goal when confession stimulated by the priest is finished. The performance of the meritorious good works is presumed to consist in the penitent's performance of the satisfactions imposed by the priest, generally conceived as prayer, almsgiving, restitution, service, and the like. When the absolution is pronounced, the process is presumed to be complete: the sinner has become a righteous man and is in 'a state of grace'.

It was at this point that Luther rent the medieval fabric of thought. He had done all that was required of him, had gone beyond even that devotion and discipline demanded of a dedicated monk. He had had the opportunity to study and master the entire Scholastic theory and practice of justification. Yet he never knew the real sense of pardon for which he yearned with his entire being; he never learned the peace and comfort of God's love towards him. For all his spiritual striving, for all his intellectual effort, he met uncertainty, a cold comfortless darkness. Finally he realised he had it all the wrong way: it was not a matter of the holy righteous God being far off and creaturely man having to do all he could to reach him; rather, it was a matter of the sinner being far off because of the alienating power of sin (not simply because of sins of commission or omission, but because of the sheer tyranny of an essentially sinful nature), and of God's having himself come *all the way*, and at his own costs having fought and prevailed in Christ.

When this faith was kindled in his mind and heart, Luther was overwhelmed by the grandeur of God's costly love, and knew not only pardon and peace, but the quickened desire to serve and love his fellowmen in the everyday demands of the common secular life. I myself know a distinguished and respected national figure who once said that as a boy of eight he had told his father a lie. The father simply looked at his son and without saying a word burst into tears. When the boy had become a man, he was able to say that, having learned how his father felt about untruth, he was sufficiently shocked and mortified to have carried the lesson all his life. The effect of being met with tenderness when he deserved punishment gave him a kind of glad wonderment and a new relationship to his father. This little illustration is a sort of parable on Luther's experience. German theologians may express it in far more profound theological language, but truth may enter in at lowly doors, as the Master taught us. No theologian since Christ saw the evangelical truth so clearly and vividly as Luther; he almost rivals Christ in his powers of conveying truth through homely parable, warm illustration, and in words 'understanded of the people'.

SALVATION BY WORKS AND SALVATION BY FAITH

There are two ways of salvation in the Bible. On the one hand, there is salvation by faith in Christ only, which was promised in the Old Testament, which Christ himself made possible, and which he commissioned the Apostles to proclaim after it had been effected. On the other hand, there is salvation by obedience to the Law. This was the Judaism in which Christ and his disciples were brought up, and of which St. Paul before his conversion was the zealous defender over against the Gospel. Salvation by works can be understood only in relation to salvation by faith.

Christ moved men beyond this doctrine of salvation by works, as Paul was to do after his conversion. He came to call not the righteous, but sinners to repentance. He came not as a rabbi to teach the Law, but as Christ to show men who loved the Law that it was only a preparation for the Gospel: if they had understood the righteousness of the Law, they would have seen the necessity of the righteousness of the Gospel. When Christ spoke to them of the relationship between God and man, it was in terms of a lost son (Luke 15) who was saved not by his righteousness, but by the mercy and goodness of the father. The son could never on his own have restored the relationship he had broken. Similarly the labourers in the vineyard (Matt. 20) were rewarded not in proportion to their work, but by the graciousness of their master. The Pharisee (Luke 18.9ff.) was not justified for all his virtue and goodness, solid though these were, whereas the publican was justified, because even though he was aware of his sin and hopelessness, he nevertheless maintained hope—not in himself, but in the merciful God to whom he cried. No man can have any claim on God. The message was proclaimed to all alike: repent and believe the Gospel. The truth of Christ's Gospel lies in the fact that man is estranged from God in sin, that man is even rebellious, and that this estrangement cannot be overcome except by a move from God.

If the Old Testament can be seen as a portrait of God's gracious activity, the New Testament can be seen as its perfect fulfilment. This point can be illustrated by comparing the ministry of Christ with that of John the Baptist.

John preached a mission of repentance, but there was a paralysis about his message. When his bewildered converts asked him what they were to do now that they had repented and been baptised, all that John could offer was ethical advice; even John, though 'greatest of all born of women', was in another world, a religion of Law, merit, ethics. 'He that hath two coats, let him impart to him that hath none; and he that hath meat, let him do likewise' (Luke 3.11). To the publicans he said, 'Exact no more than that which is appointed you' (Luke 3.13). To the soldiers, 'Do violence to no man, neither accuse any falsely; and be content with your wages' (Luke 3.14). Rather feeble doctrine for such a fiery preacher.

With Christ it was different. He showed his hearers that it was not advice they needed, but the saving Word of God. They had had the finest advice ever given to any people, the Law, but they could not keep it for they were in sin. He spoke of a repentance that brought them into the Kingdom of God, of a God who throughout all the centuries had been gracious and merciful, of a God who loved them and sought them while they were yet sinners, of a God who had offered the ultimate, himself as man, to win, redeem, even to die for ungrateful sinners. 'Never man spake as this man spake' (John 7.46). 'And the eyes of all them that were in the synagogue were fastened on him. . . . And all bare him witness, and wondered at the gracious words which proceeded out of his mouth.' (Luke 4.20b,22). 'For he taught them as one having authority, and not as the scribes' (Matt. 7.29). It was the self-authenticating Word of God seeking out and searching out the hearts of men. It was a new message of *salvation*, different from any they had ever heard before.

It was not a call to do more and to do it better, but a call to see more and to hear it better. 'Take heed how ye hear' (Mark 4.24) regarding what God was purposing and had purposed, regarding the saving Word that was seeking to cleanse, redeem, and enhearten men.

John could properly proclaim the prophecy of Isaiah, 'All flesh shall see the salvation of God'. And when 'all men mused in their hearts of John', he could but declare, 'One mightier than I cometh: He shall baptize you with water and the Holy Ghost' (Luke 3.4-16). This baptism was to mean not only the repentance we all need, but the new evangelical doctrine of rebirth from above as well; it meant the transition from the Law to the Gospel.

This distinction between the dispensations of John and Jesus was brought to its ultimate conclusion by the Apostles, for although Christ preached the Gospel, it could be appropriated in its totality only after his crucifixion, resurrection and ascension. That is why one finds the clearest Gospel not in the gospels, but in the epistles. A man can make almost anything he likes of Christ if he restricts himself to the Synoptic Gospels; he can find any sort of saviour he wants to find—a prophet, a preacher, a zealot, the first socialist. But in the epistles, and at its finest in Romans, Paul has fixed the content of faith clearly and unequivocally for all time, fixed it in his total sweep of what Christ has done for us men and for our salvation.

There is an important reason to pass from Jesus to Paul at this point: it was one thing for Jesus to preach the doctrine of free grace and justification by faith to dispossessed Galileans, the accursed 'people of the land', but it was quite another thing to convert the Jews obedient and loyal to the Law and the Cult, to persuade Jerusalem that the time was fulfilled and the Law fulfilled in the Gospel. Christ fought this fight, and it cost him his life. Of the Gospel writers only John saw this: he emphasised Christ's preaching and teaching in the temple at the feasts. It was in the Temple of Jerusalem that the Johannine debates declared the full significance of the Galilean preaching. It took a Hebrew rabbi, a Hebrew of the Hebrews touching the Law perfect, to tell the world that a man cannot be justified by the works of the Law (only he could fulfil such a requirement), but only by the free grace of God. This is what is meant by justification by faith in Christ only. Let us now turn to see how Paul understood this doctrine.

The phrase 'justification by faith' gives expression to what is essentially new and distinctive in Christianity, differentiating it not only from its historical origin, Judaism, but from all other religions of the world as well. Paul saw two radically distinct doctrines of salvation in conflict. One was salvation by the works of the Law, by earning merit by human effort and discipline and so making oneself acceptable to God by a human righteousness in accordance with this declared Law; this was the way of discipline, effort, ethic, self-righteousness. The other was a way for a sinner who knew he could never make himself righteous enough to be acceptable to God, and who was enabled by this very knowledge to accept joyfully the free mercy of God offered to him, a sinner. It was no longer a matter of man and his works, but of God and his work. It was no longer a matter of man and his righteousness, but God and his righteousness. It was not a case of God being far removed and of man making efforts to reach him; it was the other way round. It was man who was far removed from God, and God who had come all the way in Christ while man was in sin and opposition to him, God who had come freely offering unconditional forgiveness and a new life and a new righteousness, a life hid with Christ in God.

It is important to stress at this point the *objectivity* of this deliverance, of which St. John could write, 'that which we have heard, which we have seen with our eyes, which we have looked upon and our hands have handled, of the Word of life' (1 John 1.1). There was a very heavy cross which, had you carried it, would have filled your shoulder with splinters; there was a tomb which, had you seen it, you would have found empty; there was a Christ who in hand-to-hand combat defeated all the tyrants: wrath, sin, law, even death.

We are like men trapped in a bog: unless somebody comes along and can give a power from a base firmer than our own, we shall go under. Faith is not something inherent within you that grows; you begin with nothing at all. It is, according to Luther, 'a free surrender and a joyous wager on the unseen, untried and unknown goodness of God'.[8] 'If you believe, you possess', he said; 'if you do not believe, you do not possess—everyone always has as much of God as he believes.' In other words, God becomes effective in our life as we believe in him. Faith is a gift of God (Eph. 2.8); it is not something we put into the bargain. Nor is it something for

---

8. WA, 10, 3, 239.

which we can strive. It is not credulity, neither is it a feeling. It is not a mystical intuition, neither is it a comfortable psychological state of mind. It is not assent to propositions. It is not the case that a man has faith and that he is thereby enabled to believe the Gospel. Rather it is that when this Gospel is proclaimed, faith is called out, created, given by God; a man is literally confronted by God. It comes as a new kind of self-understanding—not a change of opinion, nor an act of the unconscious, but a movement in man's existence brought about through an encounter with God. This is what Paul meant when he described the Gospel as the power of God unto salvation. It wins, compels, changes, arrests: it makes a man aware of a new dimension. The hearing of the Gospel is an *event* in a person's life such as being confirmed, or getting married, or having a baby. It *happens*. That is what is meant by objectivity.

When the Gospel is declared and heard, it brings faith with it. The Gospel is primary: when it is preached it *awakens* faith in us. When one hears the Gospel, and is conquered by it, that is faith. Hans Küng writes, 'In justification the sinner can give nothing which he does not receive by God's grace. He stands there with his hands entirely empty—like Abraham in Genesis 15.6 and Romans 4.3, and like the Israelites before Moses in Exodus 4.31: 'And the people believed; and when they heard that the LORD had visited the people of Israel and that he had seen their affliction, they bowed their heads and worshipped.' This sinner is a man who knows that he has nothing to build for God, but he accepts God's word like David: 'Would you build me a house to dwell in? . . . Moreover, the LORD declares to you that the LORD will make you a house' (2 Sam. 7.5,11). This sinner is a man who will not dash off on a charger, but whose power lies in quietness and trust (see Isa. 30.16), who receives the kingdom of God like a little child (Mark 10.15), and who says nothing more than a Marian: 'let it be to me' (Luke 1.38). This sinner is a man who expects nothing from himself, but expects all from God, who is completely open to that which is his only refuge. This sinner is a man who does not work his own righteousness, but believes and therefore radically excludes any 'self-boasting': 'Then what becomes of our boasting? It is excluded. On what principle? On the principle of works? No, but on the principle of faith. For we hold that a man is justified by faith [alone] apart from works of law' (Rom. 3.27-28).[9] 'Yet we know that a man is not justified by works of the law but through faith in Jesus Christ, so even we have believed in Jesus Christ, in order to be justified by faith in Christ, and not by works of the law, because by works of the law shall no one be justified' (Gal. 2.16).

When Paul wanted to make this doctrine unequivocally clear, he wrote ʿΟ δὲ δίκαιος ἐκ πίστεως ξήσεται: 'He who is justified, by faith shall live' (Rom. 1.17). This text had played a remarkable role in Jewish history and was to play a still more remarkable role in Christian history. We meet it first in Habakkuk 2.4. Confronted by the Chaldean invader who was to devastate their land and take the people of God into captivity, the prophet went into his tower to hear what God was to say to him. God reassured him that the proud conqueror would one day fall, but that 'the righteous shall live by His faithfulness'. Pride, pillage, and war lead a people to its own destruction: Chaldea would walk the path of Assyria. Nevertheless, in his faithful devotion to God, the Jew as Jew would be preserved and survive, while the proud conqueror would go the way of all aggressors, who show their unbelief by working against God.

In the synagogue the text played the significant role of a summary of the Law. The Talmudic tradition says that on Sinai Moses received 613 commandments; King David summed them up in eleven (Ps. 15), Isaiah summed them up in six (Isa. 33.15f.), Micah summed them up in three (Mic. 6.6-8), another Isaiah summed them up in two (Isa. 56.1), and finally Habakkuk summed them up in one: 'the just shall live by His faith'. The synagogue considered this commandment, then, to be summing up of righteousness by the Law and its works; to keep it was to hold on to life: by such a faith the faithful would live.

Paul takes the prophetic and hallowed word to show that though originally righteousness came by faithfulness to the Law and its works, it was yet designated *by God* that righteousness should come not by the Law but by faith. How could a rabbi handle the Word of God with such liberty, if not perversity? He justified his case in

---

9. Cf. Romans 4.2, 5-6; 5.11; 9.30-32; 10.4-6; and also 1 Corinthians 4.7, and 2 Corinthians 12.9.

this way: Scripture has many meanings, not all of them immediately disclosed in the original context. First there is the plain, incontrovertible, obvious, historical meaning attached to the event, and this must never be doubted or questioned. From the text of the book of Exodus, for example, we can know that the Israelites were saved from hunger in the wilderness by the gift of manna from heaven. But the text is not exhausted by its first plain meaning. When those who sat in Moses' seat refused to believe Christ, arguing, 'Our fathers did eat manna in the wilderness', Jesus replied, 'Moses gave you not that bread from heaven, but my Father giveth you the true bread from heaven. For the bread of God is he which cometh down from heaven, and giveth life unto the world. . . . I am the bread of life (John 6.31-35).

Scripture was not exhausted by what God said and did to and with the original recipients. Paul knew it had a further word to say to his contemporaries, 'upon whom the end of the ages has come' (1 Cor. 10.11). To express it differently, we might say that the events of Scripture happened forward, but have to be interpreted backward from Christ, their Omega point. As Luther was later to say to Erasmus, *Tolle Christum e scripturis quid amplius in illis invenies?*: 'Take Christ out of the scriptures, and what else will you find in them?' 'Scripture, foreseeing that God would justify the Gentiles by faith, preached the Gospel beforehand to Abraham, saying, "In thee shall all the families of the earth be blessed" (Gal. 3.8). Or as Christ expressed it, again to unbelieving recipients, 'Your father Abraham rejoiced to see my day: and he saw it, and was glad' (John 8.56).

When that promise was first made to Habakkuk, it had its own meaning, but its fuller meaning was yet to be disclosed. The veil over Scripture was removed by Christ. God purposed to say through Habakkuk what he was now saying through Paul. Paul combines the two ideas of the righteous man (*dikaios*) and faith (*pistis*) into one — he who is justified by faith — and it is this man who 'shall live'. Habakkuk is, of course, speaking of righteousness by faithfulness to the Law; Paul is saying that its ultimate meaning is fulfilled in a righteousness of faith in the Gospel of Christ.

Of course, Paul's case was not based on one text; he taught that the entire Old Testament spoke of, prophesied, and was ultimately fulfilled in a righteousness by faith, not works. The significance of Abraham, who is the father of us all, is that he 'believed God, and it was counted unto him for righteousness' (Rom. 4.3). He was the man who 'was not weak in faith', and 'staggered not at the promise of God through unbelief . . . being fully persuaded that what God had promised he was able to perform. . . . This was all written not for his sake alone . . . but for us also to whom righteousness shall be imputed if we believe' (Rom. 4.19-24). All this happened centuries before the Law was given. It had been God's clear intent all along that man should be justified not by obedience to the Law, but by faith, trust, and confidence in God and his promises.

Paul further deepened the truth of justification by faith by showing that it could never rest on man's faith, but only on God's faithfulness. He expressed this theologically by showing that salvation was by God's promise and election: 'it is not of him that willeth nor of him that runneth, but of God that sheweth mercy' (Rom. 9.16). This he argued by showing that not all the seed of Abraham are the children of promise, 'that the purpose of God according to election might stand, not of works, but of him that calleth' (Rom. 9.11). Jacob was chosen, whereas Esau was not — and they were twin brothers.

The doctrine of justification by faith has led to certain misunderstandings. It has, for instance, been a common ploy of Roman Catholics to seek to discount the theology by quoting James when he argues that faith without works is dead, and that Abraham was justified by his works (James 2.14ff.). The answer is simple. The word *works* in James and in Paul means two entirely different things, as does the word *faith*. To James in this context, *faith* means orthodoxy, assent; to Paul it means the total commitment of body and soul to Christ. James is saying that unless a faith *issues* in the fruit of good works directed to one's neighbour, it is no faith at all. Paul contends the same thing, and Christ before him. The word *works* in Paul means the works of the Law, the doing of which some men claimed to be a means unto justification, unto acceptance by God. This was the clash of Christ against Judaism, and of Paul against the Judaisers, even when they included Peter and James and the pillars of the Church. James is protesting against a formal orthodoxy, the mere holding of opinions that bear no fruit in Christian conduct. Paul is protesting against Judaisers who make the Law a precondition of the Gospel. Luther was always sensitive to this distinction: 'faith alone justifies', he said, 'yet faith is never alone'. It is never without love and the works of love. 'Where there is not love, neither is there faith, but mere hypocrisy.'

A further point may be added here: what gives force to the appeal to James is that Roman Catholicism has always demanded the performance of meritorious works and good deeds alongside the receiving of God's saving work in Christ. This modifies the simplicity of justification by faith in Christ only. Roman Catholic theologies have never felt easy with the Pauline doctrine. It is worth reminding ourselves that the natural man does not take easily to the doctrine either, particularly if he is cultivated, educated, and moral. The natural man has a tendency (similar to that of Rome) to believe that it is essentially his own decency, his own efforts, and his own doing that restore him to God, or at least go a long way towards it. This is why Roman Catholicism tends to emphasise the Church, whereas the evangelicals emphasise Christ. Paradoxically, however, preaching Christ only gives a purer doctrine of the Church as well as the power of the Gospel. The Gospel always tends to dissolve the institutional Church, and sadly, the institutional Church tends to destroy the Gospel. Perhaps the true Church will have to tolerate the empirical church till the end of time.

Another passage not infrequently raised against the Pauline doctrine is the parable of the Last Judgment (Matt. 25), in which people are ultimately divided on a basis of works done. This does not argue that a man is justified by his works, however, for such a view is plainly contrary not only to Matthew's parable of the labourers in the vineyard (Matt. 20), but to all of Christ's teaching on forgiveness, mercy and grace as well. It is simply saying what James emphasised later: the acid test of faith is the fruit of good works; a faith without works is empty talk.

Evangelical and Catholic theologians can be distinguished from one another on the grounds that the evangelicals teach that the plain and only meaning of the word *justify* is 'to be accounted or deemed righteous' — that is, to have righteousness imputed to one so that a relationship made abnormal by sin may be made normal — whereas the Catholics teach that justification is not by 'faith alone', but by faith furnished with love, *fides caritate formata*. They do teach, however, that it is by the grace of God that a man is led to faith (by which they essentially mean that the man assents to the faith of which the Roman Catholic Church is custodian and interpreter); it is taught that he is then ready for sanctifying grace, which, if lost, may be restored throughout the sacrament of penance. The necessity for justifying faith to be furnished with love is explained by the fact that though God forgives a sinner, that sinner cannot enter into fellowship with him in a sinful state. God the righteous cannot countenance man the unrighteous. Hence, in justifying the sinner, God *makes* the sinner righteous. Righteousness is not imputed, leaving the sinner sinful; instead, it is *imparted*. God grants the sinner the love that is the fulfilling of the Law, whereby he is made acceptable, and in short, he is justified not by faith alone, but by faith and love.

Luther's teaching seems closer to the New Testament, truer to experience. The sinner cannot ever attain any righteousness of his own: he merits or deserves only condemnation. But God in his mercy, while we were yet sinners, freely opted to receive us to Himself and to restore us to his side, to a fellowship that we from our side had broken and could never mend. Luther used to express it as *simul justus et peccator* ('at one and the same time both righteous and a sinner'):[10] as *semper peccator, semper penitens, semper justus* ('always a sinner, always penitent, always justified'),[11] and as *ignoranter justi et scienter iniusti; peccatores in re, iusti autem in spe* ('in a way we do not understand, we are justified; though, at the same time, in a way we do understand, we know we are unrighteous: sinners in deed, yet righteous in hope').[12]

The story of his discovery of this precious truth is one of the loveliest of all time. He describes how he went into the monastery to save his soul, and how none of the disciplines, the confessions, or the absolutions ever answered his need or spoke to his condition. The more aware he was of God's purity, righteousness, and transcendence, the more keenly he became aware of his own creatureliness, unrighteousness, and mortal finitude. He knew he could never attain the righteousness God demanded, and that one day he would be bound to face God's destructive wrath. Then he realised, by long study and prayer, that it was not a matter of Martin and his righteousness, but of God and his righteousness — not a matter of

10. WA, 41, 272, 17.
11. WA, 41, 442, 17.
12. WA, 41, 269, 30.

Martin's work, but of God's Work. God knew this all the time, and had so loved the world that he gave his only begotten Son, that whosoever should believe in him should not perish but have eternal life. Martin realised that the meaning of Christianity was not a matter of works of merit, pilgrimages, fastings, good works, and so on, but a simple capitulation in faith to God's work of salvation. 'When I saw that Law meant one thing and Gospel another,' he said, 'I broke through.' Faith to Luther meant being 'in utter despair of everything save Christ.' When a man realises that in the matter of his own salvation he has nothing and can do nothing, he is then received by God, considered acceptable, and justified only on the grounds that he accepts what is proffered.

It is important in this connection to remember that when we use the word *faith*, we mean 'faith in Christ'. We are justified *per fidem propter Christum*. Faith is simply taking what is offered. As Calvin put it, 'Faith is only the instrument by which righteousness is received and cannot be confounded with Christ, who is the material cause, and at once author and dispenser of so great a benefit'. Perhaps it could be argued in a spirit of reconciliation that the righteousness first imputed merges into a righteousness active, and therefore, is in part imparted.

It would be a mistake to treat this debate as an ancient disputation of the theological schools, and therefore as having no contemporary relevance. The phrase 'justification by faith' continues to sum up the true nature of the Gospel, continues to be the secret of spiritual growth. Roman Catholic theology tends to confuse justification with sanctification. It seeks to make a man *grow* in justification by teaching works, disciplines, fastings, almsgivings, and so on as human works that are a necessary part of man's justification. But sanctification is the work of the Holy Spirit raising a man already justified by faith, not a contributing factor to man's justification. Sanctification like justification is by grace alone through faith alone.

Luther, too, allowed for the process of growth, as he did for the contrary process of atrophy, particularly in the context of the doctrine of man. Nevertheless, he considered such growth to be always and only the work of the Holy Spirit who liberates one continuously from the dominion of sin, for man, though redeemed, is yet a sinner, and remains a sinner. In a fascinating disputation on the nature of man that Luther conducted with the theological emissaries of Henry

VIII at Wittenberg in 1536, he said in his Thirty-ninth Thesis[13] that 'man lives in sin, and from day to day is either in a continuous process of justification, or in a continuous process of corruption'. At this point Luther appears closer to the traditional Catholic position, but he would not concede that good works help the process along. Only the Holy Spirit effects that work: true good works are not those works we devise for ourselves, but are the result of the work of the Holy Spirit. Nevertheless, this appears to be a highly significant admission, for Luther himself wrote as well as defended this thesis.

Perhaps the Protestants would find themselves to be much nearer to the Catholics if they were to regard the whole matter more in dynamic terms of growth and progress and life (as Catholics tend to do) than in the more static and conceptual and intellectual terms of definitions, phrases, and formulae that they characteristically hold to. Certainly, the debate should be removed from the area of polemics. When all is said, we are not defining doctrines but are laying ourselves open to Christ and his work, and that is all that should matter. It is not how we *think*, but how we *live* that is of the essence. Protestant scholars have rightly always been deeply concerned and unreservedly committed to this point of doctrine, but we may now note with some satisfaction that many Catholic scholars are studying the matter in fresh, creative, irenic ways.

THE CATHOLIC DEBATE OVER JUSTIFICATION BY FAITH

Some Catholics have suggested in a recent debate that took place in France that the divergence between the Catholic and Protestant points of view becomes more apparent when the matter of justification is looked at from man's angle, rather than from God's;[14] we might almost say that the difference is as much psychological as theological. Another suggestion that emerged from these dialogues is that an underlying philosophical difference has contributed to the differing theological positions. It was suggested that an Aristotelian

---

13. WA, 39, 1, 44-62.
14. See C. Moeller and G. Philips's *The Theology of Grace and the Ecumenical Movement*, trans. R. A. Wilson (Patterson, N.J.: St. Anthony Guild Press, 1969).

anthropology would see man as a self-sufficient entity enclosed within himself, whose highest functions will never surpass the limits of his nature; consequently, any elevation to a higher mode of life and action, as described in an adoptive sonship to God, will entail the addition of an extra 'supernatural' quality. A Platonist anthropology, on the other hand, does not see a clear barrier between 'natural' and 'supernatural'; it will not therefore think of elevation to divine sonship as entailing an additional quality, but rather in terms of progress or advance along a course that is quite open-ended. It is true that in both cases such an elevation will only come about as the result of divine intervention, but the former view will focus on the created effect in man, whereas the latter will concentrate on the uncreated source of this elevation. It is not suggested that this philosophical approach will explain the divergent views on justification, but it does throw a little light on the matter with regard to the question of *how* man appropriates the benefits of Christ. We might simply say that the difference between the Catholic and the Reformer on the doctrine of justification arises partly from their differing views of human nature.

In his book *Justification* (1964), Hans Küng offers a useful clarification of terminology by pointing out that Catholic theologians normally use the word *justification* in the subjective sense — that is to say, in referring to the effect wrought in man — and that they prefer to use the word *redemption* or *atonement* for the objective sense, referring to what Christ did. If this point is accepted, then the area of divergence is reduced (though not wholly removed) because the subjective and objective aspects of the active and passive aspects of the process of justification are two sides of the same thing and are necessarily complementary. The use of the words *subjective* and *objective* perhaps evokes the chief area of disagreement, because the forensic view of justification, which holds that the Christian appropriates what Christ has won for him purely by faith, seems to the Catholic to exclude any subjective or real change in the man himself. This is the essence of the distinction between '*imputing* righteousness' and '*imparting* righteousness'. The Catholic, following Trent, holds that the righteousness won by Christ is not merely *imputed*, but *imparted* — that is to say, it is communicated to man in such a way that a real *transformation* takes place in the believer.

Küng gives support to this position, pointing out that the idea of a 'transfer' from the state of being a son of Adam to being an adoptive son of God must have both an active and a passive sense: *active*, alluding to the God who brings about this transfer of his sovereign, justifying act; and *passive*, alluding to the really changed situation of man, who has been transferred from one situation to the other. Commenting on the question of how a man is indeed *simul justus et peccator*, Küng argues that this righteousness (which we do really possess, for it actually dwells in man) is by its very nature always alien and extrinsic; we must constantly receive it afresh from Christ as a grace that never originated in us.

With respect to the part played in man's initial justification by free will, Küng takes the Catholic line of granting free will and leaving room for merit and cooperation. In support of this position he quotes from St. Bernard's *On Grace and Free-will*:

> What then is free-will for? It is to be saved. Take away free-will and there will be nothing to save; take away grace and there will be nothing by which salvation is wrought. The work cannot be accomplished without these two—the One by whom it is done, the other to whom or in whom, it is done. God is the Author of salvation; free-will has only the capacity for salvation. Only God can bestow salvation; only free-will can receive it.

Küng's own comments underscore the point: 'God who justifies in Christ remains the God of the covenant; He wants a true partner and not a robot, responding to Him with a personal, responsible, active and heart-felt 'Yes!' For this purpose He has, in His prevenient grace preserved in the perishing sinner, the power, the understanding and the ability to choose. He renews the offer of His grace with urgency, but not with compulsion.'[15]

It is seen that the Catholic, in line with Trent, insists on the reality of human merit and the doctrines associated with it. The Catholic argues that merit is concerned with what one *is*, not with what one *has*: merit is inseparable from the work of the Holy Spirit within us and participation is based on the active presence of God within the soul. The Catholic insists that man's active cooperation with the justifying grace of God is significant and meritorious. On this point Küng argued in an earlier essay,

15. Küng, *Justification* (1964; London, 1981), pp. 266, 265.

The legal character is of fundamental significance for justification. Since it is a question not merely of some physical occurrence in man but of a statement that he is just, a declaration of justice, a court judgment, a nonreckoning of sins, and a reckoning of Christ's justice (imputation: Rom. 4; Gal. 3.6) through God — for that reason the gravity of the situation, in contrast to all sinful frivolity, becomes evident: what is involved is God, his personal anger, and his personal grace. But precisely for that reason, in opposition to all the faintheartedness and despair of the tormented conscience, the overriding consolation of the situation is manifest. It is not I myself who must strive in vain to cast off my burden of guilt. No, it is God himself who lifts it off because he forgives us, whole and entire, through his gracious word. It has been shown elsewhere that Catholic tradition not only does not exclude the legal character of justification, but actually includes it. Catholic tradition, however, lays great stress on this: God's justification must be taken seriously; God does what he says. When God declares a man just, he draws him into the righteousness of God and thus he effects a transformation of man's very being. When God says a man is just, since it is God who says it, man is simultaneously made just. From this it follows that justification includes in itself all the effects which touch the very being of the man who is justified, and his effective transformation, and thus also includes a positive sanctification effected by God. But it remains true that biblical and especially the Pauline act of justifying ('justification') does not say this explicitly. [16]

Other contemporary Catholic theologians have addressed and are addressing themselves to this matter. Harry McSorley is of the opinion that Luther was reacting against the semi-Pelagianism of Biel and Ockham, whose *devotio moderna* was a departure from traditional Catholic thought, and that decadent scholasticism was wrong in teaching that to be acceptable to God, a man had to do 'all that in him lies' and thereby merit forgiveness. Luther's protest was in full accord with Augustine, Anselm, Bernard, Gregory of Rimini, and the second Council of Orange: Aquinas, Trent, Vatican II are quoted to support McSorley's views. In his book *The Christian Dilemma* (1952) Willem van de Pol makes a similar argument, suggesting that the Reformers were battling against a dom-

---

16. Küng, in *Christianity Divided: Protestant and Roman Catholic Theological Issues*, ed. D. J. Callahan, H. O. Obermann, and D. J. O'Hanlon (London, 1962), pp. 315-16.

inant semi-Pelagianism that they understood to be implicit in Catholicism and that there is nothing incompatible between Luther's doctrine of justification and Roman orthodoxy. Louis Bouyer makes similar claims in *The Spirit and Forms of Protestantism*, asserting that Luther's view of salvation 'is in perfect harmony with Catholic tradition, the great conciliar definitions on grace and salvation, and even with Thomism.' And in his book *Protestantism* (1959), Georges Tavard states that there is no real contradiction between Roman Catholic theology and Luther's gospel; he refers to the eclipse of the gospel in Luther's day, and asserts that Luther's doctrine of justification is compatible with Catholicism. Küng's researches show that McSorley, van de Pol, Bouyer, and Tavard are essentially right in arguing that the rampant semi-Pelagianism of Luther's day was also condemned by the Catholic Church.

In the assessment of the present debate between Catholics and Protestants, I have cited only Roman Catholic theologians, and in this group only those who have engaged over many years and very deeply in Luther research. I could of course have cited many leading Protestant ecumenical theologians as well, but the fact that the case can be made nicely by reference only to Catholic theologians is itself a matter of no small significance. It is also signally important to note that at the plenary meeting of the Lutheran World Federation meeting in Helsinki in 1963 it was concluded that it can no longer be said that the Catholic teaching on justification is wrong, or against the Gospel. The 1972 Malta Report of the International Lutheran/Roman Catholic Study Commission came to the same conclusion. Does this not suggest that already Luther is being brought back within the framework of Catholicity? It is within this living organism that Luther's protest will be fully understood and finally effective in achieving the ends to which God called him in the sixteenth century. Luther's stress was always on the free, unmerited, sovereign grace of God, and it is to this that the doctrine of justification by faith alone *refers*, and that it safeguards. It belongs to Catholicism as much as it does to Protestantism.

CHAPTER EIGHT

THE AUTHORITY OF THE BIBLE

LUTHER'S AIM WAS never to create a new Church, and certainly not a *Lutheran* Church.[1] For Luther there was only one Church, the Church of Christ. It was his opinion that what had gone wrong with the Church was that it had long ceased to be catholic and had grown papist. He never accepted the misnomer 'Lutheran' with reference to the Church reformed, however. He simply sought to reestablish the true original Church as it had been instituted by Christ and represented by the Apostles. Time had eroded the original design of the founder. Important doctrines of the original Church had simply been allowed to decay—justification by faith, proclamation of the pure Gospel, the true meaning of the Lord's Supper, the priesthood of all believers, the right conception of the ministry, the authority of Scripture, a New Testament Christology, the doctrines of the Church, of society, of the last things, and many others. Not only had much fallen away, but much had been added—penance, the Mass, papal infallibility and authority, indulgences, the interdict, all the Catholic cultus of external aids, and perhaps, worst of all, a secularised Church. All that Luther sought was to bring the Church in its beliefs and practice to the vision and intent of Christ its founder.

To find this original plan, one has to go back to the New Testament. Where else? There it is described how Christ founded his Church and what he wanted it to be; and, most vital, it is there that the apostolic witness is given concerning the nature of Christ, God's purpose in him, and how Christ interpreted his own nature, mission, and message. This was the ultimate reality to Luther: no man can get nearer the source than that. It was the ultimate, ob-

---

1. Nor did Cranmer, who was always at pains to distinguish between the ancient Catholic Church and the recently corrupted Church.

jective, historical authority, the criterion of all judgment, the canon or norm by which we are to live.

To bring the Church back to this original scheme means to destroy and abolish all the humanly devised innovations and novelties that spoil the old plan, and to rebuild those essential parts of the Church that had collapsed in the course of time. This Luther tried to do in the sixteenth century. But re-formation of this kind cannot be limited to the sixteenth century. *Ecclesia reformata semper reformanda* — 'the Church once reformed must remain in a constant process of reformation'. The existing Church must always and continually examine her life and work to see whether it is in harmony with Christ's original foundation, and must constantly be prepared to strengthen or rebuild essential things that have been weakened or eroded and to abolish abuses, additions, and innovations that have seeped into its life. This constant clearing out of all practices and ideas that are not a direct outcome of the original commission is both painful and disturbing; nothing less than the perpetual reference of all we think, say, and do to the apostolic witness is what Luther meant by Reformation: it was the *re-formatio* of that which had suffered *de-formatio*, and owing to the sin of the natural man, would always be in a process of *de-formatio*, whether it was the so-called 'reformed' Protestant Church or the so-called 'unreformed' Catholic Church. Christ's Church must always be penitently willing to be reformed by Christ its founder: Christ is the Great Reformer. And the mind and will of the founder is in the New Testament.

Going back to the Early Church does not mean copying its forms in any slavish way, or seeking to reintroduce its ways, its worship, its customs, or any other of the merely temporal marks of its first-century existence. Luther did not want to go back 1,500 years to some idyllic pattern of church life (which never existed in any case as Luther knew and as anyone who reads 1 Corinthians knows), but he argued that no age and no circumstance can be allowed to tamper with the Gospel as expressed in apostolic terms. Luther was convinced that St. Paul and the other Apostles would have completely agreed with him had they been able to travel to the sixteenth century. He saw the Apostles as Lutherans, or, expressed in his own terms, the Lutherans were the legitimate successors to the apostolic Church; the papists were not. If anything in Lutheranism could be shown not to be apostolic, then Lutheranism had to reform itself, or rather, allow God to reform it: 'If error in his writings were to be proven by the Word of God, then would he gladly revoke it . . . consign it to the flames, and tread it underfoot.'[2]

Returning to Christ and the apostolic Church does not entail confining oneself to the *New* Testament; it also encompasses the *Old*. It was not only that the Old Testament had authority for Christ as he himself read it and expounded it, but more important, it testified of him: 'the scriptures . . . are they which testify of me' (John 5.39). A great deal of Christian doctrine is a fulfilment of Old Testament theology and prophecy, as Christ frequently argued, and can be understood and expressed only in those terms. The Apostles claimed that the Christian interpretation of the Old Testament is the only true interpretation. The decisive interpretation of the Gospel cannot be seen except in relation to Law. In other words, Re-formation to Luther meant setting the Church in a living relation not only to the New Testament, but to the *whole* Bible. For all his powerful evangelical preaching and writing, it is salutary to recall that Luther was a professor of Old Testament studies, not New Testament studies.

Luther, and with him all the Reformers of the sixteenth century, German, Swiss, and British alike, believed that God spoke to them in the Scriptures in exactly the same way he had spoken to his prophets and apostles. They believed that if the common people had the Bible in their hands in a language they could read and understand, God himself would speak to them, to comfort, reassure, guide, and strengthen them. What this means, of course, is that every man, woman, and child could have immediate access to God. The Scriptures would be for them a personal rather than a dogmatic revelation. They would reexperience a fellowship with God enjoyed by his saints in past ages, a fellowship into which they might enter with the saints.

The Reformers spoke of two voices: the voice of God speaking to man in love, and the voice of the renewed man answering in faith to God. We are not speaking of buried history, but of a living communion, which the faithful reader of the Bible enjoys here and now. Every Reformer's concern was to put the Bible into a man's hand and let God do the rest. 'Let the man who would hear *God*

---

2. *D. Martin Luthers Werke: Kritische Gesamtausgabe* (Weimar, 1883 ff.), 8, 867ff. Hereafter abbreviated WA (Weimar Ausgabe).

speak read Holy Scripture.'[3] Or, as Luther memorably proclaimed in his second Wittenberg sermon in 1522, preached when he re-turnd from the Wartburg to restore peace in Wittenberg;

> I will preach [the Word of God], teach it, write it, but I will constrain no man by force, for faith must come freely without compulsion. Take myself as an example. I have opposed the indulgences and all the papists, but never by force. I simply taught, preached, wrote God's Word; otherwise I did nothing. And then, while I slept, or drank Wittenberg beer with my Philip and with Amsdorf, the Word so greatly weakened the papacy, that never a prince or emperor inflicted such damage upon it. I did nothing; the Word did it all. Had I desired to foment trouble, I could have brought great bloodshed upon Germany. Yea, I could have started such a little game at Worms that even the Emperor would not have been safe. But what would it have amounted to? A fool's play. I did nothing; I left it to the Word.[4]

When John Eck came to Germany to do battle with Luther it was this new situation he met. 'Things have come to a pretty pass', he said, 'when even the women answer back doctors of theology by quoting the Bible at them.'

'HEARING' THE WORD OF GOD

The expression 'the Word of God' rings an alien note in the mind of contemporary man. Indeed, many theologians and even some biblical scholars are uneasy with the term, often hostile to it. In criticism, it is often implied that theologians who use this term (a most honourable term in the whole of the Old Testament and on the lips of Jesus himself) claim a divine authority for their own words and for their own preaching. But we are not absolutising the human possibilities of the intellect at all. We are saying that originally and irrevocably, the Word of God means that originally and irrevocably God speaks: he addresses man at a known time, in a known place, in words that proceed from him to man. 'God's Word' means 'God speaks'. In other words, God acts. Any further statements must be regarded as exegesis, not as imitation or negation of this proposition.

---

3. 'Papacy at Rome' (1545), WA, 54, 263.
4. *Works of Martin Luther*, ed. Henry Eyster Jacobs (Philadelphia: Muhlenberg, 1943), 2:399. Hereafter abbreviated *WML*.

We must then think first and foremost of the spirituality of the Word of God: we are under the work of the Holy Spirit and are not discussing a historical or natural event, *in eo ipso* (even though there is no Word of God without a physical event). The Word of God is an embodied Word, in that it comes to us mortal and natural men in our creaturely sphere, and cannot come otherwise. Exactly in the same perfect way as when 'God, who at sundry times and in divers manners spake in time past unto the fathers by the prophets, hath in these last days spoken unto us by his Son' (Heb. 1.1-2), so did he give expression to his Word in the form of the Word made flesh in Jesus of Nazareth. In this way no Word is expressed but in its creatureliness. In Christ, we see the Father; in Jesus, we hear God. Just as Jesus was tied not only to the corporality of men, but also the spirituality of God, so we must understand his Word primarily as spiritual and secondarily as natural. The Word is written, spoken, communicated by the familiar physical means of paper and ink and speech, and is carried in the hand as any other letter. It has to be heard, listened to, and understood like any other word, document, or letter; and yet it is faith given by God that enables a person to hear God's Word in it, to understand it, to obey it. We must never lose sight of its spirituality: we are hearing God through the internal testimony of the Holy Spirit.

Just as importantly, when we say that God speaks, we make reference to the personal character of the relationship between who he is and what he says. God's Word is not an objective thing, to be discussed and analysed; nor is it a concept man may define, as he may define, say, the concept of justice. It is not to be understood in terms of content or ideas: it is not anything objective at all. It is what it says, God speaking. It issues forth in a most concrete event, an event that can neither be anticipated nor repeated. The Word is made known and true for no other reason than that he says it; in other words, he himself is in that Word, and he himself accompanies that Word. In short, what God utters is never in any way known and true in abstraction from God himself.

It is a shallow mind that sees this language of personalising the Word of God as anthropomorphic. The problem is not whether God is a person; the problem is whether *we* are. Is there a single person in the world who is fully a person in the sense that God is fully a person? In a disputation in 1536, Luther argued that 'Theology describes man fully and perfectly'.[5] Man only begins to grow into full personhood when, under God's Word, he begins to move from his slavery to self to a glorious liberty and freedom under God. It is God himself who comes to us in his Word: precisely in his Word God is a person.

Not only is the Word personal as it addresses us, but it is purposive: whenever and wherever God speaks to a man, it is in a purposive relatedness or pointedness in his life, expressed in terms that are eloquently appropriate to his circumstances, words that go straight home to him in the most concrete terms, and only to him in that way. Therefore, the real content of God's speech can never be expressed in general terms at all. We may express what God said to Jeremiah, or even what we think God is saying to us at the moment, only in general terms. Both are legitimate exercises, but we may not confuse our own words with the fulness of God's Word itself: our words only point to his.

Four things seem clear:

(1) The Word of God directed to us is first of all such a word that we do not and could not speak it to ourselves. The Word of God tells us something new which otherwise we could never have heard from any one. It always has the nature of a thunderbolt: 'it is the boulder of a Thou which does not become an I, that is here cast in your path.'[6] It is an otherness that is yet related to us, that makes itself known to us in a way no other word, no matter how true or noble, could ever strike us. Whatever God may say to us, it will always be uttered in this way — it will be uttered as the Word of the Lord.

(2) Since it is the word of the Creator to his creature, it aims at us and touches us in our existence. No word of man can reach us in our very existence, and no word a man speaks can hurt that existence; only God the Creator can reach us there (and destroy us there).

(3) Since it is the Word of the Creator directed to us, it is that very Word necessary to restore the original relationship between us and him. God speaks to us, and therefore reveals himself to us, which means that he turns himself wholly and anew towards us. As

---

5. WA, 39, 1, 175-80.
6. Barth, *Church Dogmatics* (Edinburgh: T&T Clark, 1955-), I, 1, 160.

the Unknown, he is making himself known to us. This signifies that he is criticising the relationship existing between us and him, but is declaring by that criticism that his purpose is to maintain it and establish it anew from his side. No man can do this; only God, who created this relationship, and confirm and renew it if it has been disturbed or destroyed. This means that his Word is the Word of reconciliation, issuing from the Reconciler. It is the Word from God, who by a second creation sets up his covenant anew with us in judgment, but yet in grace.

(4) As a Word of reconciliation directed to us, it is the means by which God announces himself to man. In other words, he promises himself as the content of man's future; He promises to meet man on his way through time and to meet him at the end of all time, as the hidden Lord of all times. His presence through the Word is precisely *his* presence, the presence of him that should come, to fulfil and complete the relationship founded between us and him at Creation, now renewed and confirmed at the reconciliation. This Word cannot be a word of man. Only God's Word is the guarantee and means of actualising the full, genuine presence of the speaker.

It was because Karl Barth had found such a theology of the Word that his commentary on Romans burst like a bombshell in the playground of the theologians. Nothing has been the same since. Luther had the same, though more effectual experience, and Barth derived his first from a deep confrontation with Luther. Yet it is true to say that unless this experience is understood and appropriated, the reader can neither understand the Bible, nor ever hear those awful rumblings from Heaven when God addresses us that emerge eventually as his creative, reconciling, redeeming Word, which takes us out of our present earthly existence and transplants us into the Kingdom of his dear Son, in which Kingdom we truly belong.

For Luther, to read Scripture was to be confronted by God. His contemporaries realized this as well: they realised that it as not merely a matter of their handling a book called the Bible, but of God handling them when they read it. What was at issue was not the authority of a book, but the authority of God. Nevertheless, as clear as this is to a student of the Reformation, this simple point has become obscured in history. Catholics opposed this important concept in the interests of papal authority from Trent onwards; and

Protestants have allowed secularisation and liberalisation to alienate them from it. It is important that such changes or developments be distinguished, and that the controversial differences be clarified before twentieth-century man attempts to comprehend or reassess the Reformation argument. It is in this way that the real significance of Luther can emerge.

Luther taught that the authority of the Bible lays in the fact that it is the vehicle by which God addresses the penitent and faithful heart in *his* own way and in *his* own words. Luther spoke not of the authority of a book, as we have seen, but about the authority of God. This truth cannot be stated too strongly. It shocked the sixteenth century enough; post-eighteenth-century man cannot easily bridge the gulf between the religious climate that lasted to the *Aufklärung* and the contemporary secularised, liberalised, de-Christianised climate that began to develop in the eighteenth century. Yet it is important to understand the sixteenth-century mind in this respect: it was galvanised not by a holy book, but by a holy God. As Luther expressed it, 'Whenever a man reads the Word of God, the Holy Spirit is speaking to him.'[7]

There are many difficulties that beset the reader seeking to understand precisely what Luther's view of the Bible really is. The first is that he always intended to write a book on the subject, but never did so; consequently we are left with many statements and views expressed throughout his writings, some of which are open to different interpretations. More critically, controversialists and apologists have engaged in much polemic concerning this subject, and as a result Luther's position has been seriously misunderstood. Furthermore, Lutheran theology has changed and developed, particularly since the rise of higher criticism, modernism, and liberalism, so that sometimes modern Lutheran scholars will claim that their view is Luther's in spirit, even when it is a far cry from Luther's in fact. And in response to that, certain Lutherans who are fundamentalist in approach (particularly Americans, such as those belonging to the Missouri Synod) tend to resist all development and to hark back to a precritical position. The position needs clearing up, and in my judgment can be considerably simplified, even if it means leaving aside a fuller discussion of disputatious points. It is

---

7. WA, 47, 184.

possible for a good Lutheran scholar to state Luther's view on Scripture with some precision, and this is what I will now attempt to do.

LUTHER'S VIEW OF SCRIPTURE

It is certainly a basic principle for Luther that Scripture be considered the only authority. *Sola scriptura* is indelibly written across the pages of the early sixteenth century: what cannot be proved from Scripture has no authority in the Church. He faced the Emperor at Worms in 1521 with these words:

> Unless I am convinced by the testimony of Scripture, or evident reason [*convictus testimoniis Scripturae aut ratione evidente*] (for I put my faith neither in Pope nor Councils as authorities in themselves, since it is established that they have often erred and contradicted one another), I am bound by the scriptural authorities cited by me, and my conscience is captive to the Word of God; I will recant nothing and cannot do so, since it is neither safe nor honest to do aught against conscience. Here I stand! I can no other! God help me. Amen.

No statement was ever clearer; and the clarity was matched by the courage. Nobody in the hall had any doubt about Luther's position. Nonetheless, this statement has been interpreted in many ways. Some have argued that Luther is putting reason alongside the Bible as an equal authority. This is not the meaning to be given to *ratio evidens*, as anybody who knows his Luther will agree: he could speak of reason as 'the Devil's whore'. Rather, he speaks here of the proud reason that sets itself over against God as being the wiser, a reason that is foolish enough to invent doctrines or laws outside God's revealed Word. Luther said nothing disparaging about man's powers of logical ratiocination, but only about the unredeemed reason of proud unconverted man, the magisterial use of reason in discoursing about God. Reason of this kind is for him the sign of human pride in unregenerate souls; it is the original sin. [8]

Luther had an altogether different opinion of the humble reason of regenerate man, however. This converted reason is open to the truths of the Word of God and accepts them with a joyous sense of adventure. It may combine different parts and draw legitimate con-

---

8. See the important disputation *On the Nature of Man*, WA, 39, 1, 175-80.

clusions (e.g., the doctrine of the Trinity). This reason of the converted man seeks to serve and understand and grow in the Word of God, but never to rule over it. Moreover, human reason is crucial in the assessment of the significance or importance of the nonessentials, the external ceremonies or customs neither demanded nor forbidden by the Word of God; it enables a man to distinguish the things that are different, and to put them in their proper place, as, for example, rules about what one may eat on Fridays, and what one should wear on Sundays. Reason could well function as a handmaiden to theology in matters as, say, criticising variant readings in the text, in assessing the errors of copyists or discrepancies between the records of Kings and Chronicles or similar human errors. Nevertheless, Luther made it abundantly clear that man could never have arrived at the truth of the Gospel by dint of reason alone, and that the revealed truths of the Incarnation, of the Cross, of the Resurrection, and many others, are an offence to human reason, a scandal and a stumbling block. Here he taught as his master had taught so often (e.g., in Matt. 11.6, 13.21, 15.12, 24.10, and 26.31; in Mark 4.7 and 6.3; in Luke 7.23, and in John 6.61 and 16.1), as Paul had preached (in 1 Cor. 1.17-18 and 2.12-14, and in Rom. 9.33), and as Peter had believed (1 Pet. 2.8). Similarly, Luther contended that it is not the claim of an individual to his right of private judgment, to his own conscience, so beloved of modern Western democratic man (as justified as that is in a sociological or political context), but of a conscience *captive* to the Word of God (i.e. ruled only by Scripture) that ought to an individual's actions.

The moment Luther claimed that the authority of the Bible supersedes that of the tradition of the Church, he invited the criticism of his contemporaries that it was the tradition of the Church that had been responsible for the selection of those very books that now formed the canon. It was the Church that had written and approved the actual constituent books; without the Church there could have been no Bible. It was then asked how he could justify his acceptance of one line of tradition, but not the whole.

Luther argued that the Church is a witness to, not judge of, the Bible: 'The Church cannot give a book more authority or dependability than it has of itself, just as it also approves and accepts the works of the fathers, but thereby does not establish them as good or make them better.'[9] He pointed out the discrepancies between the corrupted Church of his own day and the relatively uncorrupted early Church, suggesting that the former had strayed from the Word. He never argued that there had been a Golden Age, for even the inner circle of the Twelve had had its traitor. He did argue, however, that his own line of interpretation went back to the apostolic witness, and that it was the apostolic witness to Christ and God's purpose in him for mankind that constitute the source of all doctrine and the permanent criterion by which to judge all that the Church believes and practises. For Luther, this witness was the witness to ultimate reality, to which all doctrine, all customs had to be submitted, no matter how ancient or venerable they were. In 1519, at the disputation with John Eck at Leipzig, he surprised the Roman Catholic protagonists, by showing that this interpretation went right back to the Greek Fathers (about whom the Latin West knew nothing) and was in accordance with the certain line of the great Church Fathers, Latin and Greek, whereas the Pope's was not. In fact, the Pope's claim was relatively recent and actually an innovation.

Luther went further. He argued that there were disputed books as well as rejected books at that time and that, of the approved canon, four books had remained doubtful (namely, Hebrews, James, Jude, and Revelation). He admitted they all contained some sound apostolic doctrine as well as good moral teaching, but that they nevertheless contained grave errors and that their emphases could be misleading. They certainly could not claim full authority in the Church. For instance, on internal evidence it was shown that Hebrews had not been written by an Apostle; it is a fine work, sound overall, but the argument in chapters 6 and 9 that a lapsed Christian has no second chance runs counter to the unanimous witness of the undisputed New Testament books. Luther further contended that the author of James, again no Apostle, argues against Paul, and was a Jew who had heard the Christian bells ring but did not know where they were hanging. When Luther translated the Bible, he translated these four works, but put them at the end of the New Testament, and without pagination.

In any case, when it is suggested that Luther placed an infallible Book, the Bible, in the place of an infallible Church, and transferred

---

9. WA, 2, 325.

the same kind of infallibility that had been supposed to belong to the Church to this book, the issue is merely obscured. In medieval times, men accepted the decisions of popes and councils as the final utterance on all matters of controversy in faith and morals. At the Reformation, it is said, the Reformers set the Bible where these popes and councils had been, and declared that the final appeal was to be made to the Bible. There is, of course, some truth in this statement, and everybody recalls how Luther said that a miller's maid or a boy of nine with the Bible knew more about divine truth than the Pope without it. Yet, that is less than the whole truth. The Protestants and the Catholics did not mean the same thing by *Scripture*; nor, for that matter, did they mean the same thing by *infallibility*. A look at these two words will help the argument along.

When Luther put Hebrews, James, Jude, and Revelation in a class apart, he was not assuming an authority over the already approved canon of Scripture of the Early Church. He merely submitted all decisions — those of the Early Church as well as those of the medieval Church — to his one criterion of the apostolic witness to Christ. In his view the Early Church acted as a kind of tribunal bearing witness about which books contained the true Gospel and which did not. The authority of the canon does not derive from the authority of the Early Church, but from the authority of their 'inner' testimony to Christ. This inner authority still carried the same weight for Luther (as it does for all time) that it did for the Early Church. This 'inner' argument must be allowed due weight alongside the 'historic' argument.

There is no contradiction among the undisputed canonical books; although there are wide differences of outlook and emphases among them, they nevertheless bear a common witness to Christ. The point from which they are all to be considered is the revelation of God in Christ Jesus. From this point of view, Law and Gospel are understood and the entire Bible holds together: 'It is on this point that all the divinely created holy books speak with one voice, namely, that they altogether preach Christ and His claim. That is the real touch-stone which evaluates all books of the Bible, whether they preach Christ or do not.'[10]. This does not mean that Luther *selects* certain parts of the Bible that he prefers and rejects other parts that

---

10. *Vorreden zur Heiligen Schrift*, p. 107; cf. WA, 40, 3, 652, 12ff.

do not confirm his preferences. He believes that *all* the books of the Bible point to Christ, that *all* find fulfilment in the Gospel of Christ. It is in fact a modern development to set the Old Testament on a kind of lower level of revelation. Luther found his most powerful witness to Christ in Genesis and in the Psalms, in the Law and in the Prophets, and even in the minor prophet Jonah. It is this principle that made him reassess the disputed books of Hebrews, James, Jude, and Revelation. He never extracted the undisputed writings from the canonical writings. His principle was one not of selection, but of interpretation.

It is true that this principle caused him to make pronouncements concerning the value of certain books relative to others, as we all do. He grew to treasure St. Paul's writings and 1 Peter as specially valuable, almost as keys to the Gospel; he valued St. John's Gospel above all the Synoptic Gospels, even above all other books of the Bible, without suggesting that the others were not authoritative. He valued these specially treasured writings for throwing light on the others, for rendering their meaning more clear. As Calvin was later to say, it is St. John's Gospel that shows the inner meaning of the Synoptic Gospels.

I suggested earlier that the Protestants and the Catholics do not mean the same thing by Scripture. A single point, often overlooked, is that the Scriptures to which the Catholics appeal include the Apocryphal Books of the Old Testament; furthermore, Protestant scholars characteristically appeal to the original Hebrew and Greek texts of the Old and New Testament, not to the Latin translation of Jerome. This is less significant than it was in the sixteenth century, for Catholic scholars are now highly competent biblical scholars, and at university level this difference hardly arises. If there is one thing for which we can all be thankful, it is the importance of the Bible in the contemporary Roman Catholic Church. The Vatican II documents make most refreshing reading on this point.

There is another point to be made concerning the authority of the Bible for the Catholics in conflict with Luther, however. Every medieval theologian declared that the whole doctrinal system of the Church was based upon the Scriptures of the Old and New Testaments. The Reformers were doing nothing unusual, nothing in opposition to the common medieval practice in which they had been born, educated and lived, when they appealed to Scripture. Luther was serenely unconscious of any contradiction to his position when he put the believer's experience of Christ as set out in the New Testament over against the vulgar hawking of pardons for money. His opponents had no answer to his appeal to the New Testament, though they were later to devise spurious ones. They made, at first, the same appeal themselves; they believed they could meet Scripture with Scripture. They were, at first, confident that the authority appealed to, namely Scripture, would decide against Luther. But this did not happen.

It was not simply that Luther had a unique grasp of Scripture in the original languages, but that he had grasped it as a whole and as a unity, that insured his success. His opponents brought out texts as from a huge warehouse, unrelated commodities; Luther quoted them as a living, organic whole, every reference throwing light on the other. The unity that Luther saw was the living unity of the Bible as a whole: every statement had its own authentic intrinsic biblical ring of authority. The unity that Rome eventually imposed was the dogmatic authority of the Church: every statement had to be approved by the Church and bear its stamp of approval. Eventually at Trent (1545-63) this was promulgated by the decrees that placed Scripture and tradition alongside each other as equal authorities, a decision disputed by many of the Roman participants when *partim . . . partim* (i.e., partly in Scripture and partly in tradition) was changed to *and* i.e., in Scripture *and* tradition).

The schema *Concerning Divine Revelation* opens up fresh possibilities of coming to a closer understanding of the relationship between Scripture and tradition, a matter that has caused and causes sharp division between Catholics and Protestants. The schema argues that there is a 'close connection and communication between sacred tradition and sacred Scripture' on the grounds that they originate in the same divine spring; it also states that the teaching office is not above the Word of God, but rather that it serves it (this was precisely Luther's argument, though rejected by Rome in the sixteenth century). Nevertheless, there is a point that separates us: Scripture is never understood by the Catholics as standing over against the Church, in confrontation and in criticism of it, face to face with it.

This confrontation did not and could not arise in the apostolic age, but it did arise in the postapostolic ages, and has existed ever since. The relation between Scripture and tradition must be defined and understood in a different way when we are referring to the apostolic age than when we are discussing the postapostolic age. In the second century the apocryphal gospels were playing a more important role than the canonical gospels, and this fact was the historical cause of the fixation of the canon. The fact of the formation of the canon brought about a change in the relationship between Scripture and tradition.

At the time of the formation of the apostolic tradition, the eyewitnesses—those who confessed this faith and those who taught this faith—were one and the same people (which means that during the apostolic age, tradition, Scripture, and the teaching office were intermingled). On the other hand, since the formation of the canon, the eyewitnesses and those who confess the Christian faith are no longer the same. They are separated. In this connection Oscar Cullmann argues that it could clarify the debate if, instead of using the word *Scripture*, which sometimes relapses into the idea of a 'dead letter', we should use the phrase *biblical salvation history*, which could help to relate the historical events with the present living tradition of the contemporary age. [11] Certainly salvation history continues, but Cullmann asks whether it is authoritative in the way that biblical history is normative. The very existence of the canon shows that the revelation given by eyewitnesses about the central event of salvation history (i.e., its culmination in Christ) has ceased: after that there can only be the unfolding or exegesis of these events. Nevertheless, the very existence of the canon also indicates that salvation history *continues* as the unfolding of the decisive events. The characteristics of the apostolic age are admittedly the same as the characteristics of the postbiblical days, but there is one decisive difference, and that is that the eyewitnesses are no longer with us. This is the ground for arguing that after the apostolic age the Church must always be 'confronted' by Scripture, brought under its sovereign criticism as the norm or canon of judgment for all time. The postapostolic age and the postapostolic teaching office are no longer on the level of Scripture and may never be so considered. This point must be debated between Catholics and Protestants; the essays of

---

11. Cullmann, *Vatican Council II: The New Direction* (New York: Harper & Row, 1968), pp. 40-50.

Father Danielou with his insistence on 'salvation history', and Father Congar's reference to 'living tradition' give us hope of a happy outcome.

It is because of the existence of this 'superior norm' that the idea of reform in the Church is at all possible. This is the importance of the canon in the life of the Church. The Bible should be seen as a creative, corrective, and dynamic norm. At the very moment when it calls forth reform, it also gives the criteria by which the Church may distinguish between legitimate development and distortion. In the postapostolic Church, the Church in and of itself is not capable of discerning between the true and the false. That is why there are so many traditions in the postapostolic period that are patently false, or at least contrary to the Bible. It is necessary for the Church's healthy existence that the Scripture stands over against it as a superior norm. [12] If there is not this confrontation, a great danger exists for the Church: that of self-justification, of considering all the traditions that have persisted, even triumphed in the life of the Church, to be authentic simply because they are old and established. It is then but a short step to argue that such truths, if not explicitly in the Bible, are contained therein implicitly. (Many such traditions are older than Christianity itself!) We might well ask in what sense the bodily assumption of Mary is implicit in the Bible, however. It is more honest to state that it is a mere tradition (albeit a deviant one).

It is as necessary to bring the postapostolic teaching office as it is to bring the postapostolic traditions under the authority of the Bible. The postapostolic Church needs an authoritative teaching office, but it must be a teaching office subject to the norm of Scripture. The Bible must be interpreted in the Church, for it is the same Holy Spirit who inspired Scripture who now inspires the living Church. But if the magisterium is not subjected to the norm or canon of Scripture, then the teaching office itself may become a source of error more dangerous than if there were no teaching office at all.

Nevertheless, there is a clear way forward in this debate on Scripture and tradition. The argument thus far has been directed

---

12. For a detailed study of this theme, see Hans von Campenhausen's *Ecclesiastical Authority and Spiritual Power in the Church of the First Three Centuries*, trans. J. A. Baker (Stanford: Stanford University Press, 1969).

mainly to Catholic *theory*; we might, then, do well to note that in Catholic *practice* the Church often subjects itself to the Bible. In the pronouncements of Vatican II the Bible is referred to on every page as the authority under which the Church is working and thinking, and in Catholic preaching today a refreshing rediscovery of the Bible is evident. Perhaps what is most needed in the present dialogue is for Protestants to recognise the value of the living tradition in the postapostolic Church as well as the value of the teaching office, and for Catholics on their part to concede the confrontation of Scripture as a norm and criterion for the Church. Cullman makes a plea for the replacement of the time-honoured *sola scriptura* of the Reformers with the formula *scriptura, traditio, magisterium, sed scriptura sola norma superior* (Scripture, tradition, and the teaching office — but Scripture alone as the superior norm). [13] This original suggestion could move the dialogue on to new ground, as could the schema on the place of Scripture in the Church, which offers declarations that unite Catholic and Protestant completely in a common attitude to the Bible — including a statement of such startling simplicity and rugged truth that it might have graced the lips of Luther himself: 'In the sacred books the Father who is in heaven meets His children with great love, and speaks with them.' Does this not say everything?

In this connection a common assumption or generalisation has established itself — namely, that Luther's emphasis on the centrality of the Word of God was the cause of the Roman Church's alienation from the Bible. This is only a half-truth, however, and has brought much misunderstanding. It is a known fact of history that the early protest movements such as the Cathars, the Waldenses, and the Albigensians had turned from the secularised and institutionalised Church to the simple purity of the Bible. It is equally clear that from the decrees of thirteenth- and fourteenth-century councils to the Syllabus of 1864 (in which Pius IX condemned Bible societies along wih freemasonry and communism), the official policy of the Church had been to regard unrestricted access to the Scriptures on

---

13. On this point Cullmann goes on to say, 'In the ecumenical context the dialogue about the problem of tradition will progress if from the Protestant side we can recognise the value of the living tradition in the post-apostolic church and the value of the teaching office, and if from the Catholic side the confrontation of the Scripture as a superior norm in relation to the Church is acknowledged' (*Vatican II*, p. 50).

the part of laymen as both a danger to their souls and a challenge to the authority of the Church. Nevertheless, it must be recalled that the Church had often responded to such early evangelical challenges not by denying the authority of the Bible, nor by keeping it away from the faithful, but rather by issuing approved versions of it along with commentary. Eighteen such versions appeared during the period from the year of Luther's birth, 1483, to the year he published his own translation of the New Testament, 1521. It could be argued that the Church was not so much against the Bible as against the fundamental fallacy of private interpretation. Yet, when all that is granted, it remains the case that Luther had never seen a Bible before he entered the monastery, and when there, he was discouraged from reading it by his mentor Nathin, who told him that it 'only breeds unrest', and who tried to divert him with the old Fathers — that is to say, with tradition. Notwithstanding widespread interest in the Bible, ultimate authority remained vested in the Church rather than in God's Word.

The point at issue between Luther and Rome was less the authoritative status of the Scriptures (on which both sides were agreed) than how that authority was to be interpreted — that is, whether, as Trent was later to affirm, the Scriptures could be properly interpreted by the Church alone in the light of sacred tradition, or whether, as the Protestants maintained, the individual believer by virtue of his faith and the guidance of the Holy Spirit, had the right and duty to interpret Scripture as God addressed him in it. It could be argued that the Reformers did not so much rediscover the authority of the Bible as they invested the actual words of Scripture with an *independent* authority. It was not so much a matter of the words they read as of the Word they heard when they read; that Word was the Word of God and had the authority of God. This fact accounts for the great wave of Bible translations in the sixteenth century (some two hundred in German-speaking lands during the Reformation period and as many as thirty-eight in England).

The *sola scriptura* of Luther was hardly a new cry in Europe, though its emphasis was. The doctrine can be found in Marsilius of Padua (d. 1343) and in Ockham (d. 1349); Wycliffe (d. 1384) and Huss (d. 1415) went further and proclaimed the Bible as the only touchstone on matters of faith and doctrine. Men began to turn away from the secularised ambitions of the papacy and the despiritualised Church with its concomitant immorality of the clergy in order to find an authoritative spirituality in the Bible. Some few turned to mysticism. In the second half of the fifteenth century the Christian Humanists were everywhere busy in Europe editing, translating, and expounding the Scriptures. For example, Valla (d. 1457) compiled his *Annotations of the New Testament*, which proved a stimulus to biblical studies as well as a challenge to the authority of the text of the Vulgate. Wessel (d. 1489) anticipated Luther both in setting the authority of the Bible above that of popes and councils, and in his perception of justification by faith. Ximenes (d. 1517) fostered the New Learning in his new university of Alcalá in Spain, where the first printed text of the Greek New Testament was completed in 1514, followed in 1522 by the famous Polyglot Bible. In France Lefèvre was editing the Psalms (1509), the Epistles of St. Paul (1512), a commentary on the Gospels (1522), and his translations of the Psalms and the New Testament (1523-25). John Colet (d. 1519) startled his Oxford students and later his London congregations with his biblical teaching and Pauline preaching. In the Empire at large, men such as Jakob Wimpheling (d. 1518) and the distinguished Hebrew scholar Reuchlin (d. 1522) devoted their high philological learning to finding fresh interpretations of the Bible.

Erasmus's Greek New Testament was perhaps the most significant achievement in this area. Published in 1516, it exploded the myth of the perfection of Jerome's Vulgate and extended to the scholar the right to examine biblical texts critically. It proved of immense value to Luther. It is interesting to note here that Erasmus had more than an academic interest in doing this work; in his preface he stresses the importance the Humanists attached to reading the Bible:

> I wish that all men might read the Gospels and the Epistles of Saint Paul. I wish that they might be translated into all tongues of all men, so that not only the Scots and the Irish, but also the Turk and the Saracen might read and understand. I wish that the countryman might sing them at his plough, the weaver chant them at his loom, the traveller beguile with them the weariness of his journey. . . .

When Catholic contemporaries blamed Erasmus for begetting Luther, saying that Luther hatched the egg that Erasmus had laid, they were giving indirect testimony to the value of the work of the Humanists to the cause of the Reformation in the field of biblical studies.

For the medieval theologian the Bible certainly was authoritative: it was a sort of spiritual law-book, a storehouse of divinely communicated knowledge, of doctrinal truths and rules for moral conduct. In fact, without Luther's principle, it could be little more than that. Luther and all his followers found in the Bible an altogether new life, a life of fellowship with God: God had met them there, God had come to them, and in Christ the Holy Spirit had made his abode with them. They were not talking about doctrine, nor even of corruption and abuses, but quite simply of God. Herein lay the power of the Reformers, their awesome certainty. It was not a matter of superior scholarship or greater ability, nor of any power proceeding from man; it was an experience of God given by God himself which could be neither gainsaid nor betrayed. What Paul could say of himself—'it pleased God . . . to reveal His Son in me' (Gal. 1.15-16)—each Reformer could say of himself. That revelation occurred in the Bible, and continues to occur insofar as the Church submits to the Bible.

What gave the Reformers a powerful advantage over the Catholics was their grasp of the historical revelation recorded in the Bible. Medieval biblical scholars laboured under the supreme difficulty of being debarred from much of the biblical content. There was abundant material provided for the construction of doctrines and for moral guidance, but as important and as clear as that is, it is all rather a small portion of the total text. There are long genealogies, pages of detail about the tabernacle and temple, wars and battles, sieges and deputations, simple tales of simple folk, details of national history, and the like. What was the medieval theologian to make of this? Either he had to discard it, or somehow he had to transform it into doctrinal or moral teaching. He did this very simply by allegory.

As firmly set as the modern mind is against allegory, it should be recalled that one great benefit that accrued from the use of the allegorical method was the conservation of the biblical text itself: no part of it was jettisoned. Furthermore, a good deal of the biblical material is already in the form of parable and proverb and is amenable to allegorical interpretation; so long as such interpretation is not presumed to be 'authoritative', and is kept on the level of private meditations, no harm is done. Concerning Matthew 13, for instance, Origen writes that the mustard seed is *literally* an actual seed; *morally*, it is faith in the individual believer; *allegorically*, it is the kingdom of God. Regarding Canticles 2.15, he suggests that the little foxes are *literally* fox cubs; *morally* they are sins in the individual heart; *allegorically*, they are the heresies that tear apart the Church. Augustine proceeds in the same manner; in expounding the parable of the Good Samaritan he allegorises every detail, even going so far as to suggest that the two pence represent the two sacraments. One can even see a beginning of this tendency in the New Testament itself, when, for instance, the parable of the Sower is interpreted.

Apart from the benefits of preserving the historical text and deepening the spirituality of the reader, the application of this technique is wholly destructive of the historical character of revelation. It further produces total uncertainty of what the passage originally meant and intended. In Luther's day the technique, as explained by Nicholas de Lyra, was '*Litera gesta docet, quid credas Allegoria / Moralis quid agas, quo tendas Anagogia*' —that is to say, the literal meaning tells you what happened, the allegorical what you should believe, the moral what you should do, and the anagogic what will bring you to heaven. This four-fold sense tends to destroy the meaning of the historical character of revelation, and leads to complete uncertainty concerning what the passage actually means. One could never arrive at Christ's meaning if one were to see the two pence as two sacraments. In fact there could be no serious critical study of the Bible at all.

Along with this idea of a four-fold sense of Scripture, which brought bewilderment to those who sought to understand what the Bible actually taught, there ran the irreconcileable idea that salvation entailed holding an absolutely correct grasp of what the Scriptures did reveal about the nature of God and man individually and in relation to one another. The medieval theologians held that faith involves assent to correct propositional statements about God, man, and the universe. Such assent in turn involves the submission of the intellect to propositions that are considered to be correct by the Church (or that at least bear the Church's stamp of approval). To err in one's grasp of these propositions, or, what was worse, to differ from authoritative declarations, was to consign oneself to Hell, to join the ranks of the totally lost. The Church's claim to infallibility suggests that it can guarantee the perfect correctness of its propositions about God and man and their relation one to another. It is obvious that we are not speaking of what the Reformers meant by faith (i.e., personal trust in a living and loving active God); we are talking instead about faith as assent.

With such a theology there was actually no way a believer would find in the Bible the personal communion of God as he came to him in his reading of it. Between the God who had revealed himself there and man, the medieval theologian had placed the Church, which was really no more than the accumulated opinions of accredited theologians confirmed by popes and councils. This was not done deliberately — indeed most theologians had never noticed the process — but it had happened nonetheless. In a parallel way the Church had interposed the priesthood between the sinner and his Saviour — again, not deliberately, but indisputably nonetheless.

Luther and his followers had won their personal experience of pardon by throwing themselves on the mercy of God as revealed in Christ, and when they saw that, they swept aside the priest who was really, painful as it is to say so, an intervention between God and themselves. He stood in their way. And the traditional biblical scholar went the same way as the priest: the Reformers controverted the idea that faith was the assent to correct propositional statements, and maintained that it was the personal authoritative experience of God who had addressed them in and through his Word. They had felt and known the personal God, the God who had made them and redeemed them in Christ, who was now speaking to them in this Book, and who was making clear his power, authority, certainty, and deep concern for them. *It was less a matter of a Book than an experience of the living God.*

Of course, the peasant may not hear as much as the professor, nor be able to fit the whole Bible together as a Luther did, but all, plain man and theologian alike, and even children, could hear the Father's voice, learn the Redeemer's purpose, and have faith in the promises of God. It was, of course, a bonus if the plain man could put text and text together and build up a body of divinity to which his mind could assent; but it was not essential. It was a matter of simple trust, yielding that deep experience of God addressing them in words apposite to their own life, as he fulfilled all his promises in Christ. The one thing needful was to hear this God speak just as he had throughout the ages to his people, promising his salvation, now in words, now in pictures, or dealing with a favoured man or a chosen people.

No detail of life was any longer dead history, for every detail had become part of the continuous communion between God and his people, just as everything a child says and does, even at the level of nonsense, plays a part in the living relationship of parent and child. Each story, each incident, each word of the past took on the form of a promise that what had happened in the past would be renewed in their own experience of fellowship with a gracious God, if only their faith were of the kind that the saints of the Old Testament and New Testament enjoyed:

> The entire Bible does nothing else than give a person to understand what he was, what he now is, what behoves him, and what his works are. It informs him that he is completely undone. Secondly, it tells what God is, what pertains to Him, and what His works are, above all the mercy in Christ. *Him* it leads us to understand, and through His incarnation it conducts us from earth to heaven, to the Godhead. May God the heavenly Father grant all of us His grace and mercy to this end, through Christ, our dear Lord and Saviour. Amen. Amen. Amen. [14]

With an understanding of this kind Luther and his followers perceived the Bible to be a different book than that which had played so different a role in the hands of the medieval theologians. God was addressing them in it in a sense more real and significant than when their fellowmen spoke to them in their daily life. Therefore, it was the plain, literal historical sense that was the most important to them. The Scripture was not a warehouse of truths nor a library of doctrines and moral rules; it was the record and picture of the experiences chosen saints had had in fellowship with God throughout history since God first revealed his promise. The Bible was the story of God's revelation of himself in history. That is why it was always a priority for the Reformers to translate the Bible into the vernacular and put it into the hands of the common man; they believed that the plain man with his Bible could know more about the way of salvation than all the popes or councils without the Scrip-

---

14. WA, 48, 272.

tures—always recalling, however, that it is not the possession of a book in the hand, but the authoritative Word of God addressing the penitent believer that is of any value.

It is hardly too much to say that Luther's position almost amounted to a rediscovery of Scripture, a rediscovery born of his new insight into faith, which was less an intellectual assent to propositional statements than a recalling by God of what was a personal trust in a personal Saviour who had revealed in his life and work the fatherly mercy of God. Here was no mere theological definition, but a description of an experience that men knew to be real. It opened their eyes to the fact that the Word of God was a personal rather than a dogmatic revelation. The real meaning of the Word of God was that they had met and heard God himself, not that they had learned a little theology or a dogmatic revelation. They were not talking of an abstract truth, but of a personal Father who had made himself known to them. There were two dynamic activities in this experience, the divine and the human. On the divine side, there was God pouring out himself, revealing the treasures of his righteousness and his love in Christ, the Word made flesh. On the human side, there was the believing soul seeing right through all the works, all the symbols, all the deeds, all the words, to Christ himself, being united to him by faith in a creative, personal union.

It was this experience of being in close union with God incarnate that began to create a wholly new conception of Scripture. The medieval Church looked on Jesus as the teacher sent from God; revelation was for its members above all things an imparting of speculative truth. For Luther, however, the function of Scripture was clearly to bring Jesus near us; and since Jesus is the fullest revelation of God a human could know or appropriate, we might say that the chief end of Scripture is to bring God near *me*. It is the direct message of God's love to me myself: it is not doctrine, but promise; it is not an offering of God's thoughts, but of God Himself as *my* God. This manifestation of God, which is recorded for us in the Scriptures, took place in a historical process within the framework of actual world events, coming to its fullest and highest in the incarnation and historical work of Christ. Luther even argued that the manifestation had been so framed as to include everything that was necessary to enable us to understand the declaration of God's will in its historical context and in its historical manifestation.

In his introduction to this translation of the Old Testament, Luther made the memorable remark that the Scriptures were the swaddling clothes that contained Christ:

> I beg and faithfully warn every pious Christian not to be of-
> fended by the simplicity of the language and the stories that
> will often meet him here. Let him not doubt that, however
> simple they may seem, they are the very words, works, judg-
> ments and deeds of the exalted majesty, power and wisdom of
> God. For this is the writing that turns all the wise and prudent
> into fools, and is an open book only to the small and foolish
> folk, as Christ says (Mt. 11.25). Therefore dismiss your own
> notions and feelings and think of this Writing as the most
> sublime, the most noble of holy things, as the richest of mines,
> which can never be entirely exhausted. Do this that you may
> find the wisdom of God which he here submits in a manner
> so foolish and simple in order to quench all pride. Here you
> will find the swaddling clothes and the manger in which Christ
> lies, to which the angels direct the shepherds. Plain and or-
> dinary are the swaddling clothes; but dear is the Treasure,
> Christ, which lies in them. [15]

To Luther, and to all the Reformers, these stories were never dead histories, for they tell how God dealt with his faithful people in times past, and are promises and assurances of how he deals with his people now.

The question now arises concerning how we are to recognise the infallibility of Scripture and its authoritative character. It is clearly important that this question be answered within the context of the issues we have been considering to this point—the nature of infallibility, the idea of authority, and the confrontation by God of a believing and penitent soul who reads Scripture. The idea of Scrip-ture and the Reformation concept of saving faith belong together and may not be examined apart from their living, organic relation-ship. In medieval theology both faith and the content of Scripture are conceived primarily as intellectual and propositional (as they are still today in humanist and even in some theological circles); whereas for Luther and all the Reformers, faith was an experience, and always personal. For the Reformers, faith was a conviction awakened in the soul by the power of the Holy Spirit—*testimonium Spiritus Sancti internum*. In the same way that they found that it is God

---

15. *D. Martin Luthers Werke: Deutsche Bible* (Weimar, 1906), 5, 3.

himself who makes us know and feel the sense of pardon as a deep inner experience of faith that is all his own work, they found the same deep compelling witness of the Holy Spirit enabling them to see that it was God himself speaking authoritatively in and through the Scriptures.

Luther (and, following him, all the Reformers) drew the clearest distinction between the Word of God on the one hand and Scripture, which contains, carries, and presents that Word on the other hand. Here is a vital distinction. It is not the difference between the Word of God and the Word of God written: Luther believed that the Word of God is presented everywhere in Scripture, but that in certain places it is presented more evidently, more trenchantly. In the preface to his translation of the New Testament he shows that John (in his gospel and first epistle), Paul (especially in Romans, Galatians, and Ephesians), and Peter (in 1 Peter) preach Christ and tell us all we need to know for our salvation. He even argued that if a man were to possess these only and no other books, he could still know the way of salvation. In other contexts he said similar things about Genesis, and in particular about the Psalms, which he called the Bible within the Bible. As early as 1520, in his clarion call on Christian liberty, he wrote,

> You ask, 'What then is this Word of God, and how shall it be used, since there are so many words of God?' I answer, the Apostle explains that in Romans i. The Word is the Gospel of God concerning His Son, Who was made flesh, suffered, rose from the dead, and was glorified through the Spirit Who sanctifies. For to preach Christ means to feed the soul, to make it righteous, to set it free and to save it, if it believe the preaching. For faith alone is the saving and efficacious use of the Word of God, Roman x, 'If thou confess with thy mouth that Jesus is Lord, and believe with thy heart that God hath raised Him up from the dead, thou shalt be saved'; and again, 'The end of the law is Christ, unto righteousness to every one that believeth'; and, Romans i, 'The just shall live by his faith'.
> . . . the soul can do without all things except the Word of God. . . . Where this is not, there is no help for the soul in anything else whatever. [16]

This very real distinction between the Word of God and Scripture may easily be lost, and is often perverted by preachers' analo-

---

16. *WML*, 2: 315, 314.

gies. It is not helpful to describe it as kernel and husk, the husk (the record) being disposable once the kernel (the word) has been reached and grasped. Nor should it be taken to mean that one part of the Bible is the Word of God and another is not. All Reformers uniformly teach throughout all their works that *all* Scripture is the Word of God, and further, that anything which is not part of the record of the Word of God is not Scripture. An illustration may help: if a little child brings a simple wildflower and offers it to its parent in love, and in later years that same child offers love unlimited to the same sick or dying parent, then it is the same child, and it is the same love, and its offer brings the same deep joy; the one means more, speaks more loudly, but the parent treasures both in his heart. In the same way, Genesis speaks more loudly than Chronicles, the Psalms than Canticles, John than Mark, Paul than James—but they are all Scripture, and Scripture *is* the Word of God.

It is this word *is* that we must consider for a moment. We have distinguished the Word of God from Scripture, and yet we say that Scripture *is* the Word of God. The word *is* in this context is not being used to express logical identity; I may say, 'This book is Luther's *de servo arbitrio*', by which I mean that in my hand is the actual text of Luther's own book—and this is logical identity. On the other hand, I may say to a student of a scholar's analysis and examination of Luther's book, 'This book is Luther's *de servo arbithio*', by which I mean, and he knows that I mean, that the scholar's work *conveys* or *represents* Luther's mind as expressed in that book. It is this latter sense of the word *is*—a sense variously connoted by such words as *contains, expresses, conveys, records*, and so on—that we must understand to apply when we say that Scripture *is* the Word of God if we are going to avoid the error of denying that Scripture does indeed possess those attributes of authority and infallibility that belong to the Word of God. This distinction is not merely academic but vital, and helpful. First, it shows what is meant by the infallibility of Scripture, and secondly, it enables us to distinguish between the human and the divine elements in the Bible.

Infallibility and authority belong primarily to the Word of God and only secondarily to Scripture, insofar as it contains, expresses, conveys, records the Word of God. It is this Word of God addressing a believing and penitent heart personally, fulfilling his promises and bestowing salvation, that is authoritative and infallible. For him who had heard, it has the authority of 'Thus saith the Lord . . .', or 'Verily, verily I say unto you. . . .' Further, it speaks assuredly in the area of salvation, the area Christ kept to, and Paul, and Luther. It does not claim authority in the areas of politics and social problems, as some too confidently claim when they so easily speak of God's will for them. It is the assurance of salvation, of peace with God, of God in Christ taking up his abode in the believer's heart and mind and graciously giving the fellowship of the Holy Ghost wherein lies the assurance, the certainty.

Scripture shares the attributes of authority and infallibility only insofar as it is the vehicle of spiritual truth. All Reformers, in their books, catechisms, and liturgies, declare that Scripture is Scripture because it gives us that knowledge of God and his will which is necessary for salvation; it is Scripture because it presents to the eye of faith God personally manifesting himself in Christ. It is this presentation of God and of his will for our salvation that is infallible and authoritative. It is not a book, not letters and ink that we are discussing at all, but God in spiritual activity. God who declares himself through Scripture in his own Word is engaged on a spiritual activity, discernible only to the eye of faith. This manifestation can be apprehended only by a spiritual faculty, and that faculty is faith: no Reformer or confession of the Reformation recognises any infallibility or divine authority apprehended other than by faith. It will be readily seen that such a view of infallibility is of quite another kind than that claimed for the pontiff by Luther's contemporary Catholic opponents (or by some modern Roman Catholics for that matter). It is also quite different from that claimed by certain Protestant groups who cannot, or do not, distinguish the Scriptures from the Word of God.

For the medieval theologian, infallibility was something that granted the perfect correctness of his abstract religious propositions. For certain Protestants, it means the inerrancy of the scriptural records, that they contain no error in word or fact. But neither inerrancy nor the correctness of abstract propositional statements is apprehended by faith in the Reformers' sense of that word; they are simply matters of fact, to be rejected or accepted by the normal faculties of men, faculties we all possess. The infallibility and authority that can be perceived only by faith are, and must be, something very different: they arise from the conviction that in the manifestation of God in his Word there lies infallible power to save. This conviction is given by the Holy Spirit, by God himself. As Calvin was to express it a generation later,

> As God alone can properly bear witness to his own words, so these words will not obtain full credit in the hearts of men, until they are sealed by the inward testimony of the Spirit. . . .
>
> Let it therefore be held as fixed, that those who are inwardly taught by the Holy Spirit acquiesce implicitly in Scripture; that Scripture, carrying its own evidence along with it, deigns not to submit to proofs and arguments, but owes the full conviction with which we ought to receive it to the testimony of the Spirit. Enlightened by Him, we no longer believe, either on our own judgment or that of others, that the Scriptures are from God. . . . We feel perfectly assured that it came to us, by the instrumentality of men, from the very mouth of God. [17]

This is a religious conception of infallibility very different from that of either the medieval (or modern) Roman Catholic or the modern Protestant fundamentalist.

The distinction between the Word of God and Scripture also serves to distinguish between the divine and human elements in Scripture, and to give each its proper place. It allows for the judicious exercise of critical modern scholarship in a way that Roman Catholicism does not, and that Protestant fundamentalism cannot.

Infallibility and authority belong to the sphere of faith and to the internal testimony of the Holy Spirit, and therefore to that personal manifestation of God and his will towards us, a will conveyed in every part of Scripture. But this manifestation was given at a known time, in a known place, to a known person, in words known to all. It is a part of history, experienced in the lives of real men and peoples. It exists in a recorded form outwardly like all other historical and human writings, many of which provide their own records of the same events and peoples, the same Egyptian Pharaohs and Assyrian kings. We should constantly remind ourselves that while every part of Scripture is divine, it is also truly human. The divine energy is encased in human realities, in frail men, in perishable ink and parchment. To apprehend the divine activity requires the divine gift of the Holy Spirit; to learn the credibility of the history in Scripture,

---

17. *Institutio*, I, vii, 4-5.

it is sufficient to use the ordinary methods and tools of research common to all scholars, be they heathen or Christian.

When Luther (and the later Reformers) distinguished between the Word of God and the Scriptures that convey or present it, and when he declared that the authority or infallibility of that Word belonged to the region of faith in which God ruled and exercised his power, they made that authority and infallibility altogether independent for all time of critical questions that might *very properly* be raised about the human agencies through which the book came into its present shape. It is not a matter belonging to the domain of faith to investigate when the books that record the Word of God were written, or by whom, or in what way, or how often they were edited or re-edited. It is not a matter of faith to enquire whether incidents happened in one country or another; whether the account of Job be literal history, or a poem in which the author has developed the problems of God's providence and man's probation; whether genealogical tables give the names of men or of countries and peoples; whether there are sources comprising Genesis; whether there are three authors to Isaiah. All these, and similar problems, belong to the human side of the record, and are the province of normal critical scholarship. No special illumination of God-given faith is necessary to unravel them; they are as much subject to ordinary human investigation as any other historical problem.

Luther carved for himself a niche of liberty, which he jealously guarded and of which he freely availed himself. (This his successors have preserved, evidence for which may be found in the fact that virtually all modern biblical scholarship has issued from the German Luther tradition.) Luther never felt himself bound to accept the traditional ideas about the extent of the canon or the authorship of particular books of the Bible or even about the credibility of some of the things recorded. He said, speaking about Genesis, 'What if Moses never wrote it?' It was enough for him that it was there, and that he could read it. He openly said that the books of Kings were worthier records than the books of Chronicles and that he believed that the prophets had not always given to the king good political advice.

True as is Luther's insistence that the Bible is human literature and that it may (and indeed must) be subjected to all the scholarly rigours men apply to all other literary and historical documents, it is nevertheless also true that he insisted even more strongly that it is the record of the revelation of God, and that God had carefully guarded and protected it. This thought may be quaint to a modern scholar, but it is important that it be expressed. Luther (and the Reformers) always speak of the singular care and providence of God that has preserved the Scriptures in such a way that his people always have an abundantly full and unmistakeable declaration in them of his mind and will for their salvation from the moment Adam fell to the moment when Christ rose and redeemed man. This idea always forbids a careless or irreverent biblical criticism (or even a superior one) that might try to hide behind the liberty Luther won, or even masquerade its liberty when dealing with the records of revelation. Luther once accused the Catholic scholar Jerome Emser of going at the Bible in the way a sow tackles a bag of oats; in less homely language, as befitted his debate with Erasmus, he described the difference between that formidable scholar and himself as residing in the fact that Erasmus sat *above* Scripture and judged it, whereas he sat *under* Scripture and allowed it to judge him. Good biblical scholarship is always aware of this dimension.

We have already considered the fullness and sufficiency of the biblical revelation. No one can say beforehand how much or how little of the historic record is necessary for the preservation of the faith of the Church; certainly every person who has the faith experience enjoys its abundance as he reads now the historical record, now the poetical literature, now the prophets, now the gospels, now the epistles, now the book of Acts. It accords with the mercy and grace of God to leave his creature in full abundance and in absolute certainty. Luther's liberty should not be made to stretch to those scholars who seek to pare away the historical bases of the Christian faith; that is a different kind of activity altogether.

Zwingli, with his characteristic acumen, had the matter right in his *Sixty-seven Theses* of 1523, in which he declares that all who say that the Gospel is of no value apart from its confirmation by the Church err and blaspheme against God, and that the sum of the Gospel is 'that our Lord Jesus Christ, very Son of God, has revealed to us the will of the heavenly Father, and with his innocence has redeemed us from death and has reconciled us to God.' The idea is not to place Scripture over tradition, but rather to assert the supreme value of Scripture which reveals God's good will to us in

Jesus Christ to be received by faith alone over all human traditions that would lead us astray from God and from true faith. Luther and the Reformers were less concerned to define the authority of Scripture than to cling to the divinely revealed way of salvation and to turn away from all human interpretations and formulations. They wanted to set men in direct touch with God; to make it clear that their trust was in God, not man. That is why all of them stress the internal witness of the Holy Spirit. If a man has that, what more does he need, what more is there to have, than God himself?

Perhaps no point is more significant for, or more relevant to, the present ecumenical debate in 'the whole state of Christ's Church', than is Luther's teaching on Scripture and the Word of God. At the same time, perhaps no more significant section in the documents of Vatican II exists than the section on the Dogmatic Constitution on Divine Revelation, the expression of the contemporary Catholic mind on the Bible. And what a dramatic story of what occurred before it reached its final stage, when, contrary to the regulations, dear Pope John 'irregularly' intervened, insisting that the first draft be returned, rewritten and re-presented. Surely the Holy Spirit was at work there! All the early material about 'two sources of Revelation' (namely, Scripture and tradition) was rejected, and all the philosophical treatment transmuted into biblical and historical categories. In Article 5 of the Constitution, the important point is made, so central to Luther, that faith in the biblical sense is far more than mere intellectual assent to propositions; it is a total and obedient commitment of the whole self, freely given to God. Article 10 emphasizes the interplay and coordination of Scripture, tradition, and the teaching office, and actually says that 'the teaching office is not above the word of God'. That is not what Rome said to Luther. Here is indeed the breakthrough for which Christians have waited since Worms in 1521. Let us together walk through to the road God has so clearly opened up. Let us say with Cardinal Cushing, 'The work of the Council has not ended. It is just begun.' To complete that work, the Catholics need the Protestants—and both need Luther.

CHAPTER NINE

THE DOCTRINE OF CHRIST

IT WAS THE profound experience of God in his disclosure of the moving mystery of his purpose in Christ that captured Luther's mind; it is from this experience, this insight, this revelation of God's all-conquering love that all of his theology derives. In the opening words of his *Commentary on Galatians* (1531) he writes, 'the one doctrine which I have supremely at heart, is that of faith in Christ, from whom, through whom and unto whom all my theological thinking flows back and forth, day and night.' Similarly, when Paul sums up the epistle with its closing words, 'Brethren, the grace of our Lord Jesus Christ be with your spirit', Luther comments, 'This is his last farewell. He endeth the Epistle with the same words with which he began. As if he said, I have taught you Christ purely. *(Ego docui vos pure Christum).*'[1] With these five simple words Luther wrote unwittingly not the epitaph of Paul, but his own. No other words could sum up Luther's entire life's work so succinctly.

His main concern was to tell the world of his own experience of the great God who had shown his hand in Christ in order that men might learn of God's pardon and therefore God's peace in the living Christ, and so live in this Kingdom of God in this life within a corrupt, sinful, hostile, but temporal world, as to be received in death into his eternal kingdom. He was simply a man with a Gospel. He had a message to offer to the world because in his long, painful, single-minded search for God through his disillusionment with the medieval techniques of penance and good works, God addressed him. God spoke to him of the gospel of the sovereign unmerited

---

1. *D. Martin Luthers Werke: Kritische Gesamtausgabe* (Weimar, 1883 ff.), 40, 2, 183, 23. Hereafter abbreviated WA (Weimar Ausgabe).

and unearned free grace of God enfleshed in Christ. Luther was born again. He saw everything new.

It was when he taught what he had seen, and expressed it in his writings, that Luther found himself in a polemical position. What he described as a joyous deliverance brought him up against the secularised corruption of the Church, in the first instance by the selling of forgiveness by indulgences. In the same way he found himself opposed to the unreal and remote disputations of scholasticism, and troubled by its pagan (Aristotelian) philosophy. Erasmus and the Humanists turned against his consequent sharp evangelical and Christological theology. The radicals and enthusiasts, the peasants and the secularists were not interested in the final issue of this evangelical and Christological liberation; they spoke of social or political or personal freedom, not freedom in Christ. These latter groups either rejected or modified the sole sufficiency of Christ in the interests of tradition, learning, inspiration, human rights, social justice or similar considerations, more often than not for reasons of self-interest. In all these conflicts what impelled Luther to go on was the same experience that had caused the protest — his experience of Christ. He no more sought the polemics than had Christ before him; it was the resistance of men that brought about his great stand. Let us consider this in relation to his Christology.

Luther was condemned and later charged with heresy and excommunicated in 1521, but the condemnation arose from the fact that he would not allow the authority and tradition of the papacy to be superior to the plain meaning of Scripture as evidenced by simple reason. Luther was the most orthodox of men who accepted all the creeds (Apostles', Nicene, and Athanasian) and the traditions of the Early Church. His criticisms of theological doctrines were always confined to the theories and innovations of the Schoolmen and to the perversions of biblical theology and ancient tradition brought in by the Schoolmen under the influence of the pagan philosophy of Aristotle.

The world knows of the dramatic nailing up of the Ninety-five Theses on Indulgences in 1517, but few recall that it was an earlier Ninety-seven Theses, the *Disputation against Scholastic Theology*, that really marked the beginning of the Reformation. Luther first raised the standard of revolt in this earlier disputation, which was directed against scholastic theology in the interests of a Christology that was biblical in kind and evangelical in effect.[2]

It is interesting to study the points selected by Luther for disputation on the subject of Scholastic theology. We find the theology of Augustine defended, particularly on the matter of the bondage of the will, whereas Scotus and Biel are attacked. He discusses the nature of man and his desire to make himself God rather than to let God be God. Grace, predestination, and total depravity are discussed, and it is argued that the natural man possesses neither sound reason nor a good will. There follows a severe attack on Aristotle and his dominance in the theological schools, particularly with regard to his arguments that a man becomes good by doing good: Luther sees this as simply the foundation for works righteousness. He then discusses the religion of law and the religion of grace. It is a strong polemic against the Schoolmen and their ideas, but it is biblical throughout, and a sound exposition of the old, pre-Scholastic tradition. It is already powerful, biblical, evangelical thinking, in which Christ is both centre and circumference.

He brought two main charges against the Scholastic theology: first, he denounced it as being committed to the idea of works righteousness and thus heedless of the pure New Testament doctrine of justification in Christ by faith only; and second, he described it as sophistry. This was more than an epithet of abuse; he meant that the Schoolmen 'played' with the externals of doctrine and never got to their inner meaning. They raised questions nobody ever asked, and found answers that helped nobody. It was a kind of intellectual gymnastics, or keep-fit, of no use to anybody except to sharpen the mind. He found this imposing intellectual edifice to be hollow within; he found that the God they referred to was not the God and Father revealed in Jesus Christ, the God who could never be arrived at by intellectual ratiocination bounced off a few biblical texts, for the product of such thinking amounted to no more than the abstract entity of pagan philosophy: it certainly was not the God of the Bible; at its best it was no more than an idol.

It is well known that down to the time of Augustine the centres of intellectual life were Antioch and Athens, Alexandria and Car-

---

2. See my *Luther: Early Theological Works*, Library of Christian Classics, no. 16 (Philadelphia: Westminster Press, 1980), pp. 251-73.

thage. In medieval Christendom the centres moved northwards to the courts of Theodoric and Charlemagne into the cities of Canterbury and Oxford, Paris and Cologne. This shift meant that medieval Christendom had to acquire a language, a culture, a philosophy, a theology quite new to its traditions, and in addition master the patristic corpus of the East. This whole activity is what we now call Scholasticism. In essence it was a system of learning and of ordering, an assimilation by the Frankish-Nordic mind of that immense and alien corpus. Its strength was its rationalism. It sought to combine faith and reason in order to preserve for rational man a religion based on revelation and lived by faith.

Luther was some distance from the Schoolmen concerning the meanings they presumed to attach to the words *faith* and *reason*. In this context, *faith* to the Schoolmen meant the sum of patristic teaching about the truths of the Christian religion extracted by the Fathers from the Scriptures, and *reason* meant the sum of philosophical principles extracted from the writings of ancient philosophers, of whom Aristotle was supreme. The great Schoolmen took it upon themselves to construct a system of Christian philosophy by combining patristic doctrinal conclusions with the conclusions of human reasoning, which they thought at its highest in Aristotle. Consequently, Christianity lost its most important characteristics. The Schoolmen spoke of God as 'the Absolute', as 'the Prime Mover', 'the First Cause', 'the Intelligence that ordains all created things', and so on. Such terms can never capture the biblical realism of a personal God who in his love sent his beloved Son for us men and our salvation. Furthermore, Aristotle's teaching on ethics eventually entailed a works righteousness. For Luther, Scholasticism was inimical to true Christianity as taught by Christ, embodied in the apostolic witness, and preserved by the Fathers: It was sophistry. Luther protested against such teaching and swept it away.

As I noted once before, I am not alone in having discerned a parallel between Athanasius and Luther. Athanasius found himself opposed to the unbiblical element of the thought forms of his times, which could see Christ and the Holy Spirit only as *creatures*, and which sought to interpret Christianity in terms of the alien categories of gnosticism, or Arianism. To this there is clearly a parallel in Luther's dispute with Scholasticism. Luther was arguing for a dynamic, personal, biblical, historically based theology, in contrast to the academic, static, conceptual, propositional, intellectualised theology of the Schoolmen. This also serves to shed some light on our current theological climate. Today the conflict is not between Roman Catholicism and Protestantism at all, but between the contemporary radical, non-Theistic, non-Incarnational theologians on the one hand, and the biblical, believing theologians on the other hand, among whom Roman Catholic and Protestant theologians are of the same mind and the same heart. Here unity already exists.

Luther remorselessly pushed men's theology away from the priority of *thought* to the priority of *being* — that is, away from theology expressed in intellectual categories to truth as objectively experienced in history and life. Rome sought the security and certainty of identifying truth with its own authoritative interpretation and approached what was tantamount to a theology of assent. Luther argued that the unredeemed man must be converted before he can see and know, that man had to be freed from himself and his own interests, freed from his own prejudices and presuppositions, before he could know the truth in Christ, *as it comes and reveals itself to him, not as he thinks it is.* True knowledge of this kind requires obedience to God and total submission to the ways he has revealed himself to us in history. Luther's theology was shattering to the church precisely because he carried through his theological perceptions into the sphere of church practice and everyday living. He set Christ in the centre in the theological schools, in the centre of man's everyday life. Had his Christology remained a debate among schoolmen, Luther would have had no more significance than any other of his many contemporaries among the German professoriate. By pursuing it to its proper end, he lifted Christianity off its hinges and rehung it, his plumbline being Christ as interpreted in the New Testament and by the old Church Fathers.

The main rebuttal of the Scholastic theology lay ironically with the weight of tradition: Luther stood where the old Catholic Church has taken its stand; his theology was that of the old Fathers, rooted in the faith in a truine God and in the belief in the person of Christ, the revealer of God. He reached right back through the Fathers to the Bible, and found his theology rooted in his experience of Christ, his redeemer and mediator. He was Christ-centred, and Christ-mastered. He would cry out at table and in the garden to the birds of the mercy of God in Christ. For that reason he was staunchly opposed to any worship of the saints, any invocation of the blessed Virgin Mary. The saints were not colleagues of Christ, nor was Mary an 'easier' to 'more approachable' mediatrix. Luther insisted on the necessity of Christ alone for all believers, and also that Christ alone was the sole revealer of God, our only mediator (and advocate).

It has been argued that in his doctrine of the person of Christ, Luther was orthodox and traditional, but there is one point of special interest that Luther emphasized, namely, the old patristic term the *communicatio idiomatum* (i.e., the 'sharing of attributes'). Luther argued that the attributes by which the human and the divine nature may be described are to some extent interchangeable in the person of Christ. For example, it is an attribute of God that he can be everywhere, whereas man can only be at one place at any given time; thus, insofar as Christ was a man, he could function only in a given place at a given time (e.g., Palestine), but insofar as Christ is God, he can be everywhere—but even the human nature of Christ, even his body as seen and touched by the disciples after the Resurrection, possesses the qualities of the divine nature and can now be everywhere. The Transfiguration, the Resurrection, and finally and perfectly the Ascension marked the progressive revelation of a mystery 'kept secret' by Christ.[3] Be that as it may, certainly the full exaltation took place at the Ascension.

It is not easy to be precise here on Luther's thinking, for he hated theological speculation, and in his extempore statements he will support sometimes one view, sometimes another; nevertheless, his doctrine of the omnipresence of both natures of Christ brought him into opposition to the medieval idea that heaven is 'some kind of place up there'. Christ sits at God's right hand, true, but God's 'right hand' is not restricted to any one location: God is everywhere. Luther said that we act with our right hand. Everywhere God is active, there is his right hand, and so Christ also, not only his divine nature, but also his transformed, resurrected body.

At first sight it may appear that such speculation is alien to

---

3. It later became a matter of dispute among Lutheran theologians as to whether Christ 'kept secret' [*krypsis*] certain divine qualities during his earthly ministry, or whether he experienced 'emptying of himself' [*kenosis*], as described in Philippians 2.7.

Luther, but it is a means by which he is taking the historical accounts seriously and drawing some important conclusions for the faith of the Church and in relation to scientific development. He held that it is essential to know that Christ's body can now be everywhere, for instance, because in this way only can we understand how Christ's body could be present at the same time at every altar throughout the land—and Luther firmly believed in the real presence of the flesh and blood of Christ in Holy Communion. His speculation allows him to formulate a biblical and traditional explanation of the real presence, while rejecting the Aristotelian doctrine of transubstantiation. Many Catholic scholars (e.g., Edward Schillebeeckx) are now also seeking a fresh interpretation of the real presence apart from the later and unsatisfactory theory of transubstantiation.

In this connection we can welcome the use of the word *transignification* in the Protestant/Catholic debate today. It approaches very nearly the thinking of Cranmer and Ridley in Luther's days. Cranmer, in his fine work A *Defence of the true and catholic doctrine of the sacrament of the body and blood of our Saviour Christ* (1550), spoke of 'sacramental mutation', of 'the sacramental body and blood', and of 'corporally eating the bread and wine and spiritually feeding on the flesh and blood of Jesus Christ his Saviour and Redeemer'. At the same time he rebutted in great detail the doctrine of transubstantiation, with its Aristotelian philosophy of substance and accidents. He carefully distinguished between the doctrine of 'the old catholic Church' and that of 'the lately corrupted Romish Church'. Latimer expressed similar views before his judges: 'that which before was bread now has the dignity to exhibit Christ's body. And yet the bread is still bread, and the wine still wine. For the change is not in the nature, but the dignity'. 'The dignity to exhibit Christ's body' is a highly expressive phrase. Rome eventually held out for the late medieval doctrine of transubstantiation, and condemned the English Reformers and later the Elizabethan Anglican Church Settlement.

This use of the word *transignification* (and similar coinages such as *transvaluation* or *transfiguration*) delivers us out of the dangers that the late medieval theology introduced with the use of the term *transubstantiation*. In the earlier use of the word (i.e., before 1215), the word *substantia* carried a metaphysical rather than a material meaning. With this sense the Reformers had no quarrel;

even Luther used it in this sense. It was Thomas who had filled the word with Aristotelian philosophical sense, and it was this meaning that Trent adopted, and that caused the rift. In his conservative use of the idea of *substantia*, Luther held the bridge open to the Catholics. Zwingli, and later Calvin, finally and effectively burned the bridge.

It is a most welcome development that Catholic scholars are discussing these ideas and opening up a new vocabulary. Vatican II, with its new teaching on the liturgy containing fresh emphases within the Eucharist on 'the opening up of the treasures of the Bible' and, most important, on the Word of God in the homily, has opened the door to fresh, creative thinking on this central doctrine. A measure of the distance we have together travelled is that in the Agreed Statement of the Anglican/Roman Catholic International Commission of 1971, published in the Final Report 1982, we note that the doctrine of transubstantiation (for the rejection of which people were burned at the stake in the sixteenth century) has now been relegated to a footnote.

In addition to helping Luther to define an acceptable explanation of the nature and significance of Holy Communion, his speculation concerning the omnipresence of Christ also served to distinguish the Lutheran from the Anglican fellowship. Many Lutherans thought that in their Reformation the Anglicans had rejected Luther's emphasis; they justifiably pointed to Article XXVIII and in particular to the 'Black Rubric', which states that 'The natural body and blood of our Saviour Christ are in heaven and not here: it being against the truth of Christ's natural body to be at one time in more places than one.' Later Lutheran theologians have felt that these views were directed not only against transubstantiation, but against Luther's doctrine itself. They have also suggested, not without foundation, that the Thirty-nine Articles are patently Calvinistic interpretations, and that at the time Lutherans were not desirous of having intercommunion with the 'Calvinist' Church of England.[4]

Furthermore, a quite unexpected bonus of Luther's speculation was that when he 'delocalised' heaven, he enabled Lutheran theo-

---

4. This matter arose not only in the sixteenth century, but whenever the English royal family intermarried with Lutheran royal families, as in the case of Prince George of Denmark in the eighteenth century, and of Prince Albert in the nineteenth.

logians to accept the new Copernican theories that the earth revolved around the sun. This was unexpected in that Luther himself rather poked fun at the 'new-fangled' ideas of Copernicus, but his theology gave a measure of scientific freedom which Catholics did not enjoy. Galileo was imprisoned by the Jesuits for spreading such views in Italy even a century later. This could not have happened in Lutheran countries.

On the matter of the work of Christ, Luther was emphatically orthodox and traditional. In no sense did he have any leanings to the 'subjective' theories of atonement, exemplified by Abailard's work (and later developed by Rashdall and the modernists). Such views claimed that Christ's work was a supreme example, the strength of which was its subjective appeal to the individual —*subjective* in that it effected nothing objective, it changed nothing. According to Luther, on the other hand, the Cross is not merely an instructive revelation; he believed that something *happened* there, that a mighty battle had been fought and won by Christ, a battle sealed by God himself when he raised Christ from the dead. For him the Cross signifies a real act, a genuine change in God's attitude, a transformation of God's wrath into grace: it was the supreme battle between life and death; everything was changed there, for the entire relation of man to God was resolved once and for all in the crucifixion Christ suffered and the resurrection God effected.

Again, Luther was loath to speculate, preferring to accept the simple biblical narratives, but two main lines in his thinking emerge. The first is associated with what older theologians used to call 'satisfaction'. Luther disliked abstract nouns and preferred to deal with hard facts as experienced by ordinary human beings. He knew the purity of God's holiness and justice, and knew equally that God can have no relations with man in his sin and disobedience except to work against him by handing him over to self-chosen sin and disobedience (i.e., the wrath). There could be no escape of God's punishment. According to Luther, Christ faced the punishment man deserves, and when Christ took our sins upon himself, he faced the ban and condemnation of God in our place. Luther was convinced that upon being condemned as the lowest criminal to face the most degrading and humiliating death on a cross, and judged as the worst sinner, Christ actually experienced what it was to be condemned of God, forsaken of God to the extent that he experienced that foul death. His cry, 'My God, my God, why hast Thou forsaken me?' was the cry of a man who felt and knew that he was condemned and forsaken by God. In bearing the consequence of sin, though sinless, he experienced the full depths of every sinner who in his sins feels alienated from God, rejected by God, forsaken and condemned, sentenced to death. 'Him who knew no sin He made to be sin on our behalf' (2 Cor. 5.21). He suffered the depths of despair that sin dispenses and man suffers and deserves to suffer in order 'that we might become the righteousness of God in Him.' God had to assume humanity and face the rejection and condemnation of sinful humanity before he could unite humanity with Himself. There was no other way. Only God could do that. As Gregory of Nazianzus expressed it, 'What Christ has not assumed he has not healed, but what has been united with God is saved.'[5] Or as Luther so charmingly expressed it, 'God became man in order out of proud and unfortunate gods to make real men.' There's the truth. We think of ourselves virtually as petty gods, but Christ will convert us to true men, at peace with God and in harmony with his creation: 'God so loved us as to be willing to pay the price of His only, dearest Child. Him He sent into our misery, hell, and death, and let him drain these to the dregs.[6]

It is true that Luther stood foursquare with all the creeds and with all the orthodox trinitarian formulas. He felt that he was one with the great leaders in the ancient Church, who had all seen with crystal clarity that in order to build any theology of God it is first of all necessary that one know God himself, and He is to be known only through Jesus Christ. He had been through the same experience as they, and he could identify with the theological expressions of their faith. Their doctrinal formulae were not dead conceptualisations, but expressions of a living faith. He could take these old dogmas and make them live again in an age when they seemed to have lost all their vitality.

Yet, in a characteristic way Luther was never bound to the old technical language; sometimes he even expressed a distaste for it (as Athanasius had done). He could express these profound theologies in everyday language. Speaking of the Incarnation once, he said that

---

5. *Epistola*, 101, 7.
6. WA, 10, 3, 161.

it was like knowing a man, but not knowing how he felt about you, until one day he showed himself in deed to be a friend: God had shown his true face in Christ. All his language expressed the great biblical themes and spoke to the souls of men with the warmth and imagery of his master. He washed his hands of all the Scholastic sophistries and expressed the profound truths of the New Testament in language understood by the people and within the terms of their own experience.

Although Luther accepted gladly all the old theology about God and the person of Christ, he put a new and richer meaning into it. He said over and over again that the only thing worth considering in theology is the divine work of Christ and the experience we have of it in faith. He believed that apart from Christ man can have no real knowledge of God. Of course, he granted a certain amount of natural knowledge—namely, that God exists, that he created the world, and even that he punishes evil and rewards good— but such knowledge is no saving knowledge, no God *pro me.* In order truly to know God, it is necessary to know him through the Jesus of history. Luther discounted the unknown conceptual God of philosophical paganism, the God whom pagans and nominal Christians worship. For Luther, Christ fills the whole sphere of God: 'He that hath seen me hath seen the Father'; and conversely, he that has not seen Christ has not seen the Father. The historical Jesus is for Luther the revealer—the *only* revealer—of God: he hath revealed Him. The revelation is given in the wonderful experience of faith in which Jesus compels us to see God in him—the whole of God, who has kept nothing back that he could have given us:

> Here God pours out not sun or moon, nor heaven and earth, but His own heart and His dearest Son, and even suffers Him to shed His blood and die the most shameful of all deaths for us shameful, wicked, ungrateful people. [7]

It is questionable whether any framers of the old creeds, any of the Church Fathers, had ever entered such depths of incarnational thinking or ever spelled it out in such telling imagery and warm language. With Luther all theology is Christology. Luther knew no other God than the God who had manifested himself in the historical Jesus, and made us see in the miracle of a faith kindled and

---

7. WA, 36, 426, 34ff.

given by God that he is our salvation. This is at once a liberation as well as a simplification, and cuts itself loose, finally and for all time, from sophistry new or old. With such a faith, and such an experience, what is the significance of language that sees God as the prime mover, the first cause, the effective cause . . . ? What?

Writing on the place of the three Ecumenical Creeds (1538) Luther, in oft-quoted words, argues that a recognition of the centrality of Chirst is a safeguard against heresy:

> I have found and noted in all histories of the whole Christian Church that all those who have had and have maintained the central doctrine of Jesus Christ in its integrity have remained safe and sound in the true Christian faith. Although they erred and sinned in other respects, yet they were finally saved. For if any one stands firm and right on this point, that Jesus Christ is true God and true man, all the other articles of the Christian faith will fall in place for him and firmly sustain him. So very true is St. Paul's saying in Eph. 1.22 that Christ is the chief treasure, the basis, the foundation, and the sum total of all things, in whom and under whom all are gathered together, and that in Him all the treasures of wisdom and knowledge are hidden (Col. 2.3). . . . On the other hand, I have also noted that all errors, heresies, idolatries, offences, abuses, and ungodliness in the church have originally arisen because this article, or part of the Christian faith concerning Jesus Christ, has been despised or lost. Clearly and rightly viewed, it is plain that all heresies militate against the precious article concerning Jesus Christ. . . .
>
> Some have attacked Christ's divinity [Modernists, Mohammedans, etc.]. Others have made his humanity the object of their attack [Manichaeans, Docetists, Modalists, etc.]. The rage of such people never ceases where the love of Christ is preached in harmony with the Apostles' Creed, namely, that He, true God and true Man, died for us and rose again; that Christ is the seed of the woman who bruises the serpent's head and into whose heel the serpent in turn thrusts his venomous fang. Hence enmity continues until the final judgment.[8]

Or again, in his commentary on Galatians (1531), Luther writes (as Middleton has translated him),

> Here ye see how necessary a thing it is to believe and to confess the article of the divinity of Christ, which, when Arius denied,

---

8. WA, 50, 266f.

he must needs also deny the article of our redemption. For to overcome the sin of the world, death, the curse, and the wrath of God in himself, is not the work of any creature, but of the divine power. Therefore he which in himself should overcome these, must needs by truly and naturally God. For against this mighty power of sin, death and the curse, (which of itself reigneth throughout the world, and in the whole creature), it was necessary to set a more high and mighty power. But besides the sovereign and divine power, no such power can be found. Wherefore, to abolish sin, to destroy death, to take away the curse in himself: and again, to give righteousness, to bring life to light, and to give the blessing, are the works of the divine power only and alone. Now, because the scripture doth attribute all these to Christ, therefore he in himself is life, righteousness, and blessing, which is naturally and substantially God. Wherefore, they that deny the divinity of Christ, do lose all Christianity.[9]

Luther never ceased to emphasise the divinity of Christ. Of numberless instances, here is a short one from a sermon on Colossians 1.15 preached in 1537:

Christ is the kind of 'Image of God' which has the Godhead or the divine essence in itself. Other images or facsimiles do not in themselves have the essence of the person or the object of which they are an image. . . . Christ is the Image of the Father in such a way that He is the Image of the divine Essence and did not originate out of another essence or nature . . . but is a divine Image, fashioned from eternity of the divine Essence and nature . . . and has the same divine Essence the Father has.[10]

In more striking language on Christ as 'the image of God', he said 'A crucifix is a wooden [hölzern] image of God, but Christ is a 'Godden' [Göttern] image of God.'[11] He repeats over and over again that if you want to believe in God, you must believe in Christ. If we cannot say that it was God who died for us, but think it was but a good man who suffered death on the cross, then we are lost. Like Athanasius, Luther found his salvation in the deity of Christ.

Certainly previous theologians had spoken of the two natures

---

9. Luther, quoted in A Compend of Luther's Theology, ed. Hugh Thomson Kerr, Jr. (Philadelphia: Westminster Press, 1966).

10. WA, 45, 277ff.

11. WA, 50, 227, 21.

of Christ, yet Luther went far beyond this language; he even found it dangerous. He discouraged the idea that there were two natures and that we could look at them separately. In fact he did not start with the theological premise of the person of Christ as a doctrine we can examine by the intellect. He began with justification by faith, recognising that he was saved not by his good works but by the work of Christ: God was working out his salvation. He approached the person of Christ through his mediatorial work. He builds from the fact of his experience of Christ's work to his person; he does not start with the theological premise of the nature of the person and descend to his office.

On this very point Oliver Quick wrote a very penetrating passage on Luther's Christology:

> With Luther Christology makes a fresh start, and most modern theories on the subject may trace their origin to him. The main value of Luther's doctrine lies in his refusal to allow preconceived doctrines of the nature of deity, whencesoever derived, either to modify the witness borne by the New Testament to the Saviour's manhood or to suggest (as did Calvinists) that the divine nature of Christ remained external to the incarnation. Very modern his langue sometimes sounds.

> The Scriptures begin very gently and lead us on to Christ as to a man, and then to one who is Lord over all creatures, and after that to one who is God. So do I enter delightfully, and learn to know God. But the philosophers and doctors have insisted on beginning from above; and so they have become fools. We must begin from below and after that come upwards.

Brunner remarks that no one after Irenaeus had taken the *vere homo* so seriously as Luther.

> Luther spoke quite openly about our Lord's childhood, about his gradual growth and development, even in the spiritual sphere, pointing out that, so far as his humanity was concerned, 'Like any other holy man he did not always think, speak, will everything, like an almighty being, which some would fain make him out to be, thus mingling unwisely the two natures and their work; for indeed he did not always see all clearly, but was led and aided by God.'

Again Luther writes: 'He endured good and evil things like anyone else, so that there was no difference between him and anyone else, save only in this, that he was God and had no sin.' At the same time Luther returns uncompromisingly to the scriptural and primitive emphasis on the reality of God's victorious act through Jesus, which involves the truth that Jesus himself is God.

> For to conquer the sin of the world, death, the curse and the wrath of God in his own person *(in semet ipso)* is not the work of a creature but of the Almighty. Out of this there necessarily results that he who personally *(in semet ipso)* conquered is truly and by nature God. . . . Because the Scripture ascribes all this to Christ, therefore is he himself life, righteousness, and blessing, which is the nature and substance of God. . . . Therefore when we teach the people that they are justified through Christ, that Christ is the conqueror of sin, death and the eternal curse, we bear witness at the same time that in his nature he is God.

In other words, God's nature consists not only in what he unchangeably is but also in what he triumphantly does. Luther will allow no separation between God's nature and his work, or between divine nature and divine person. He who does God's work in person *(in semet ipso)* is thereby shown to be both by nature and personally God.[12]

Here again, in this central theme of Luther, namely his doctrine of Christ, Catholic and Protestant theologians can find together a theology deeper than we have ever known, a Gospel more apposite than we have ever given. In his penetrating and moving teaching on the doctrine of Christ, Luther shows to the whole of Christendom Christ in all his truth, all his glory, all his splendour. Luther echoes the voice from heaven—he is the voice from heaven: 'This is my beloved Son, hear Him.'

---

12. Quick, *The Doctrines of the Creed* (London, 1938), pp. 127-28.

CHAPTER TEN

THE DOCTRINE OF THE CHURCH

THE SUGGESTION THAT Luther's theology of the Church could be the source of a fuller and truer catholicity seems on the face of it to be absurd. One might protest that since Luther, after due process of examination and hearing, was banned, excommunicated, and declared a notorious heretic by the official procedures of the Catholic Church to which he belonged, the matter is closed and ought to be considered closed for all time. It may with propriety be asked whether such a suggestion does not imply that the Roman Catholic Church ought to rescind her official and conciliar promulgations — decisions confirmed and endorsed for nearly five centuries. It may be added, the point at issue is not some disputable matter such as indulgences or celibacy, which could conceivably be open to revision or reconsideration or debate at any time; rather, it is a central issue of the Faith, even *the* central issue. The Roman Catholic Church may not reverse decisions of this kind, for they are final and irrevocable. Further, during the centuries of division, the positions of the two communions have become fixed and hardened, and marked differences of practice, tradition, and even of belief and morals are apparent. Catholicism and Protestantism have now each developed their own ethos. How can Catholic ecclesiology accommodate Luther? What new factors could have arisen to justify the reopening of the Luther affair? Is there really any reason for Luther's doctrine of the Church to be reconsidered?

One reason is that the Dogmatic Constitution of the Church promulgated by Vatican II strikes a wholly new note: it is pastoral and strongly ecumenical, Christocentric, biblical, historical, and eschatological. It is wholly different from anything that has been written by the Roman Catholic Church from the Council of Trent in 1545 right up to our own times in the *Mystici Corporis* of Pius

XII in 1943—that is, until Pope John called the Roman Catholic Church to *aggiornamento*, mainly to consider the nature and role of the contemporary Church. Before we discuss this document, *Lumen Gentium*, however, we should look at Luther's doctrine, since all the fresh creative points promulgated by the Council Fathers are already outlined in Luther's appeal to the Church of his day. That the Roman Church disregarded Luther, condemning him and his theology in the sixteenth century, impoverished both its theology and witness. The fresh biblical streams of Luther must be allowed to flow through these channels not cleared, and a new catholicity be allowed to develop. It is happening already; we must facilitate that movement and open ourselves up to the divine activity.

LUTHERS TEACHING ON THE CHURCH

Luther's teaching on the Church is dispersed throughout his writings, but we might single out the tract 'The Papacy at Rome' (1520) and the important book *On Councils and Churches* (1539) for special attention—the first because it came early in the struggle and was written for the laity, and the second because it is representative of the mature Luther writing to the situation created by the calling of a general council.

As early as 1519 Luther had declared that the spiritual preeminence claimed by Rome had been founded on false and forged decretals of the previous four hundred years, and that against this there stood the testimony of the authentic history of the eleven hundred years following the Crucifixion, the text of Holy Scripture, and the decree of the Nicene Council. For this Luther was heavily attacked; after the Disputation of Leipzig (1519), Augustine von Alveld of Leipzig wrote a Latin work claiming to justify the divine right of the Apostolic Chair, a work of shaky scholarship that was abusive of Luther. This Luther ignored, but when Alveld came out with a new work in German on the same theme, Luther was not going to let him 'poison the defenceless laity', and so in great haste he put together the booklet 'The Papacy at Rome' (some sixty pages long).

On one level, the booklet is simply a refutation of the arguments in Alveld's book, but Luther has all of Catholicism in mind as he writes, and in fact the work becomes something of an explanation *to the laity* at this critical juncture of 1520 of the real position:

'I welcome the opportunity to explain something of the nature of Christianity to the laity he writes. '. . . I must first of all explain what these things mean, the Church, and the Head of the Church.' Neither in civil government nor in the Church is there need of a single monarchical head, Luther argues. The Roman government managed without a single head, as does the Swiss confederacy.

Against the modern demand that the Church must socialise itself, that it must organise as the public centre in a community of the people's civic life, that it should provide moral uplift to the nation's political activities, and that ministers become 'preachers of dreams in material communities', Luther says,

> On this point we must hear the word of Christ, Who, when Pilate asked Him concerning His Kingdom, answered, My Kingdom is not of this world. This is indeed a clear passage in which the Church is made separate from all temporal communities. Is not this a cruel error, when the one Christian Church, separated by Christ Himself from temporal cities and places, and transferred to spiritual realms, is made a part of material communities?

Against the view that Christianity should be a single worldwide visible ecclesiastical order, Luther declares that the Church is already a spiritual community composed of all the believers in Christ upon earth, that it is not a *bodily* assembly at all, but a truly *spiritual* thing, 'an assembly of the hearts in one faith'; that 'external unity is not the fulfilment of a divine commandment', and that those who emphasise the externalisation of the Church into one visible or national order 'are in reality Jews':

> All those who make the Christian communion a material and outward thing, like other communities, are in reality Jews, who wait for their Messiah to establish an external kingdom at a certain definite place, namely, Jerusalem; and so sacrifice the faith, which alone makes the kingdom of Christ a thing spiritual, or of the heart.

There are many Christians outside the unity of the Roman Church who are nonetheless within the true Church. We cannot call those people heretics and apostates merely because their priests and bishops are not confirmed by Rome:

> Such are the Muscovites, Russians, Greeks, Bohemians and many other great peoples in the world. For all these believe

> as we do, baptise as we do, preach as we do, live as we do,
> and also give due honour to the Pope, only they will not pay
> for the confirmation of their bishops and priests . . . they will
> not submit to extortion and abuse with indulgences etc. Fur-
> ther, they are ready to hear the Gospel from the Pope.

Nevertheless, though Luther attacks the supremacy of outward organisation in the Church, he also disputes the supremacy of man's own thinking and reasoning over the theology of the Church. By 'reason' he means the ability to defend, or even to establish, divine order by means of the intellect. Unless that same faculty of reason has previously been established and enlightened by faith to attempt to employ it would be as foolish as to attempt to throw light on the sun by means of a lightless lantern. Scripture provides the only rule of faith, and he ridicules those who play with Scripture to make it say what they want it to say.

Set against the external unity of human ecclesiastical organi-sation and against the internal rule of purely human thinking, Lu-ther is equally against any human visualisation or dramatisation of divine worship. Spiritual edification must never be turned into out-ward show. The word Church may not be applied to an assembly in which 'the external rites are in use' — rites such as chanting, read-ing, vestments, and, where the title 'the spiritual estate' is given to men in holy orders, not on account of their faith (which perhaps they do not have), but because they have been ordained, wear dis-tinctive dress, lead prayers and sit in the choir:

> The word 'Church', when it is used for such external affairs,
> whereas it concerns the faith alone, is done violence to; yet
> this manner of using it has spread everywhere, to the great
> injury of many souls, who think that such outward show is the
> spiritual and only true estate in Christendom. Of such a purely
> external Church, there is not one letter in the Holy Scriptures.

There begins to emerge in this booklet the sharp opposition to the popedom of Rome, though such thinking had already expressed itself in Augsburg in 1518, and in Leipzig in 1519. At Leipzig Eck had laid emphasis on the passages 'feed my sheep' and 'Thou art Peter, and upon this rock I will build my Church' (Matt. 16.18). With regard to feeding the sheep, Luther deplores the lack of pastoral care shown by Rome, which shows no love for its flock, but simply fleeces it. Regarding the second text, he shows that in the same

Gospel the power of the keys was given to all the disciples: this power belongs to the Church and not to Peter's person alone:

> These words of Christ are nothing but gracious promises, given to the whole Church (*Gemeinde*) in order that poor sinful consciences may find comfort when they are 'loosed' or absolved by man. . . . They are not given to strengthen and establish papal power. . . . The Rock does not signify authority. . . . It signifies only Christ and the faith in Him, against which no power can prevail. . . . Even some of the popes themselves have forsaken the faith wantonly and without struggle, and live under the power of Satan. . . . Some of the popes were heretics themselves and gave heretical laws. These Roman knaves come along, place the Pope above Christ and make him a judge over the Scriptures. They say that he cannot err.

In this booklet Luther insists that none are to be regarded as heretics simply because they are not under the pope, and that the pope's decrees, to stand, must endure the test of Scripture. He made good on a promise to Frederick's secretary that he would appeal to the Emperor and to the German nobility if the Pope did not reform: he called for a general council and suggested a programme of action. In 1524 the project was taken up by the German Diet, then meeting at Nürnberg. It demanded that the Pope call 'a general, free, and universal council of Christendom to be held as soon as possible and on German soil.' The purpose of the proposed council was to settle the matters raised by Luther, and at the same time, to remove the abuses outlined in the 'Complaints of the German People', presented at Worms and reiterated at Nürnberg. The plea was never actually dropped, but it was mentioned at every diet after that, and each time consideration of it was postponed. The Emperor supported it, and saw it as the best way of restoring peace within the Church and remedying the evils within it. The call was issued in 1536 to meet in Mantua 1537, and for this meeting Paul III commissioned his cardinals to report on the state of the Church, and to propose measures for reform.[1]

It was this action by the Pope that compelled Luther and his

---

1. See the *Consilium delectorum Cardinalium . . . de emendanda ecclesia* (1538) in Kidd's *Documents Illustrative of the Continental Reformation* (Oxford: Clarendon Press, 1911), pp. 307-18.

supporters to define their position towards the council. Early in 1535 the Pope had sent Paul Vergerius, papal nuncio in Germany, to sound out the Protestants and seek their cooperation. The Schmalkald League laid down four conditions for their participation in the council: (1) it would have to be a free council, not a papal council; (2) the Protestants would have to be invited to it as full participants, not as heretics; (3) the decisions would have to be based on the authority of Scripture, not of the pope; and (4) it would have to be held in Germany if at all possible. These conditions were wholly unacceptable to Rome.

Meanwhile, the plans for the council had run into other difficulties, chiefly caused by the worsening relationship between Charles V and Francis I. It was postponed, not once, but twice, eventually being scheduled to meet in Vicenza in 1538. By that time the Emperor and the King of France were at war, however, and the meeting was impossible. Finally, in May 1539, the council was indefinitely postponed.

It was at this moment of indecision and uncertainty that Luther wrote his book *On the Councils and on the Churches* (1539). All the early hopes that he had envisioned in 1520 of the reformation of the Church had faded in these twenty years. Discouraged, but not disillusioned, he still hoped for the reformation of the Church, and still wrote in a vigorous and robust style. In the area of ecclesiology this work was probably Luther's most important.

The work falls into three parts. The first part presents the following argument: the Church cannot be reformed according to the councils and the fathers. There is no hope in the Pope, and the world must despair of any possibility of reformation from that quarter. Deserted by the Pope, who will neither seek reformation nor hear advice on the matter, church folk have no other course than to seek reformation from Christ in prayer: we must not despair of Christ, says Luther, nor leave the Church. Why should we not hold our own council, if necessary—without pope, without ecclesiastics, without lay lords—and then see what comes of it? He demonstrates from history that the true foundation of the Church is not the ancient councils and the Fathers, but the Scriptures; that the first four general councils only declared the faith as taught in the Scriptures; that in matters of faith their powers were strictly limited by this fundamental principle; and that only a council representing the true Church (rather than the false papal Church) can bring about a real reformation. By this Luther does not mean that Protestants are the true Church and the Catholics the false; when he speaks of the 'true Church' he means that 'hidden' group of faithful believers who are in both the Catholic and Protestant Churches. It was the papist and Romanist claim he was criticising, the claim of the body that had presumed itself infallible and placed it above Christ, the body that was steeped in unbelief and soaked in immorality, and that sought to un-Church the Protestant faithful.

In the second part of the book, Luther examines the proceedings of the first four General Councils in order to substantiate his contention that in matters of faith they took the Scriptures as their sole standard. In all the controversies and heresies concerning Christ's person, they formulated no new articles of faith, but simply vindicated the teaching of Scripture. Many subsequent papal councils have departed from the fundamental principle on which the first four based their contentions. The reason for this lies in the pope's claim to have an authority superior to the Scriptures, and to put himself in the place of Christ. Eastern bishops never conceded this; the Patriarch of Constantinople emerges as no more than a peer and equal. If the Pope will not call a *true* council, Luther argued, but persists in calling a few of his own bishops and clerics who, after wasting years in fruitless argument, will eventually finish up only by burning a couple of heretics; if the Pope persists in this policy and will not call together a council of faithful men from all over the world, laymen included, then let the Emperor give a lead by calling a German council: the other nations will follow.

The third part of the book is the most important for our enquiry, for in it Luther develops afresh his conception of the Church. He answers the question, What is the Church? and what are the marks by which we might recognise it? As in the Apostles' Creed, he defines the holy Christian Church as the fellowship of saints, 'the mass or assembly of such persons as are Christian and holy': they are those who believe in Christ, and are sanctified by the Holy Ghost; in short, they are God's people. If these words had been used in the creed — 'I believe that there is a holy Christian people' — we would have avoided all the misery that has come from the use of the word *Church* instead of *God's People*. In and through these people Christ lives, works, and rules through his redeeming grace, and the Holy Spirit operates through his sanctifying, renewing power. This is what constitutes the holy catholic Church — a very different thing from the holy Roman Church. According to Luther, the marks of this Church are the effective preaching of the Word of God, the ministration of the sacraments of baptism and communion in accordance with the Word, the exercise of pastoral care and discipline in the congregation by the power of the keys, a regular ministry, public worship and prayer, and the marks of the Cross.[2] Luther further stressed the operation of the Holy Spirit in the heart bringing constant sanctification and vivification in Christ, of growing in Christ, and of abounding more and more in grace (2 Pet. 3.18; 1. Thess. 4.1).

Besides this Church, the holy Church built by God, Luther quaintly says the Devil builds his own chapel, the counterfeit or false Church, the marks of which are holy water, salt, herbs, candles, bells, images, pallia, altars, tonsures, and all the like external tomfooleries with which he seduces and deceives his votaries. Some of these Luther granted, may be used for popular folk piety, any value they might assume in such contexts is purely accidental; in no circumstances do they serve to sanctify the soul. One can preach in the street as well as in a pulpit and dispense the sacraments without an altar, even if pulpits and altars are normally expedient and harmless. On the other hand, the tyranny of the multitude of regulations by which the popes and the canonists enslaved the Church and displaced Scripture should indeed be banished from the Church and relegated to the shelves of libraries for relics of the old papal domination. He makes a strong plea for the maintenance of schools to train pastors and preachers and public servants. Schools are more important than councils. Next in importance the Christian household and the civic authority: Church, school, family, state. This is God's order, which is meant to preserve us all against any encroachments of the devil and all his works. The pretended law or government of the pope leads us away from the blessed and divine estates instituted by God. 'He will endure it no longer, but act according to the teaching of SS. Peter and Paul and Augustine,' he concludes.

---

2. In saying that 'the marks of the Cross' serve to identify the true Church, Luther meant to suggest that the Church, like its founder and master, must seek to serve the sinful world, and that this will inevitably bring persecution and hatred down upon it; no Church that enjoys the prerogatives of a lordly and dominating class can suppose itself to bear the marks of the Cross.

VATICAN II ON THE CHURCH

Expressed in these terms, Luther's doctrine of the Church seems very reasonable; it is certainly historical, biblical and pastoral. Yet, as one of the most respected of Catholic scholars, Christopher Butler, argues,

> The official response was the counter-Reformation Council of Trent, in which the Church acknowledged and met the need of some moral and organisational reform, but was less successful in accomplishing a theological renewal in any deep sense. The Council of Trent dominated the ensuing centuries of Catholic history and the Church assumed a fixed attitude of counter-protest. The idea of the Church tended to be restricted to her institutional and authoritarian aspects, seen by some of her ablest and most devoted sons as primarily a bulwark against change. Not only the sacred tradition of the gospel but the forms in which it was currently presented were endowed with an aura of absoluteness, and changes were presumed to be anti-Catholic, anti-Christian, even impious.[3]

Modern interest in ecclesiology is largely a result of the Reformation and of the attack of Luther on the Church as it really was in the sixteenth century. In consequence, Catholic theological writings on the Church has tended to be controversial or polemical, and has concentrated on the visible, authoritarian, juridical, and legal aspects of the subject, these being the aspects most often criticised by Protestants. A lot of time was spent (in fact, wasted) by Catholic theologians refuting the concept, often emphasised by extreme Protestants, of 'the invisible Church': they should have remembered that Luther's phrase was 'the hidden Church', that faithful few on both sides of the divide known only to God. The emphasis of Vatican II on the 'mystery' of the Church was an enormous liberation and would have gladdened Luther's heart; we are now speaking the same language.

The last major official pronouncement on ecclesiology before Vatican II was the encyclical of Pius XII, *Mystici Corporis* (1943),[4] in which the idea of the Body of Christ is treated not merely as an image but as a concept; it is applied without qualification to the

---

3. Butler, *The Theology of Vatican II* (London, 1967) pp. 11-12.
4. A shortened version can be found in Anne Freemantle's *The Papal Encyclicals* (New York, 1956, 1963), pp. 270ff.

Church on earth, although it is recognised that it includes the saints in heaven. More important still, the Church as the Body of Christ is simply and materially identified with the Roman Catholic communion:

> If we would define and describe this true Church of Jesus Christ—which is the One, Holy, Catholic, Apostolic, Roman Church—we shall find nothing more noble, more sublime, or more divine than the expression 'the mystical body of Jesus Christ . . .'[5]

From this material identification of the Church as Christ's Body with the institutional Church visibly united under the Vicar of Christ, the encyclical infers that 'only those are to be accounted really members of the Church' who have been baptized, profess the true faith, and 'have not cut themselves off from the structure of the body by their unhappy act or been severed therefrom, for very grave crimes, by the legitimate authority.' The suggestion here again is that the structures of the Roman Church are univocally the structures of the mystical body. 'It follows that those who are divided from one another in faith or government cannot be living in the one body so described and by its one divine spirit.' The encyclical allows sinners who have not apostasised to remain members of the Church. What this amounts to is that a simple dichotomy is established between those who belong to the Roman Catholic communion and every one else, be he Christian or non-Christian, religious or irreligious. This view is still widely prevalent, particularly among Roman Catholic laity.

All this was changed by Vatican II, and it is from this breath of the Holy Spirit we can all take fresh inspiration and make a new start. None can deny that on studying these documents we are being introduced to a new way of thinking that changes everything. It would be out of place here to attempt to summarise the Dogmatic Constitution of the Church; it is much too significant a document, too tightly packed with pregnant words. Nevertheless, a few general remarks may be offered, and a few conclusions suggested.

First, it is significant to recall that few documents have ever gone through more drastic revision than this one, between the first scheme and the finally approved text. In his first encyclical, *Eccle-*

---

5. Ibid., p. 271.

siam Suam (1964), Paul VI had stated (Art. 33) that the Church was 'the principal object of attention of the Second Vatican Ecumenical Council'. It might not be too much to say that in one way or another the entire work of the Council is centred about the theme of the Church. Certainly, mighty and significant changes were made in the text, indicating a striking development in the understanding of the Church experienced by the Council fathers, which resulted from dialogue (or is it too much to claim, from the work of the Holy Spirit?).

The original scheme, prepared by the Theological Commission before the first session in 1962, was the stale old stuff of yesteryear, anti-Protestant, with heavy emphasis on the hierarchical and juridical aspects of the Church, including the supremacy of the pope. When the Council Fathers, met, in the fellowship of the Holy Spirit, however, they were immediately moved to set forth a radically different vision of the Church, a vision more biblical, more historical, more vital and dynamic. An entirely new document was drafted. This scheme was itself subjected to thorough revision in the light of debate at the second session (1963). The debate was closed at the third session, and the document approved and promulgated (1964).

No new dogma is defined. It simply sets forth, with all the weight of conciliar authority, the Church's understanding of its own nature. As Pope John requested, the document is essentially pastoral: there are no anathemas, no condemnations. Here is the Church (in Pople John's words) 'the loving mother of all', spreading everywhere the fulness of Christian charity. There are no rigid definitions, no scholastic or juridical subtleties; there is instead strong and vivid biblical language. Here is the Church seen as continuing the ministry of the good shepherd, who came to serve and not to be served, and who gave his life for the sheep. Here is the serving and loving and suffering Church, the handmaid rather than the mistress. Nevertheless, the Church is shown as 'the little flock' of frail and sinful men. Humble and weak, it stands there in constant need of purification and renewal. At the same time, it stands there confident of God's loving help and continual guidance.

Throughout, the Constitution approached the mystery of the Church in incarnational terms—that is to say, in terms of the paradoxical union between the human and the divine. Because the Church is human, it exists in time and is subject to all the forces and tensions of history. Yet, because of its divine element, it sees its ultimate goal beyond history: it never forgets the glorious vision of the final kingdom.

One senses that the orientations of the Constitution on the Church are pastoral, Christocentric, biblical, historical, and eschatological, and that its tone is strongly ecumenical and evangelical. It speaks in a language that will be readily understood by other Christians, even by non-Christians, and explains the Catholic viewpoint without giving offence to non-Catholics.

Instead of beginning on the old pattern of treating the structures and government of the Church, the encyclical introduces us to the idea of the Church as a people to whom God communicates himself in love; it prepares us at once to understand the Church to be the people of God, and in this context it places a new emphasis on the role of the laity. The responsibility and role of clergy is considered, yet always in the role of service and of ministry, not domination. It is in this context that the Council broke through to its doctrine of 'collegiality'. In this connection the Council divides its considerations under the three headings normally associated with Christ, namely, the offices of prophet, priest, and king: authority is seen as being exercised in the ministry of preaching, of making holy, and of governing the people of God. The Church as a whole, including the laity, is conceived of as having a total task that might suitably be summarised under the three New Testament words *witness, ministry,* and *fellowship.* Only in the treatment of Mary is the Constitution open to serious Protestant criticism: here the Immaculate Conception and the Assumption are taught (59), as well as the invocation of Mary as Mediatrix (62); 'the faithful flee prayerfully to her for protection' (66), and the cult of the Virgin is to be 'generously fostered' (67); prayers are to be offered to her to intercede with Christ in heaven (69). All this is extrabiblical and open to serious theological objection.

Nevertheless, as Father Dejaifve expressed it, 'The greatest merit of the Constitution is that, far from canonising the past, or even consecrating the present, it prepares for the future.'[6] And perhaps the first thing to be said about this document in relation to the theme of this book is that almost all the fresh discoveries are those that Luther begged the Church of his day to reconsider and to reform.

---

6. 'La "Magna Carta" de Vatican II', *Nouvelle Revue Theologique*, 87 (Jan. 1965):21.

This fact sets Luther in this true ecumenical significance as a reformer addressing the Church catholic, 'the whole state of Christ's church', to use an Anglican phrase. Luther must be brought out of the confessional Protestant position into which history has forced him and his movement, and into the catholicity of the whole Church.

Secondly, it should be remembered that, strange as it may seem, this document is the first conciliar exposition of the doctrine of the Church in Christian history. Here was an unprecedented venture in self-examination and self-understanding. The Council Fathers knew that any significant renovation of the Church's witness and ministry to the world would have to begin with a valid doctrinal statement concerning her basic nature. It was this emphasis on the Church and its renewal for mission in the world that gave Vatican II its most distinctive character as a council.

Thirdly, the powerful pastoral tone, expressed in generous and sensitive ecumenical terms, is highly signfiicant and helpful. Gone are the hostile polemical and autocratic tone of Trent and Vatican I. Here the Church invites ecumenical dialogue in love and respect. Here the Church is capable of self-criticism, expressing a deep responsibility in terms of the *whole* Church to the *whole* world of the mission entrusted to it by God: in this context it enters a *dialogue* with the world rather than a *monologue*, and shows itself capable of historical development and fresh thinking. Above all, there is the characteristic Catholic call to holiness, and with that, to Christian witness and service.

Fourthly, the thinking is neither partisan nor immobilist. It recalls the days of Regensburg (1541), when the scholarly and irenical Melanchthon and his supporters were working with men of the stature of Gropper, von Pflug, and Contarini to formulate peace in the Church. In actual fact, Vatican II represents a vast advance on Contarini and the best of the sixteenth century Catholic peacemakers. It cannot be denied that the Constitution on the Church has reopened the way to a serious and fruitful discussion of Christian unity, the first since Luther. This must be seen, appreciated, and acted upon.

When the Constitution scrapped its first scheme and began with the Church as a mystery, it at once elevated the discussion from the levels of organisation, structure, and management to that of the awareness of the Church as of divine origin, of the need to maintain its relationship with God, and of its ultimate eschatological destiny with God. This was the most crucial of all steps. We are all too too aware of the human face of the Church, of its materialism, its worldliness, its instinct for self-preservation; we need to be reminded that its true dynamic is in other hands. The gates of Hell have not prevailed against us because of God: it is only he who has preserved the Church throughout history, and it is to him any effective witness in the world is due. If we preserve this language of 'mystery', it keeps open our awareness of God's constant sovereignty and of the fact that we Christians belong to his Church, rather than his Church belonging to us. It also preserves the powerful New Testament idea that the whole Church is mysteriously present in each local congregation where 'two or three are gathered in Christ's name', but that no congregation, nor any single communion for that matter, exhausts the fulness of the Church catholic.

Immediately, in its second chapter, the Constitution introduces the fine biblical theme of the 'People of God'. Here we find two main ecumenical implications. The first is that the 'people of God' includes the entire Christian community, and this on the basis of baptism (one recalls Luther's emphasis here, *Baptisatus sum*). In using this phrase rather than 'the Mystical Body', a great liberation was effected, for it allows us to understand that unity need not be destroyed even if the separated brethren 'do not profess the faith in its entirety or do not preserve unity of communion with the successor of Peter': separated brethren may remain separated *Christian* brethren. The second implication is that the people of God have not been immune to faults and failings, and therefore are open to self-criticism and self-correction.

The development of the idea of 'collegiality' in the hierarchy is also significant. It restores the older patristic notion of the sharing of the entire episcopacy in the leadership of the Church seen as a worldwide community. It further offers relief from the sterile and unacceptable Ultramontanism, and from the rather restrictive and older conciliarism. This decreases the authoritarian claims of Rome and at the same time increases the authoritative nature of its leadership.

The notion of the laity as the presence of the Church in the world restores yet another biblical emphasis that Luther had early stressed—the priesthood of all believers. It provides the doctrinal foundation of the basis for the ministry or apostolate of the laity in and for the world.

A further welcome note is the universal call to holiness, a dimension largely lost in Protestantism and certainly more faithfully preserved within Catholicism. This meant a great deal to Luther, and ought to mean more to Christianity, for in the world at large, Christian men and women hardly seem to think or behave in ways different from those of their national, social and cultural associates. The notion of 'higher' and the 'lower' levels of Christian faithfulness was certainly refuted by Luther; he wanted as high a quality of holiness in the layman as on 'the spiritual estate'. His whole idea of the role of the religious is near to that of Vatican II. He gave a special emphasis to the living and organic relationship between the Church militant and the Church triumphant in his teaching of the communion of saints.

Quite certainly the Council Fathers intended this Constitution to be a working basis for the renovation and reform of the Catholic Church, and perhaps as a basis for ecumenical dialogue. Vatican II has been taken very seriously, not only by Catholics but by all Christians, and it is important that it be not implemented piecemeal by enthusiasts for the aspects they most favour, but as a whole and by the whole state of Christ's Church. No single factor could serve to facilitate the complete implementation of its principles more strikingly and effectively than a fresh appraisal of Luther as the pioneer to a fuller and truer Catholicity. Therein is Luther's significance for Christendom. This is what Vatican II is telling all of us. 'He that hath an ear, let him hear what the Spirit saith unto the churches.' (Rev. 2.7.)

Yet, it is precisely at this point that Catholics turn sharply from Luther. How can there be any discussion with a Luther who calls the Church of Rome 'a false Church', 'a counterfeit Church', 'the Devil's chapel'? For a Roman Catholic the Church is an ultimate, infallible authority, to which is given the very keys of heaven. By what authority does Luther make such assertions, assertions that strike the Catholic as abuse, pure and simple? Before we turn finally to the new thinking emanating from Vatican II we must look at such objections, for if there is to be any really creative debate with Rome, such questions must be answered.

At the beginning of his protest and before any hard battle lines were drawn, Luther simply claimed the right to speak as a called Doctor of Theology duly instituted in a chair of Theology at Wittenberg. His authority was Scripture, patristic tradition, and sound reason. He owed it to his Church and his university to teach these authorities. In no sense was this the taking of a 'Lutheran' line. Luther was always a man under the authority of God's Word. Step by step he disclosed all the evidence for his thinking, always inviting the academics to debate, always putting the laity on their own theological feet. The response of Rome was simply to refuse to listen to him or enter into any kind of debate with him; instead, it chose to condemn him unheard and to silence him. Luther, stupified by such response, realised that there was to be no way forward by open and free examination of the evidence.

In the aftermath of the rejection he received from the Church, a new factor began to take shape in Luther's thinking, a factor discernible from the beginning in his biblical commentaries that emerges more explicitly only relatively late in his life, owing to the opposition he incurred from both the Catholics and the radical Protestants: it was the idea of the true Church, alongside which existed the false Church, which hated and persecuted the true and faithful Church. He often referred to this as the church of Abel and the church of Cain. Luther's criticism of the Roman Church, therefore, should first be set in these prophetic categories: he was a prophet who loved his Church, speaking a Word from God, sometimes harsh, most times warm and loving.

It was after he was not only excommunicated, but declared an outlaw, and after many years of opposition, attack, and abuse, that he began to express in his commentary on Galatians (1531) and his commentary on Genesis (1535 to his death) that there was a parallel between Paul's experiences and his own. He expressed the conflict between the true and false Church as the recurring contest between true and false prophets, between true and false apostles. This was no figurative or poetic truth; Luther anchored these truths in historical events. He once said that the Devil never sleeps and human nature never changes, and so the struggles he was engaged in were no different from those with which Adam was assailed.

Luther believed that from the Fall onward an enmity had existed between the seed of the woman and the seed of the serpent. The seed of the woman was Christ, that is, the true Church; the seed of the serpent was the false church. The struggle between them proceeds apace in every age. It began when Satan persuaded Adam and Eve to forsake their pure faith in God, and it continued into

Luther's day. Abel was the founder of the true Church, Cain of the false church, and the sons of Cain had continued their persecution until God had destroyed them, saving only Noah, 'the herald of faith and of righteousness'. Throughout history Satan had killed the prophets sent by God and finally Christ himself. In Luther's day, just as Abel had done no harm to Cain, Luther's followers did no harm to the Catholics who harassed them; instead they accepted the persecution as belonging to what Luther had characterised as the marks of the true Church. Christ had argued for a similar restraint in the face of the Scribes and Pharisees, whom he described as the sons of those who had slain the prophets and were to slay him, even though they garnished the tombs of the prophets (Matt. 23. 29-31).

Luther had a unique propensity for identifying his own personality with that of the biblical figures he was describing. A man once said that while hearing a sermon that Luther had preached on Elijah, he was so moved that he actually believed it was Elijah himself speaking from the pulpit. It is interesting to note that Luther identified himself more closely with Noah than with any other person, the reason being that he saw in Noah a strength of conviction that enabled him to stand against an unbelieving secularised world and through faith endure all its scorn as well as his own haunting doubts. Was he alone right, and all the world wrong? Was he alone the man of faith? Were all his fathers and predecessors wrong? The stand of a lone man confronting the world with nothing to rely on save his faith in the Word of God fired his imagination and gripped his mind. He once ruminated that it was just one hundred and twenty six years that elapsed between the death of Adam and the birth of Noah, exactly the number of years that separated Hus from himself.

Towards the end of his life, as he clearly realised that the Church was going to reject wholly and utterly his biblical evangelical theology, and as his health failed, he had gloomy forebodings of the eschatological end. He often reflected that Christ himself had predicted that the end would be like the last days of Noah before the flood. He moved from the emphasis on the faith of Noah to the times of Noah, suggesting that God had in these last days restored again the Gospel before the end. He believed that the insignificant remnant that had laid hold of the Gospel, the true and hidden Church, was in its last and most terrible struggle with a world of unbelief. In the eyes of the world they were the most insignificant of groups, but in the eyes of the great assembly of heaven, they were the significant remnant, God's own people. This is the language of a prophet. Here is no heretic: here is the man of faith.

In his commentary on Galatians, Luther gives poignant expression to the view that not only did his call parallel that of Paul, but that his experiences paralleled those of the prophets and apostles of the Old and New Testaments:

> In like manner say I of myself, that before I was lightened with the knowledge of the Gospel, I was as zealous for the papistical laws and traditions of the fathers, as ever any was, most earnestly maintaining them and defending them as holy and necessary to salvation. . . . I punished my poor body with fasting, watching, praying, and other exercises. . . . I honoured the Pope of mere conscience, and unfeignedly, not seeking after prebends, promotions and livings: but whatsoever I did, I did it with a single heart, of a good zeal, and for the glory of God. But those things which were then gainful to me, now with Paul I count to be but loss for the excellency of the knowledge of Jesus Christ my Lord. . . . I sought for peace and quietness of conscience which in so great darkness it was not possible to find.[7]

He interprets Paul and relates his confession to his own:

> I persecuted the Church of God, I was an enemy to Christ, I blasphemed His Gospel, and to conclude, I was the author of shedding much innocent blood. . . . In the midst of this cruel rage, I was called to such inestimable grace. . . . The abundant grace of God, who calleth and showeth mercy to whom he will, pardoned and forgave me all those blasphemies; and for these my horrible sins, which then I thought to be perfect righteousness, and an acceptable service to God, he gave unto me his grace, the knowledge of his truth, and called me to be an Apostle.

> We also are come at this day to the knowledge of grace by the self-same merits. I crucified Christ in my monkish life, and blasphemed God through my false faith, wherein I then continually lived. Outwardly I was not as other men, extortioners, unjust, whoremongers; but I kept chastity, poverty and obedience. . . . I fostered under this cloaked holiness and trust in mine own righteousness, continual mistrust, doubtfulness, fear, hatred and blasphemy against God. . . . I was more contu-

---

7. Commentary on Galatians 1.14 (Middleton), p. 80.

melious and blasphemous against Christ and his Gospel, than Paul himself, and especially I. . . .[8]

Luther claims that as Paul was rescued by God, so he was himself rescued. As both had been the staunchest defenders of the old faith, so both came to preach another Gospel. In the face of determined opposition and persecution by members of the old faith, Paul had argued that he had received his doctrine and his commission from God direct and not from men. Luther did the same:

> So we can also boast, that we have not received our doctrine from the Pope. The Holy Scripture and the outward symbols we have indeed from him, but not the doctrine, which hath come unto us by the gift of God alone. Whereunto hath been added our own study, reading and inquiry.[9]

The parallel was not only with the call and the doctrine, but also with the sufferings. Luther compared Paul's temptations and tribulations to the stigmata of a St. Francis, dismissing the latter as monastic follies. The *true* stigmata were stripes, imprisonments, hunger and thirst, cold and nakedness, persecution and accusation from false brethren (2 Cor. 6:5; 11.26-28), which are inflicted on one, not cultivated. They are the work of false apostles pretending to be apostles of Christ, as Satan pretends to be an angel of light (2 Cor. 11.13-15). Luther asked whether Paul had not suffered the same temptation which he was suffering:

> Paul . . . was marvellously troubled with this enormity, that after the preaching of his good and wholesome doctrine, he saw so many sects, commotions which caused so many evils and offences. He was accused by the Jews to be a pernicious fellow, a mover of sedition in his whole nation, and to be an author of the sect of the Nazarenes (Ac. 24.5). . . . He preacheth such things whereby he not only overthroweth the Jewish commonwealth, excellently well ordered and established by the laws of God; but also abolisheth even the Ten Commandments, the religion and service of God, and our priesthood, and publisheth throughout the world the Gospel (as he calleth it) whereof are sprung infinite evils, seditions, offences, and sects. He was compelled to hear of the Gentiles also, which cried out against him in Philippi, that he was a troubler of the

---

8. Commentary on Galatians 1.15 (Middleton), pp. 81-82.
9. Commentary on Galatians 1.17-18 (Middleton), p. 86.

city, and preached customs which were not lawful for them to receive (Ac. 16.20f).

We are also constrained at this day to hear the same spoken of us, which was said of Paul and the other Apostles; to wit, that the doctrine of the Gospel which we profess, is the cause of many and great evils, as of seditions, wars, sects, and inumerable offences.[10]

Similarly, both Luther and Paul had to deal with those who argued that since they were not justified by the Law, they should be able to live without the Law. Writing on Galatians 3.19, he says, 'This happened to the Apostle. And the self-same happeneth at this day unto us.'

In the same way, both St. Paul and Luther had to endure the hatred not only of those who were of the old faith, but also of those who were once their followers and had now turned into enemies. Luther refers to the false brethren (Sacramentarians and Anabaptists) who at the beginning of the evangelical cause were glad to hear him and to read his books, but who were quickly seduced by the fanatics, after which they 'showed themselves more bitter enemies to our doctrine and our name than any other; for although they hated the papists, they hated us yet more'.

Both Luther and Paul found their authority to be questioned: both were attacked for being individual human beings who presumed to oppose a long and venerable institution ordained of God. The false teachers of Galatia crept in after Paul had left, boasting that they were the holy people of God, the seed of Abraham, with the promises of their fathers, the Jews. They were the disciples of the apostles; who was Paul, and on what authority did he speak? They had seen Christ, heard him preach. They were Jews: God would never abandon his chosen people. They were many: Paul was but a single person.

Yet for Luther the marvel was that God had preserved the Church and the Gospel using only one person. It was Paul alone who stood up to Barnabas and to Peter. In this connection Luther pointed out that Julius, Celsus, Porphyry, Jerome, and Erasmus all accused Paul of pride in having the audacity to rebuke Peter, the greatest of the Apostles, before the whole Church. Luther replied that such comment showed a failure to understand the issue. What

---

10. Commentary on Galatians 4.17 (Middleton), pp. 407-08.

Paul was defending was the supreme article of Christianity, justification by faith alone. This article could neither be corrupted nor modified; Paul would rebuke an angel from heaven who sought to do so. Paul's critics were considering the importance of the person, Peter, whereas Paul was considering only the importance of the article of faith.

Luther's certainty in judging his opponents as false teachers arose not from any conceit in himself as critic and judge, but only his determination to please not men but God. To lay any foundation other than Christ laid was to Luther anathema, as is stressed in the paraphrases of Paul:

> I teach only those things which are commanded me from above: neither glorify myself, but him that sent me. Besides that, I stir up against myself the wrath and indignation of both the Jews and the Gentiles: therefore my doctrine is true, sincere, certain, and of God, neither can there by any other, much less any better, than this my doctrine is. Wherefore, whatsoever doctrine else teacheth not as mine doth, that all men are sinners, and are justified by faith only in Christ, must needs be false, wicked, blasphemous, accursed and devilish; and even such also are they which either teach it or receive it.

He goes on to say,

> So we with Paul do boldly pronounce all such doctrine to be accursed as agreeth not with ours. For neither do we seek by our preaching the praise of men, or the favour of princes or bishops, but the favour of God alone, whose only grace and mercy we preach, despising and treading under foot whatsoever is of ourselves. Whosoever he be, then, which shall teach any other gospel, or that which is contrary to ours, we are bold to say that he is sent of the devil, and hold him accursed.[11]

Later still he says,

> Our stoutness therefore in this matter is godly and holy; for by it we seek to preserve our liberty which we have in Christ Jesus, and thereby to retain the truth of the Gospel; which, if we lose, then do we also lose God, Christ, all the promises, faith, righteousness, and everlasting life.[12]

---

11. Commentary on Galatians 1.10 (Middleton), p. 72.
12. Commentary on Galatians 2.4f. (Middleton), pp. 100-101.

At the very end of the exposition he writes, on the matter of Paul inveighing against the false apostles,

> In like manner, when we call the Pope Antichrist, the bishops and the fanatics a cursed generation, we slander them not, but by God's authority we judge them to be accursed, according to that which is said in the first chapter: 'If we, or an angel from heaven, preach otherwise than we have preached unto you, accursed be he', for they hate, persecute and overthrow the doctrine of Christ. [13]

By the time he had written his commentary on Galatians, Luther had come to believe that he occupied in his day and generation the same role that the Old Testament prophets and the New Testament apostles had occupied in biblical times. This does not mean for a moment that Luther put himself on the level of such men but merely that he saw his role in similar terms. He knew he bore the same stigmata that Paul had borne: doubt, temptations, afflictions, persecutions. He felt in his bones that when he died Germany would enter a time of war, distress, and disorder, and that false teachers would rise to subvert all he had done, as had happened in the days of Paul. The quite startling parallel he drew between his background in Catholicism and Paul's background in Judaism suggests that he practically identified himself with Paul.

Luther argued that he was able to understand Paul only because he had experienced similar sufferings. Once he saw himself in the role Paul had occupied, he found an explicit model for his behaviour towards opponents, and, what is more, he found a quiet certainty and authority for his words and deeds. He justified his polemics by pointing to Paul. He justified his stubbornness on points of doctrine in the same manner. When Catholic critics speak of his immodest polemics and his lack of charity, of his individualism and subjectivism, of his egocentricty and his pride, they are making superficial judgments from the perspective of established Catholic practice. We can understand such judgments, but for a deeper understanding we should bear in mind more carefully how Luther saw it all, and how he explained it all, on the pattern of Paul.

By standing in the role of the Old Testament prophet and the New Testament apostle, Luther strengthened his own authority and

---

13. Commentary on Galatians 6.77 (Middleton), p. 554.

validated both his teaching and his mission. He was a prophet: his teaching was God's, and therefore true. By equating his evangelical opponents with the biblical false prophets and apostles, he discredited them and their doctrine with them. The role of the true prophet and the false prophet are implicit in Luther's conception of the true Church and the false Church, the Church of God and the chapel of the Devil, and of the never-ending and never-changing struggle between them.

This whole matter of the Church should be reconsidered by both Catholics and Protestants, so that both may discover together the prophetic role Luther played in the sixteenth century, and see to what extent that prophetic voice may speak to the twentieth. An exceptional opportunity to do just this has been given by Vatican II in its own prophetic promulgations.

CONCLUSION

IN THE FIRST CHAPTER of this text we gave consideration to the four centuries of hostility and destructive criticism from 1517 to 1939 when Catholicism sought to devalue Luther's theology and denigrate his person. In the second chapter we noted with much gladness the Catholic revaluation of Luther following the work of Joseph Lortz in 1939-40, which introduced a period of respect and interest that culminated in the highly creative and prophetic advances of Vatican II.

In subsequent chapters we have considered Luther in his role as a prophetic reformer addressing the Catholic Church that rejected his biblical and evangelical theology and allowed him to maintain them in a confessional position only outside the fellowship. This had the effect both of reducing genuine Catholicism to *Roman* Catholicism and of rendering the Reformation movement polemical and confessional. I have suggested that the work of Luther can only begin to be appreciated properly when it is seen as a reformation of Catholicism — that is to say, Catholicism needs Luther in order to be fully catholic, and Protestantism needs Catholicism to fulfil its *raison d'être*.

As evidence for the thesis that Luther is a prophet to the whole state of Christ's Church, Catholic and Protestant alike, we have considered Luther's religious experience and some of the major emphases of his theology and the relevance for today's world of both his understanding of the Christian religious experience and his theological grasp of the essentials of the Christian message.

The examination of over four centuries of criticism has to this point been confined to the work of Catholic scholars only, but to make the case complete, it is now necessary to note the vast number of scholars and universities, city-states and countries that have hailed Luther's protest from the beginning and have supported his cause in the face of hostility, deprivation, persecution, and even death. It is no new idea to see Luther as a prophet sent by God: that was how most of his contemporaries regarded him from the beginning, even when he was still in the monastery. It is worth studying how those who knew and loved him were prone to estimate him, however. Admirers have compared him favourably with such personages as the Apostle Paul, the Angel of the Apocalypse, and even Christ himself. Perhaps the most significant application he has received is that of 'The Prophet'.

No less a person than Grotus Rubeanus, the distinguished humanist, in a letter to Luther in 1519, compared him to Paul, even to his similar conversion experience. His own professor at Erfurt, Nathin, described him as the second Paul, converted to holiness. Other equally distinguished and varied writers and scholars named him *vir apostolicus* — 'the apostle' (1520); 'the one and only true Pope and Apostle' (1520); *apostolus Christi* — 'Christ's apostle' (1521); "the apostle through whom we know the Gospel and Christ" (1521); 'the most distinguished Apostle of Christ in these stormy times' (1522); 'our own Paul' (1522); and 'the Apostle of Germany' (1524). Hans Sachs described him as 'a Christian teacher, the greatest since Paul' (1524). And a medal, stamped 1524, describes him as 'apostle'. [1]

When Luther tossed the Papal Bull into the flames in Wittenberg before the university and city on that dark, cold December morning of 1520, the report described him as manifesting himself before the world as 'the angel of the Living God'. In a pamphlet of 1523, he was figured as 'the angel whom God had sent to mankind'. In a dialogue of Peter with a peasant, a kind of simple question-and-answer affair, Peter is made to say that 'I come from Wittenberg, from the prophet, Angel and Apostle of Jesus Christ, sent specially from God to thee'. To the amazed peasant, Peter goes on to justify these descriptions, and describes Luther as a 'tool (or instrument) of God', 'a preacher sent by God to give His saving Word to the poor lost sheep of Germany'. Poems and hymns composed in 1521 describe him as the Angel of the Apocalypse 'flying in midheaven, with an eternal gospel to proclaim to those who dwell on earth' (cf. Rev. 14.11).

---

1. The sources for these descriptions can be found on pp. 37ff. of Hans Preuss's *Martin Luther — the Prophet* (1933). I acknowledge a great debt to Preuss and his fine scholarly work on Luther.

Those who drew the parallel between Luther and Christ made a strong point indeed—too strong, in fact—but part of the force of that comparison derived from the opinion that the Pope was the Antichrist and Luther the one who truly preached Christ and his Gospel. The parallel began to develop when men described Luther as 'the man sent by God', which is of course how Christ described himself (John 5.24, 30, 36ff.; 6.29, 38ff., 44, 57; 7.16, 18, 28ff., 33; etc.). The scholar Erbelin von Guenzburg wrote, 'I believe that Luther has been sent to cleanse the Bible of its shallow exposition . . . and sent also to teach the theology of the cross and the doctrine of faith. He was called by God for this very purpose, and God gives him the wisdom, the art, the mind, the strength and the heart, to do this' (1522). Other descriptions of him at the time include 'God's elect', 'Sent from heaven', and 'the chosen one of God'—all phrases from contemporary poems and hymns.

His journey to Worms was described by many as his Palm Sunday procession. Pictures and poems appeared in Worms, when it was said that Luther's pilgrimage was like that of the holy prophets and of Christ himself, that the secular power would do with Luther what Pilate did to Christ, and the Pope would do to him what the Jews did to Christ: 'Luther in fact stands before the Papists exactly as Christ, Paul, Peter and the saints stood before their authorities'. The full Latin text shows quite clearly that Worms was interpreted as Luther's passion narrative. From the crowds at Worms a woman's voice had cried, "Blessed is the womb that bare thee, and the paps which thou didst suck", a parallel the crowds accepted.

The book *The Passion of Dr. Martin Luther* (1521) makes remarkable reading. For example, the Archbishop of Mainz, who had sparked off the Reformation with his granting of indulgences, is described in the work as Caiaphas, who in his palace gathers the Pharisees who plot the death of Luther 'but not at the Reichstag lest we have an uproar of the people'. Aleander is said to give Luther the kiss of Judas, and Luther claims, 'I have taught daily in the Temple, yet you never took me'. Further on, he holds the supper with his disciples, one of whom says, 'The Saxon [i.e., Frederick the Wise] will never betray thee', and Luther replies, 'Before the cock crows twice he will deny me thrice'. The Archbishop of Trier, who tried to free Luther, is likened to Pilate; Pilate's wife (the German nation) says, 'Have thou nothing to do with this just man'. The priests attempt to burn Luther's effigy, on which is inscribed 'Martin Luther, a teacher of the Gospel', but the effigy refuses to burn, and a noble lord declares, 'This man is surely Christ!'.

The amount of evidence is overwhelming. Frederick the Wise, Luther's prince, wrote to his brother from Worms, 'not only do Annas and Caiaphas stand against Luther but Pilate and Herod, too'. The ambassador Fürstenberg from Frankfurt wrote that some people wanted to nail Luther on his cross, but if they did he would rise on the third day. Even Albrecht Dürer wrote in his diary (17 May 1521) that as God had raised his Son from the dead when the priests had slain him, so he prayed that God would quicken in the same way his disciple Martin Luther after the Pope had betrayed him. The Ulm physician Rychard suggested that mankind should begin a new calendar with Luther's birth.

Nevertheless, Luther was most significantly described as a prophet, the only title that he himself accepted, and one that time has surely endorsed. As early as 1518, Adelmann, a canon of Augsburg, described him as 'the man of God', as did many others at the time, both courtiers and clergy, including Cochlaeus. He was described as a second Daniel, and also a third Elijah, a prophet who in the strength and power of Elijah would turn many to the Lord (cf. Luke 1.17). Zwingli concurred with this assessment, referring to Luther as 'the Phoenix of the theologians' — that is to say, another Elijah. Melanchthon, too, described Luther during his absence in the Wartburg as 'our Elijah'; and it was in these same terms he announced Luther's death to his stricken students: 'Alas, gone are the chariots of Israel, and the horseman thereof'. Even Luther came to use this term in reference to himself. The image caught on: Spalatin (1521), Kettenbach (1522), Rhegius (1523), Alberus (1523), Brunsels (1523), and a whole row of leading men, princes, courtiers, politicians, scholars, along with the theologians Mykonius, Flacius, and Osiander (Cranmer's father-in-law) all refer to Luther as the third Elijah sent to reform the Church.

It was Luther's death that aroused the *prophet-motif* to its most powerful expression. Bugenhagen, the parish parson on whose behalf Luther had so often preached, stood at the side of the coffin unable to restrain the tears and spoke of his 'beloved friend, the mighty teacher, the prophet, the man sent by God as the Reformer of the Church, whom God had called away; dear Father Luther, the greatest apostle and prophet, the preacher and evangelist to Germany'. He was to write to Christian III of Denmark, in whose country Bugenhagen had been an important preacher and reformer of Denmark of the 'dear man and prophet when God had taken to himself out of this vale of misery'; and to Albrecht von Preussen he wrote, 'We give thanks to God who had given to this age so great a prophet'. Justus Jonas, a fellow professor, preached the funeral sermon at Eisleben, where Luther had died, and spoke of 'the great prophet'; when he later wrote to the Danish King, he described how every night he had taken leave of Luther and had shaken that apostolic hand, the hand that had written so many fine books but that now would write no more, the blessed prophet of the German nation having taken his leave in death.

It was at Luther's death that the description of Luther as an instrument of God sent to reform and renew the Church received its most poignant expression on the lips of Melanchthon. In his knowledge of Luther as a person and his understanding of Luther's God-given mission, Melanchthon, Luther's life-long intimate friend and co-worker in the Reformation was surpassed by no one. We are most fortunate to have charming contemporary translations of Melanchthon's works in English by Henry Bennet (1561). Bennet returned from the Continent to an England recovering from the execrable persecution of Mary and her co-religionists, an England hoping, even longing, for a fresh religious settlement under the young Queen Elizabeth, a settlement that would have done with religious wars and the burning of people for their religious views, and creatively embrace Catholic and Protestant alike. To this laudable end he compiled a small book of Reformation texts containing, among other Swiss texts, Melanchthon's *Life of Luther*, his *Death of Luther*, and his *Oration* given at the funeral of Luther, which he had translated into superb Tudor prose. Fired not by any personal allegiance, nor any party devotion, but solely by the spiritual and theological significance of the texts, as he expressed it, he wanted to open England's eyes to the great issues opened up by Luther. We could well do the same in 1983.

Standing by the coffin of his beloved friend in the church on whose door Luther had nailed up his Ninety-five Theses some twenty-nine years earlier, Melanchthon, with matchless brevity, gave a penetrating intellectual and spiritual analysis of Luther's teaching and what he effected in the Church as a man 'taught of God'. He praised his character, commended his achievements, and spoke of the man whom he 'often tymes came unawares upon . . . when he wyth teares berayning hys chekes, prayed for the universal Church'. Yet to those, even his friends, who tended to think Luther's ways and remedies were too severe, he says,

> But some (which wer not pervers) have complayned that Luther was more vehement then nede required. I wyl not dispute against any: but I aunswer this that Erasmus hath often said: God hath given this last age a sharpe Phisicion, because of the great diseases of the same, and therefore synce he hath reysed such an organe against the truthes enemies, and agaynst the proude and impudent, as he hath said to Jeremy, beholde I have placed my wordes in they mouth, to thende thou should-est destroy and edefye, and hath pleased hym to set before their beards this Gorgon or buckler, in vaine thei quarell wyth God.

In the opening passages of his *Oration*, Melanchthon strikingly describes Luther as one whom God had sent for the renewal and preservation of the Gospel:

> The Sonne of God (as Paul sayth) sitteth at the right hand of the everlasting father, and ministreth good things to men, that is, the voice of the Gospel, and the holy ghost, and to distribute these giftes, he rayseth Prophets, Apostles, Doctors and Pastors, and taketh these out of our congregacion, such as do learne, who professe, heare and embrace the Prophetes and Apostles writings. And calleth not only those to this warfare, which have ordinari power, but also he denounceth warre against them often times, by Doctours chosen of an other estate. It is moste comfortable and a pleasant spectacle to consider the Churche of all ages, and to remember the bountye of God who from time to time has sent successively godly Doctors, to thend that when the first were in battayl consumed, other might supply theyr rankes to atchieve that the former begonne.

Then, after listing the patriarchs, prophets, apostles, and the Church Fathers, he says this of Luther (and I say with him):

> Then muste we collocate hym among this select and blissful Troupe of Godly and excellent Mirrours, whom God hath sent to gether and restore hys Church, that we may understand this was the principal flower of humaine kind. Solon, Themisto-cles, Scipio, Augustus, were excellent and woorthy men, who established and governed large realmes and great Empires: yet were they much inferiour then these our Guides, Osay, John Baptist, S. Paule, Austen, and Luther.

SELECT BIBLIOGRAPHY

Abbot, Walter M., ed. *Documents of Vatican II*. New York, 1966.

Adam, Karl. *Una Sancta in Katholischer Sicht*. Düsseldorf, 1948.

Atkinson, James. *Luther's Early Theological Works*. Vol. 16 of the Library of Christian Classics. London, 1962.

_____. *Martin Luther and the Birth of Protestantism*. London, 1968, 1982.

_____. *The Trial of Luther*. New York: Stein and Day, 1971.

Bellarmine, St. Robert. *Disputations de Controversiis....* 3 vols. Ingolstadt, 1586-93.

Bouyer, Louis. *Du protestantisme à l'Eglise*. Paris, 1954. E.T., *The Spirit and Forms of Protestantism*. Trans. A. V. Littledale. London: Harvill, 1956.

Brandenberg, Albert. "Um Luthers Theologie heute," *Rheinischer Merkur*, 28 November 1958.

_____. *Gericht und Evangelism*. Paderborn, 1960.

_____. *Die Zukunft des Martin Luther*. Münster: Aschendorff; Kassel: Johannes-Stauda-Verlag, 1977.

Brecht, Martin. *Martin Luther: Sein Weg zur Reformation*. Stuttgart: Calwer, 1981.

Butler, Christopher. *The Theology of Vatican II*. London, 1967.

Clayton, Joseph. *Luther and His Work*. Milwaukee, 1937.

Congar, Yves M.-J. *Divided Christendom*. London, 1939.

_____. *Vraie et fausse réforme dans l'Eglise*. Paris, 1950.

_____. "Regards et reflexions sur la christologie de Luther," in *Das Konzil von Chalkedon*. Vol. 3. Ed. Grillmeyer and Bacht. Wurzburg. 457-86.

Campenhausen, Hans von. *Ecclesiastical Authority and Spiritual Power in the Church of the First Three Centuries*. Trans. J. A. Baker. Stanford: Stanford University Press, 1969.

Cochlaeus, John. *Commentaria de actis et scriptis Martini Lutheri*. 1549.

Cranmer, Thomas. *The Works of Thomas Cranmer, Archbishop of Canterbury* (Parker Society Edition). 2 vols. Ed. John Edmund Cox. Cambridge: At the University Press, 1886.

Cullmann, Oscar. *Vatican Council II: The New Direction*. New York: Harper & Row, 1968.

Cristiani, Leon. *Luther et le Lutheranisme*. Paris, 1908.

_____. *Du Lutheranisme au protestantisme*. Paris, 1911.

Denifle, Heinrich. *Luther und Lutherum in der Ersten Entwicklung quellenmässig dargestellt*. 2 vols. Mainz, 1904, 1909.

Ebeling, Gerhard. *Evangelische Evangelienauslegung*. Berlin, 1942.

Eck, John. *Enchiridion of John Eck against Luther and Other Enemies of the Church*. Trans. Ford Lewis Battles. Grand Rapids, Mich.: Baker Book, 1979.

Erikson, Erik H. *Young Man Luther*. London, 1958.

Evenett, H. O. *The Reformation*. London, 1937.

Freemantle, Anne. *The Papal Encyclicals*. New York, 1956, 1963.

Grisar, Hartmann. *Luther*. 3 vols. Freiburg im Breisgau, 1911-12.

Harnack, Adolf. *History of Dogma*. 7 vols. Boston, 1907.

Herte, Adolf. *Die Lutherkommentare des Johannes Cochlaeus*. Münster, 1935.

_____. *Das Katholische Lutherbild*. 3 vols Münster, 1943.

Hessen, Johannes. *Luther in Katholischer Sicht*. 2d ed. Bonn, 1949.

Holl, Karl. *Gesammelte Aufsätze zur Kirchengeschichte*. 3 vols. 1928. Darmstadt: Wissenschaftliche Buchgesellschaft, 1964-65.

Hughes, Philip. *The Reformation*. London, 1957.

————. *The Revolt against the Church: Aquinas to Luther*. 4th ed. London 1960.

Iserloh, Erwin. "Luther-Kritik oder Luther-Polemic. Zu einer neuen Deutung der Entwicklung Luthers zum Reformatot." In *Festgabe Joseph Lortz*, ed. Erwin Iserloh and Peter Manns. Baden-Baden, 1958. 1:15-42.

Janssen, Johannes. *History of the German People*. 1876.

Jedin, Hubert. *Die Erforschung der kirchlichen Reformationsgeschichte seit 1876. Leistungen und Aufgaben der Deutschen Katholiken*. Münster, 1931.

————. *Geschichte des Konzils von Trient*. 2 vols. 1950, 1957.

Kidd, Beresford James. *Documents Illustrative of the Continental Reformation*. Oxford: Clarendon Press, 1911.

Kiefl, Franz-Xavier. "Martin Luthers religiose Psyche." *Monatschrift für alle Gebiete des Wissens*, 15 (1923): 7-28.

Köstlin, Julius. *Martin Luther: His Life and Writings*. 2 vols. 1875.

————. *The Life of Luther*. 1905.

Küng, Hans. *Konzil und Wiedervereinigung*. Freiburg im Breisgau, 1960.

————. *Justification*. Rev. ed. London, 1981.

Loewenich, Walter von. *Martin Luther: Der Mann und das Werk*. Munich, 1982.

Lortz, Joseph. "Um Luther," in *Zeitschrift für den katholischen Religionsunterricht an höheren Schulen*. Düsseldorf, 1933. 193-207.

————. "Zum Menschenbild Luthers," in *Das Bild vom Menschen*. Düsseldorf, 1934. 58-68.

————. *Die Reformation in Deutschland*. 2 vols. Freiburg im Breisgau, 1939-40.

————. *Die Reformation: Thesen als religiöses Anliegen heute*. Trier, 1948.

————. *Wie kam es zur Reformation?* Einsiedelm, 1950.

————. "Die Reformation und Luther in Katholischer Sicht," in *Una Sancta*. Meitingen bei Augsburg, 1955. 37-41.

————. "Luthers Vorlesung über Römerbrief." *Trierer Theologische Zeitschrift*. 1962: 129-53, 216-47.

Luther, Martin. *D. Martin Luthers Werke: Kritische Gesamtausgabe*. Weimar, 1883ff.

————. *D. Martin Luthers Werke: Deutsche Bible*. Weimar, 1906.

————. *D. Martin Luthers Werke: Tischreden*. Weimar, 1930ff.

————. *The Works of Martin Luther*. Ed. Henry Eyster Jacobs. Philadelphia: Muhlenberg Press, 1943.

McDonough, Thomas M. *The Law and the Gospel in Luther*. Oxford, 1963.

McSorley, Harry J. *Luthers Lehre vom Unfreien Willen*. Munich, 1967. E.T., *Luther: Right or Wrong?* New York: Newman Press, 1969.

Martin, Alfred von. *Luther in Ökumenischer Sicht*. Stuttgart, 1929.

Meissinger, Karl A. *Der Katholischer Luther*. Munich, 1952.

————. "Zum Katholischen Lutherbild," in *Theologie und Seelsorge*. 1944.

Middleton, Erasmus. *Luther's Commentary on Galatians*. London, 1953.

Moehler, John Adam. *Symbolik*. 1832.

Moeller, C. and Philip, G. *The Theology of Grace and the Ecumenical Movement*. Trans. R. A. Wilson. Patterson, N.J.: St. Anthony Guild Press, 1969.

Nas, John. *Anatomy of Lutheranism as it was instituted by the Devil*. N.d.

O'Hare, P. F. *The Facts about Luther*. New York, 1916.

O'Malley, John W. "Catholic Reform," in *Reformation Europe*. Ed. Steven

Ozment. St. Louis, 1982. 297-319.

Ozment, Steven. *The Reformation in the Cities.* London, 1975.

The Passion of Dr. Martin Luther. N.d.

Pauck, Wilhelm, ed. *Romans.* Vol. 15 of the Library of Christian Classics. London, 1961.

Pelikan, Jaroslav. *Obedient Rebels: Catholic Substance and Protestant Principle in Luther's Reformation.* New York, 1964.

Pistorius, John. *Anatomie Lutheri.* N.d.

Preuss, Hans. *Martin Luther der Prophet.* Gütersloh, 1933.

Przywara, Erich. *An Augustine Synthesis.* London, 1936.

————. "Mysterium Luther," in *Die Besinnung.* Nürnberg, 1953. 303-11.

Quealey, F. M. "The Changing Image of Luther." *The Ecumenist,* 2 (1964): 36-39.

Quick, Oliver Chase. *The Doctrine of the Creed.* London, 1938.

Rahner, Karl. "Evangelische und Katholische Stellungnahmen zu Martin Luther in Katholischer Sicht," in *Una Sancta.* Meitingen, 1962. 186-97.

Reiter, Paul J. *Martin Luthers Umwelt, Charakter und Psychose....* 2 vols. Copenhagen, 1937-41.

Richter, Friedrich. *Martin Luther und Ignatius Loyola.* Stuttgart, 1954.

Rupp, Gordon. *The Righteousness of God: Luther Studies.* New York: Philosophical Library, 1953.

Rupp, Gordon, et al. *Luther and Erasmus.* Vol. 17 of the Library of Christian Classics. London, 1969.

Sartory, Thomas. "Martin Luther in Katholischer Sicht." In *Una Sancta.* Meitingen bei Augsburg, 1961. 38-54.

Schaff, Philip. *Modern Christianity: The German Reformation.* Vol. 7 of *History of the Christian Church.* Rev. ed. Grand Rapids, Mich.: Eerdmans, 1980.

Skydsgaard, K. E. *Tradition and Traditions.* 1972.

Stauffer, Richard. *Die Entdeckung Luthers in Katholizismus.* Zurich, 1968.

Strotmann, T. "Sur le theme protestant: Luther 1546—1946." *Irenikon,* 19 (1964): 318-35.

Swidler, Leonard. "The Uses and Abuses of History: Reappraising the Reformation." *Commonweal,* 81 (1964): 156-58.

————. "Catholic Reformation Scholarship in Germany." *Journal of Ecumenical Studies,* 2 (1965): 189-204.

Tappert, T. G., ed. *Letters of Spiritual Counsel.* Vol. 18 of the Library of Christian Classics. London, 1955.

Tavard, George. *A la rencontre du protestantisme.* Paris, 1954. E.T., *The Catholic Approach to Protestantism.* New York, 1955.

————. *Le protestantisme.* 2d ed. Paris, 1964. E.T., *Protestantism.* New York, 1959.

————. *Holy Writ or Holy Church: The Crisis of the Protestant Reformation.* New York, 1959.

Todd, J. M. *Martin Luther: A Biographical Study.* London: Burns & Oates, 1964.

————. *Luther: A Life.* New York: Crossroads, 1982.

Torrance, Thomas F. *Theology in Reconstruction.* London: SCM Press, 1965.

————. *Theological Science.* Oxford, 1969.

————. *Christian Theology and Scientific Culture.* Belfast, 1980.

Watson, Philip S. *Let God Be God! An Interpretation of the Theology of Martin Luther.* Philadelphia: Muhlenberg Press, 1949.

Zeeden, Ernst Walter. *Martin Luther und die Reformation im Urteil des Deutschen Luthertums.* 2 vols. Freiburg im Breisgau, 1950-52.

GENERAL INDEX

SCRIPTURE INDEX